The Mind of the Slave

EMPIRE AND AFTER

Series Editor: *Clifford Ando*

The series *Empire and After* examines the social, political, legal, and intellectual histories of the worlds united under Roman rule, and the role of imperial orders and institutions in Rome's successor states in East and West.

RECENT TITLES IN THE SERIES:

The Mind of the Slave: The Limits of Ownership in Roman Law and Society
NICOLE J. GIANNELLA

The Mind of the Slave

THE LIMITS OF OWNERSHIP IN ROMAN LAW AND SOCIETY

Nicole J. Giannella

UNIVERSITY OF MICHIGAN PRESS
ANN ARBOR

Printed and bound by CPI Group (UK) Ltd, Croydon, CR0 4YY
Published in the United States of America by the
University of Michigan Press

First published January 2026

A CIP catalog record for this book is available from the British Library.

Library of Congress Cataloging-in-Publication data has been applied for.

ISBN 978-0-472-13365-9 (hardcover : alk. paper)
ISBN 978-0-472-22240-7 (e-book)

DOI: https://doi.org/10.3998/mpub.14514947

Cover image: Portrait stele of Florus, limestone,
55 AD–70 AD, inv. no. CAR-S-709. © Landessammlungen NÖ.
The inscription is as follows:

Florus P(ublii) Vedi(i) / P(ublii) f(ilii) Fab(ia tribu) Germa/ni ser(vus) an(norum) XXVI / [h(ic)] s(itus) e(st) / [domi]nus ob meritis / [eius] fecit /
[Οὐ γάμον οὐχ] ὑμέναιον ἰδ/[ὼν οὐ νύ]νφια λέκτρα / [κεῖμαι] π(ρ)ὸς στήλῃ κεκλι/[μέν]ος παρ᾽ ὁδῷ. Χαῖρε / [Φλ]ῶρε, χαῖρε καὶ σύ, / τίς ποτ᾽ εἶ, ξένε.

Florus, slave of Publius Vedius Germanus the son of Publius and of the tribe Fabia, lies here age twenty-six. His owner made this for him owing to his merits.
Having seen neither marriage, nor wedding, nor marital bed, I lie resting by the gravestone beside the road. Greetings, Florus! And Greetings to you, whoever you are, stranger!

The authorized representative in the EU for product safety and compliance is Easy Access System Europe, Mustamäe tee 50, 10621 Tallinn, Estonia, gpsr.requests@easproject.com

For Claudia

Contents

Acknowledgments

The seeds of this project were sown in my second year of graduate school when I took Claudia Moatti's graduate seminar in Roman law and she told me to study the Edict of the Aediles. The project grew from there, entirely with her guidance, patience, and grace. This book is dedicated to her. A most appreciative thanks are also due to my committee at the University of Southern California: A. J. Boyle, Susan Lape, and Ariela Gross; as well as to old USC friends now far-flung: Hamish Cameron, Jason Harris, Ashley McIntosh, Christine Shaw, Matthew Taylor, and Lisl Walsh.

Claudia also did me the great favor of introducing me to Clifford Ando, to whom I am deeply grateful as well. Cliff has been a kind and generous mentor and friend as I began my career; I am honored to have my book in the Empire and After series.

The majority of writing took place in Ithaca; I was fortuitous enough to enjoy the wisdom of many scholars through collaborative initiatives at Cornell's Society for the Humanities. My debt is also extended to the Cornell Classics+ working group, which has advised on and read much of this manuscript over the years, as well as to various ad hoc writing groups and colleagues including Toni Alimi, Zachary Herz, Mark Letteney, Lindsey Mazurek, Éric Rebillard, and Jeff Rusten among others.

Brent Shaw, Dan-el Padilla Peralta, Joe Howley, and Suman Seth were gracious enough to not only read an early version of this manuscript but to spend a sunny spring day in Ithaca offering me many excellent "exit strategies" for the project (which I could not hope to live up to). They shaped this project as it was coming to completion. Each of them has offered support since then, and I thank in particular my colleague at Cornell, and dear friend, Suman.

I am grateful for the guidance of Ellen Bauerle, Juliette Snyder, and Marcia LaBrenz at the University of Michigan Press as well as to Sara Merker for her perceptive comments and invaluable help proofreading and indexing. The anonymous readers for the press both provided insightful and dedicated assistance as this project neared the finish line.

My greatest thanks go to my friends Damián Fernández, Murad Idris, Rachana Kamtekar, Athena Kirk, Theresa Krueggeler, Andrew Moisey, Shaun Nichols, Hayden Pelliccia, Lakshmi Ramgopal, and Abby Westervelt.

I am forever grateful for the love, support, and patience of family: my siblings, Davide, Monica, and Eric and their families; my parents, Julia and Giovanni, and grandmother, Consuelo; and my family, Charles, Sophie, Helena, and Julia.

Timeline of Jurists

M. Portius Cato	3rd–2nd century BCE
Aulus Ofilius	1st century BCE
Q. Aelius Tubero	1st century BCE
Trebatius Testa	1st century BCE
P. Alfenus Varus	1st century BCE
M. Antistius Labeo	c. 50 BCE–10/11 CE
Fabius Mela	1st century BCE-1st century CE
M. Massurius Sabinus "Sabinus"	1st century CE
C. Cassius Longinus	1st century CE
Proculus	1st century CE
Caelius Sabinus "Caelius"	1st century CE
Pegasus	1st century CE
Urseius Ferox	1st century CE
Vivianus "Vivian"	1st–2nd century CE
L. Javolenus Priscus	1st–2nd century CE
L. Neratius Priscus	1st–2nd century CE
P. Iuventius Celsus (Filius)	1st–2nd century CE
P. Salvius Julianus "Julian"	2nd century CE
Sex. Caecilius Africanus	2nd century CE
L. Volusius Maecianus	2nd century CE
Gaius	2nd century CE
Sextus Pomponius	2nd century CE
Ulpius Marcellus	2nd century CE

Q. Cervidius Scaevola	2nd century CE
Claudius Saturninus	2nd century CE
Florentinus	after 161 CE
Aemilius Papinianus "Papinian"	fl. 193–212 CE
Arrius Menander	fl. 193–217 CE
Domitius Ulpianus "Ulpian"	fl. 193–223 CE
Julius Paulus "Paul"	fl. 193–235 CE
Aelius Marcianus "Marcian"	first half of 3rd century CE
Herrenius Modestinus	mid-3rd century CE
Aurelius Hermogenianus "Hermogenian"	late 3rd–early 4th century CE

Introduction

After he retired from his position as advisor to the emperor Nero, the philosopher Seneca told a story in one of his letters about a man named Sabinus, who was immensely wealthy, but not particularly cultured—though he wished to appear so. Seneca goes so far as to describe him as having "the inheritance and character of a freedman" (*patrimonium habebat libertini et ingenium*). Sabinus' solution to his feeling of cultural and intellectual inadequacy was to buy a set of enslaved people who knew the works of Homer, Hesiod, and the nine lyric poets by heart. At his command, they were each to spoon-feed Sabinus bits of verse for him to recite to his dinner guests. Having slaves provide entertainment at dinner was not particularly unusual—flute playing, dancing, even poetry recitation—but this was a bit eccentric. Following what must have been a tedious supper of stilted poetry recitation by the slaves and butchered verse by the freedman, Sabinus comments to one of his dinner companions about the hefty price of these enslaved reciters. His companion, Satellius, responds that Sabinus could have bought as many bookcases for less expense and the same result. Seneca explains why Sabinus wanted the slaves nonetheless:

> Sabinus was of the opinion that whatever someone in his household knew, he himself knew. Satellius then began to suggest that Sabinus—a sickly, pale, and slight man—take up wrestling. When Sabinus objected, "How can I? I'm barely alive!" Satellius responded, "Oh, please don't say that! Don't you see how many slaves you have who are the picture of health?"
>
> Ille tamen in ea opinione erat ut putaret se scire quod quisquam in domo sua sciret. Idem Satellius illum hortari coepit ut luctaretur, hominem aegrum, pal-

> lidum, gracilem. Cum Sabinus respondisset, 'et quomodo possum? vix vivo', 'noli, obsecro te' inquit 'istuc dicere: non vides quam multos servos valentissimos habeas?[1]

To expose the absurdity of the notion that somehow, through ownership, a slave owner can consider his slaves' skill and knowledge to be his own, Satellius suggests that the ailing slave owner farm out his physical fitness in the same manner as he did his mind. Satellius' joke shows that Sabinus conceptualizes the ownership of his slaves' minds differently from that of their bodies: The ownership of the mind is more thorough and total. The transfer of this more totalizing ownership from the abstract—the mind—to the tangible—the body—illustrates the folly of his thinking. Nevertheless, Sabinus, who is treated rather poorly in this letter, can be pardoned for his false equivalence of knowledge and ownership since, for most goods, particularly in the Roman period, the two did go hand in hand.

While we can acknowledge the hefty dose of freeborn snobbery, Seneca's descriptor of Sabinus' *ingenium* as one of a *libertinus* suggests that there is some aspect of former slaves, despite their freedom and citizenship, which is not quite the same as a freeborn person, a remnant of their enslavement. This *ingenium libertini* is misguided insofar as Sabinus believes he knows what his slaves know (*scire*) and that whatever knowledge existed in his household was his own knowledge. Satellius compares Sabinus' idea of having ownership over the minds of his enslaved household to having ownership over their bodies, which Sabinus does have. And yet Sabinus will not entertain the idea of having an enslaved person wrestle and consider it equivalent to himself wrestling. Implicit in the purchase of something is the ability to use it as one wishes, to bend it to one's will, to sway or persuade. But despite buying and owning the body of a slave, Seneca tells us that a person can't buy a sound mind, especially the sort of mind that has the skill and discipline to commit thousands of lines of poetry to memory.[2] After all, who's to say that the Homeric slave isn't actually reciting Aristophanes in protest? Certainly not his owner Sabinus.

Here lies the difficulty at the heart of this book: Particularly for high-level or skilled slaves, an owner would want a slave with a sound mind, even though they cannot know what that slave was thinking, feeling, or possibly plotting. How a

---

1. Sen. *Ep.* 27.5–8, quote at 27.7–8.
2. Sen. *Ep.* 27.8 fin.: "Good minds are not lent or sold; and I think, if a good one were for sale, there wouldn't be a buyer: but bad minds are sold every day" (*Bona mens nec commodatur nec emitur; et puto, si venalis esset, non haberet emptorem: at mala cotidie emitur*).

slave uses their mind is beyond the bounds of ownership.[3] Seneca's deconstruction of the freedman's belief that he himself knows what his slaves know because their minds are, in a sense, his intellectual property, formulates the driving question of this book: What is the relationship between the ownership of the slaveholder and their slave's mind—that is to say, their intellect, character, and mental autonomy? This question necessitates studying Roman slavery through its legal framework, but also moving outside those parameters since slave ownership is a social relationship grounded in legal fact. In contrast to both formalistic legal studies of ownership and approaches to slavery as a form of physical domination, my book looks to the inherent difficulties that arise from keeping human beings as property. This approach reveals how Romans understood the practical limits and, consequently, the very nature of slave ownership in the first centuries of the Roman Empire (first-third centuries CE).

The Roman jurists were not partial to abstract definitions; rather, they were interested in pragmatics.[4] The term *dominium* itself does not come into its technical meaning of ownership until the first century BCE.[5] Ownership meant that the owner of a piece of property had the right to use, alienate, or destroy that good, whatever it might be, with little interference from others.[6] At times, when the jurists discuss ownership, they make no distinction between slaves and other goods as owned things (*res*). However, they recognize that slaves were different from other property and explicitly state that slaves were human beings: they were both things, like any other good, and persons (*personae*), like a slave owner's son. This was not because of some humanitarian ideal; it speaks rather to the fact that slaves in Rome were both a part of the labor force and active partners and thinkers in the economy, serving as account managers, business agents, and agricultural foremen, among other roles.[7]

While many general works on Roman law consider ownership to be abso-

---

3. Throughout the project I have tried to use, as much as possible, "they," "themself," or "their" when speaking generally about owners, slaves, or freedpersons, and "he" or "she" when gender is known or dictated by context.
4. Birks 1985, 3, "There is no attempt expressly to articulate a concept of ownership [on the part of the jurists]," and "ownership is taken for granted, continually in issue but undefined and unexamined."

   And see Nicholas (2008, 153), who, in his introductory Roman law text, remarks, "We have so far been proceeding in truly Roman fashion and have left undefined our most fundamental concept—ownership."

   See also Diósdi 1970, 122–24.
5. See Diósdi 1970, 135, for dating; he tells us that *dominus* means "owner" more generally until the time of Varro and Cicero when it comes to specify "master."
6. Birks 1985; Riggsby 2010, 136.
7. See Knoch 2005, 41–144.

lute, Roman legal scholars have revealed ways in which it was not.[8] This includes, for example, limited restrictions such as those on building on one's own land (e.g., if the construction would excessively block the light of a neighbor)[9] and people with competing claims to property (e.g., *duplex dominium*).[10] This project considers a different question that builds on the work of Peter Birks. In his article "The Roman Law Concept of *Dominium* and the Idea of Absolute Ownership," he distinguishes between the "content" of *dominium*—the scope, sanctity, and autonomy of ownership and the demands of society on ownership—and the "concept" of *dominium*—its difference from other superiorities, the singular relationship between citizen and owned thing, and its exclusive nature.[11] In his discussion of how secure the rights of Roman owners were with respect to the content of *dominium*, Birks is avowedly preoc-

---

8. Birks 1985, 1, "'Absolute' is not, properly speaking, a word which admits of degrees. Hence if Roman ownership was at all restricted in its content, as indeed it must have been and was, it was not, strictly, absolute. However, if a looser usage is admitted, a last question to be asked is whether, if some measure can be said to have been set to the extent of permissible interference with an owner's freedoms, the remaining area of inviolability was so great as to attract the word 'absolute' as a useful description of the quality of Roman ownership."

Additionally, Birks views absolute ownership as (at 1985, 1): "the relationship between an owner, or co-owners, and the thing owned was conceived as excluding all other people from all possibility of asserting a similar relationship to the same thing."

Diósdi 1970, 124, "we are led to the inevitable conclusion that Roman ownership has always been, to adopt a contemporary terminology, an absolute right." See also Diósdi 1970, 131.

In contrast, see Honoré 1961, 144: "'Absolute' is perhaps the most ambiguous word met in discussions of ownership. Sometimes it is used to deny the 'temporary' (intransmissible or determinate) character of an interest, sometimes to deny its defeasible character (liable to be divested by another, liable to escheat or forfeiture), sometimes to emphasize its exemption from social control. In the last sense, ownership has never been absolute. Even in the most individualistic ages of Rome and the United States, it has had a social aspect. This has usually been expressed in such incidents of ownership as the prohibition of harmful use, liability to execution for debt, to taxation and to expropriation by the public authority."

9. See Rodger 1972, 38–89, 140–66, on this and, in the same vein, on a neighbor not needing to accept huge amounts of run-off from his upstream neighbor. Rodger's analysis shows infringements on ownership caused by controllable (i.e., neighbors) or uncontrollable (i.e., excessive rainfall) external factors and are solved within a legal framework.

10. See recently, Giglio 2018, 76–107, who argues that the conflicts of ownership rights that arise under situations like *duplex dominium* make it clear that ownership under Roman law was a relative system even in the classical period. The literature on ownership is vast, see in particular Cortese 1988; Diósdi 1970; Capogrossi Colognesi 1969; Watson 1968a; Honoré 1961; Kaser 1956. Capogrossi Colognesi 2016, 524–36, offers a recent overview. Most relevant to this project, Birks 1985.

11. On the content, see Birks 1985, 7 (see also Honoré 1961), and concept, Birks 1985, 27. Birks concludes that while there were minimal restrictions on ownership there was no legal impediment to the creation of such restrictions; as such, ownership with respect to content cannot be deemed absolute. However, he shows that the concept of ownership was "distinct, singular, and exclusive" or absolute (Birks 1985, 31). Giglio 2018, 95–99, offers some criticism of Birks' understanding of the concept of ownership.

cupied with "legal insecurities" (e.g., compulsory acquisition). My book instead focuses on representations of "factual insecurities"[12] as my aim is to interpret the lived experience of the owner and enslaved person rather than legal theory or the legal remedies available.

A factual insecurity might be understood as a nagging feeling or concern about the place of trust fundamental to any owner-slave relationship; specifically, such insecurity manifests when an owner is not sure whether their slave will behave as they have ordered. This is where, I argue, we can see the limits of ownership. While a farmhand who spent their days in the fields and nights in their slave quarters had the ability to cause trouble for their owner through what is often called day-to-day resistance (e.g., slow productivity, feigning illness), their owner had the ability to chain them and render them unproductive, but harmless. There is little question about an owner's ability physically to dominate their slaves. Slaves who were placed in a position of trust and had access to the world outside their owner's house, however, reveal the tenuous relationship between the ownership of the slaveholder and the autonomy of such slaves. The freedman Sabinus' ignorance of whether his slave is reciting what he asked exemplifies a factual insecurity of ownership, albeit a relatively harmless one. For while few Roman owners explicitly examined the ownership of their slaves' minds the way Seneca does, fewer still would not have wondered from time to time about their slaves' characters and loyalties. The very fact that an owner must seek out, investigate, consider, and ultimately put faith in their slave raises a number of challenges for the owner-slave relationship.

As noted, studies of ownership typically fixate on transitions arising due to acquisition, alienation, or conflicts of ownership. In part, this is because such moments provide points where the law can intervene, and most studies of ownership are legal in nature. However, this approach overlooks the in-between, the generally long and mundane middle period that exists between an owner and their property. For human property, this period makes up the whole of the owner-slave relationship; it is structured around ownership but is a tenure during which there is little legal recourse between the two actors. It is helpful then to begin this book, which fixates on moments of tension and insecurity, with an analysis of the in-between, day-to-day experience of owner and slave. Alongside the freedman Sabinus from Seneca's letter, a second ancient and extralegal approach to ownership is helpful in this respect: Epictetus on what one truly owns.

12. Birks 1985, 13–14, lists a few factual insecurities.

While for those who wrote on the matter there was a consensus that slaves did indeed have minds of their own, there is no clear consensus on what this mental autonomy looked like in practice. However, what becomes evident is that people writing about the mind think in terms of ownership, and equally, those writing about ownership think in terms of the mind. In the first chapter (1.1) of his *Discourses*, Epictetus, the formerly enslaved Stoic teacher, is concerned with internal freedom. He argues that this freedom is left to the individual and cannot be controlled by others, whether that be an owner, a more powerful friend, or even the emperor. Epictetus frames his discussion of what is under a person's control, namely their will, in the language of ownership.

Epictetus' belief that nothing can take control over the internal will of a person without their consent alleviates the reality that everyone is subject to fate and circumstance. His examples of such attempts at mental control come from Neronian Rome: The emperor ordered a man, Lateranus, to be beheaded because of his involvement with the Pisonian Conspiracy, the plot to murder and replace Nero. When the freedman Epaphroditus[13]—Nero's secretary and Epictetus' former owner—asked Lateranus his offense, he responded that he would only give information to Epaphroditus' owner (i.e., Nero) and promptly presented his neck for his sentence. Tacitus' account of the death reveals that the very tribune who executed Lateranus was a part of the conspiracy as well, but Lateranus did not give him up.[14]

This tale serves as a model of behavior for those faced with bodily harm or strife. Using the examples of Lateranus and others who stood up to Nero, Epictetus takes his reader through how they ought to respond to death, exile, bondage, or imprisonment—the predictable outcomes for a conspirator. These fates are out of the victims' control as they pertain to the physical body; the only way that Lateranus or any student of Epictetus can resist subjugation is by not divulging information. Epictetus prefaces these scenarios with the question, "'What aid, then, must we have ready to hand in such circumstances?' Why, what else than the knowledge of what is mine, and what is not mine, and what is possible for me, and what is not possible for me?" ('Τί οὖν δεῖ πρόχειρον ἔχειν ἐν τοῖς τοιούτοις;' τί γὰρ ἄλλο ἢ τί ἐμὸν καὶ τί οὐκ ἐμὸν καὶ τί μοι ἔξεστιν καὶ τί

13. Tacitus (*Ann.* 15.55) refers to Epaphroditus as "Nero's freedman" (*libertus Neronis*), though there is some suggestion that he was freed by Claudius. It is not clear if he was already at this point or soon-to-be Nero's *a libellis* (secretary in charge of legal petitions).

14. Tac. *Ann.* 15.49, 60, and Epict. *Diss.* 1.1.19.

μοι οὐκ ἔξεστιν;).[15] The key is to truly understand what is under a person's control; for Epictetus that is one's *prohairesis*, which can be translated as one's will or moral purpose.[16] By keeping a hold on his *prohairesis*, Lateranus can endure what is physically done to him without any internal compromise. Epictetus discusses the relationship between a person and their *prohairesis* in terms of possession and power; he uses *procheiros* ("to hand"), which both indicates possession (as does *emos*)[17] and having something at your ready, to describe this relationship. The body, in contrast, is expendable and easily controlled by another. In each of his proposed physical scenarios (death, exile, bondage, imprisonment), Epictetus describes the appropriate reaction as being mentally at peace with the situation—"but must I die groaning?" or "but does anyone keep me from going into exile with a smile, cheerful and serene?"—yet willing to concede the vulnerability of the body—"What do you mean, man? You can fetter my leg, but not even Zeus can conquer my will (*prohairesis*)" or "Did I ever say that my neck was the only neck that couldn't be severed?"[18]

The idea of a person owning their volition is a central aspect of Epictetus' philosophy.[19] A student of Epictetus can refuse to divulge his secrets since this

---

15. Epict. *Diss.* 1.1.21. Dobbin translation with some modifications for Epictetus. See also Epict. *Diss.* 4.1.72–75 where Epictetus reasons that while one may prohibit you from taking a walk (or other physical actions) no one can force another to desire or not to desire another.

16. Long 2002, 28, suggests that *prohairesis*, a favorite term of Epictetus, be translated as "volition" or "will." On Epictetus' choice of *prohairesis* (instead of *hegemonikon*), see Long 2002, 211. It also has an element of freedom, as he says at 11, "the contrast between a mental freedom available in principle to anyone and self-inflicted slavery encapsulates his chief message throughout." See Long 2002, 207–30, for further discussion on *prohairesis*.

17. On *emos* being used for ownership, see Diósdi 1970, 60, on "*meum esse*" and *LSJ* II.3.

18. Epict. *Diss.* 1.1.22–25, "I must die. But must I die groaning? I must be fettered. And crying too? I must be exiled; but does anyone keep me from going with a smile, cheerful and serene? 'Reveal your secrets.' I refuse, for this is up to me. 'But I will fetter you.' What do you mean, man? You can fetter my leg, but not even Zeus can conquer my will. My leg you will fetter, but not even Zeus can conquer my will. 'I will throw you in prison.' My body, you mean. 'I will behead you.' Did I ever say that my neck was the only neck that couldn't be severed? These are the things that you ought to practice if you study philosophy, these are the things you ought to write down every day, the things you ought to exercise yourself in" (ἀποθανεῖν με δεῖ· μή τι οὖν καὶ στένοντα; δεθῆναι· μή τι καὶ θρηνοῦντα; φυγαδευθῆναι· μή τις οὖν κωλύει γελῶντα καὶ εὐθυμοῦντα καὶ εὐροοῦντα; "εἰπὲ τὰ ἀπόρρητα.' οὐ λέγω· τοῦτο γὰρ ἐπ' ἐμοί ἐστιν. 'ἀλλὰ δήσω σε.' ἄνθρωπε, τί λέγεις; ἐμέ; τὸ σκέλος μου δήσεις, τὴν προαίρεσιν δὲ οὐδ' ὁ Z<εὺς νι>κῆσαι δύναται. 'εἰς φυλακήν σε βαλῶ.' τὸ <σω>μάτιον. 'ἀποκεφαλίσω σε.' πότε οὖν σοι εἶπον, ὅτι μόνου ἐμοῦ ὁ τράχηλος ἀναπότμητός ἐστι; ταῦτα ἔδει μελετᾶν τοὺς φιλοσοφοῦντας, ταῦτα καθ' ἡμέραν γράφειν, ἐν τούτοις γυμνάζεσθαι).

19. On the relationship between Stoicism and property, see Long 2006, 339–40. For a very brief explanation on the relationship between *prohairesis* and assenting to a particular *phantasia*, see Bartsch 2007; and see Braicovich 2010 for a longer discussion. Epictetus is not alone in his consideration of mental autonomy as independent from status and situation; for example, Seneca tells us

control is in his power (*touto gar ep' emoi estin*); not even Zeus, let alone a mere mortal like the emperor (who can admittedly put someone in any number of grievous circumstances), has the power to affect one's will. Elsewhere, Epictetus discusses the inalienability, and thus inaccessibility to others, of the things that matter to us, namely one's will—and he does this in the language of power and domination (*dunamai* and *archō*).[20] The capability of another to rule does not extend beyond the physical. As we will see, this inalienability and inaccessibility is found in juristic discussions considering the tension between the ownership of the slaveholder and the mental autonomy of the slave: While the slave is without question under the ownership of the slaveholder, the owner cannot exert this domination over the slave's mind.

In the process of arguing that only those who have rid themselves of worldly or bodily cares are free, Epictetus defines the free person, the slave, and ownership:

> The unhindered person is free, and for them, things are to hand as he wants them. Whoever can be hindered, that is, coerced, impeded, or forced into a situation unwillingly—that person is a slave. Who is unhindered? The person wanting nothing that belongs to another. What things belong to another? The things that are not up to us: either to have, or not to have, or to have the right ones or in the right condition. Accordingly, the body and its limbs belong to another, and material goods belong to another. If, then, you covet any of these things as if they were your own, you will pay the penalty appropriate for someone wanting things that belong to another.
>
> ὁ ἀκώλυτος ἄνθρωπος ἐλεύθερος, ᾧ πρόχειρα τὰ πράγματα ὡς βούλεται. ὃν δ᾽ ἔστιν ἢ κωλῦσαι ἢ ἀναγκάσαι ἢ ἐμποδίσαι ἢ ἄκοντα εἴς τι ἐμβαλεῖν, δοῦλός ἐστι. τίς δ᾽ ἀκώλυτος; ὁ μηδενὸς τῶν ἀλλοτρίων ἐφιέμενος. τίνα δ᾽ ἀλλότρια;

---

that slaves are only slaves in body but are free in mind (*mens*), Sen. *Ben.* 3.18–21. This passage is discussed in chapter 5.

20. Epict. *Diss.* 1.9.21, "For what will they do to us? The things they have power to do will be of no concern to us; and as for the things that matter to us, these they are powerless to affect. Who, then, will rule over someone with such convictions?" (τί γὰρ ἡμῖν ποιήσουσιν; ἃ δύνανται ποιῆσαι, τούτων οὐκ ἐπιστρεψόμεθα· ὧν ἡμῖν μέλει, ταῦτα οὐ δύνανται. τίς οὖν ἔτι ἄρξει τοῦ οὕτω διακειμένου;).

See also, for example, Epict. *Diss.* 1.1.10–13: Epictetus has Zeus explain that he himself could not give the body (*sōmation*) and property (*ktēsidion*) to man to truly have ownership over, showing us the limits of Zeus, and what Zeus then did give to man. He also refers to the body as "clay" (*pēlos*)—Horace *Ep.* 2.2 describes a young homeborn slave as clay as well, discussed in chapter 1.

> ἃ οὐκ ἔστιν ἐφ' ἡμῖν οὔτ' ἔχειν οὔτε μὴ ἔχειν οὔτε ποιὰ ἔχειν ἢ πῶς ἔχοντα. οὐκοῦν τὸ σῶμα ἀλλότριον, τὰ μέρη αὐτοῦ ἀλλότρια, ἡ κτῆσις ἀλλοτρία. ἂν οὖν τινι τούτων ὡς ἰδίῳ προσπαθῇς, δώσεις δίκας ἃς ἄξιον τὸν τῶν ἀλλοτρίων ἐφιέμενον.[21]

The free person is construed as someone who only desires what they will always have control over, or what is up to them (*eph' hēmin*).[22] This, for Epictetus, is what the *prohairesis* assents to and what he describes in the possessive language of being at hand (*procheira ta pragmata*, and earlier *procheiros*). Meanwhile, the slave is hindered in various ways: coerced by the external compulsion of another person (*anankasai*), impeded by external constraints (*empodisai*, literally "to have bound someone's feet"), and forced to do something they do not want to do (*akonta eis ti embalein*), all because of a mistaken attachment to the body or worldly possessions. The slave then is not a slave for Epictetus because of legal status, but for a failure to realize what is up to them, under their power, or beyond their control. This discussion is conducted in the language of private property; Epictetus construes the inability to have complete control over the body, its limbs (*to sōma, ta merē autou*), or other worldly possessions (*ktēsis*) as a lack of ownership over those things (using *allotrios* six times in this passage). For Epictetus ownership is absolute and the slave—the person who covets these things as if they were their own (*hōs idiōi*)—is a thief.

Along with his discussion of *prohairesis* in terms of ownership, Epictetus considers its marketability.[23] People are free to do what they like with their

---

21. Epict. *Diss.* 4.1.128–130 (my translation). This view is presented in an expanded summary in Epictetus' *Enchiridion* 1.1.

22. On *eph' hēmin* in Epictetus, see Frede 2012, 44–48, as well as Frede 2007 and Bobzien 1998, 331–38.

23. Epict. *Diss.* 1.2.33, "Only consider at what price you sell your will. If nothing else, man, at least don't sell it cheap" (Μόνον σκέψαι, πόσου πωλεῖς τὴν σεαυτοῦ προαίρεσιν. ἄνθρωπε. εἰ μηδὲν ἄλλο, μὴ ὀλίγου αὐτὴν πωλήσῃς).

On selling your *prohairesis* too cheaply see, also, when Epictetus chastises those who lower themselves to flattery and genuflection of slaves in order to gain a position: Epict. *Diss.* 4.1.148: "Or when you kiss the hands of other people's slaves, making yourself the slave of slaves, all for the sake of these great and glorious honours and offices—what can you expect then?" (ἢ πάλιν ὅταν ὑπὲρ τῶν μεγάλων τούτων καὶ σεμνῶν ἀρχῶν καὶ τιμῶν τὰς χεῖρας τῶν ἀλλοτρίων δούλων καταφιλῇς, ἵνα μηδ' ἐλευθέρων δοῦλος ᾖς;).

Conversely, see Epict. *Diss.* 4.1.151 where Epictetus ties care of the body to lack of freedom: "'Are you free, then?' By God I wish I were, and I pray to be; but I still can't face my masters, I continue to value my poor body, I attach great importance to keeping healthy—though it isn't healthy at all" (Σὺ οὖν, φησίν, ἐλεύθερος εἶ;—Θέλω νὴ τοὺς θεοὺς καὶ εὔχομαι, ἀλλ' οὔπω δύναμαι ἀντιβλέψαι τοῖς κυρίοις, ἔτι τιμῶ τὸ σωμάτιον, ὁλόκληρον αὐτὸ ἔχειν ἀντὶ πολλοῦ ποιοῦμαι καίτοι μηδ' ὁλόκληρον ἔχων).

prohairesis; they can hand it over to someone or something because of desires, needs, or persuasion, but it remains up to them whether they do so or not. Epictetus, a formerly enslaved citizen-subject of the imperial government, tells his pupils that regardless of who they are and what their legal status is, they can redeem a space of autonomy in their minds. This idea that one can give over one's will can also be found in the Roman jurists' conceptions of a slaveholder's ownership and control of their slaves. Despite our author's theorizing, however, the lived experience of marketing one's will was a bit different; we should not forget that enslaved people often complied with their owners' orders and desires as a means of surviving and living in and through the bounds of domination and enslavement. Many slaves did not have the flexibility to reserve their will for self-motivated reasons.[24]

Seneca, Epictetus, and others of the philosophical class discussed a slave's mental autonomy in an attempt to show how a bound man still had the freedom to be a good man, but this has been dismissed as a merely philosophical argument and not a legal one that could be put into practice. While the letter of Seneca discussed above is a moral lesson, this same conversation regarding the absolute knowledge of a slave's internal attributes is behind some of the reasoning of the jurists and other Romans concerned with slave management. Meanwhile, if the slaveholder were to own their slave through and through as Seneca's Sabinian anecdote suggests, then a slave would never be wayward on account of his own volition or the persuasion of others, and, conversely, would never act to the benefit of the owner without express instruction. The freedman Sabinus seems to believe that owners have ownership over the mind of the slave even if they do not know the mind, while Seneca and Epictetus hold that no one, not even an owner, can compromise the autonomy of the slave's mind without their agreement.

The ancients were not alone in thinking about the mind of the slave and ownership. *Invention of a Slave*, an 1858 opinion of the attorney general of the United States, stated that the inventions of enslaved or free African Americans were unpatentable. The year before, a white enslaver queried whether he owned "the fruits of the mind . . . of his slave" and applied for a patent for a product invented by his enslaved blacksmith, Ned. The "double Cotton Scraper, and two plows" was innovative, but the patent was denied as 1857 was also the year of *Dred Scott v. Sandford*, which held that African Americans were not citizens. In

24. On agency, see below and note 43.

order to get a patent, one must be a citizen and be the original inventor. Ned was not a citizen, and his enslaver had stated clearly in his application that it was Ned who invented the machine. The brief opinion also warned that if Ned's owner were to apply for the patent in his own name, it would not be upheld in court as it was not (as he had stated) an invention of his own design. The invention of the slave does not belong to the owner in this way. The position of Ned's slave owner is a variation on that of Seneca's freedman Sabinus. As American legal scholar Kara W. Swanson puts it: "To him, chattel slavery meant ownership alike of the labor of the hands and the fruit of the mind."[25]

These scenarios contemplate the ownership of the mind of the slave and complicate the relationship between owner and slave. An owner may own their slave in body, but never know their mind. To return to Rome, what we see is not our modern questioning of the absolute nature of ownership, but how the Romans themselves considered it. While legally the *dominium* of owners over their slaves was nearly absolute, the precautions taken because of the inability to have total control over slaves revealed the anxieties of a slave society. This issue is particularly relevant in Rome as owners would place slaves in positions of trust, such as in charge of accounts and overseas affairs. This book is framed around legal scenarios such as purchase and account management that instigate and react to moments of insecurity in the ownership of enslaved people. Seneca and Epictetus were not jurists, but it is only by analyzing these literary and philosophical sources together with the juridical ones that we can approach the role of the mind and how it creates problems and tensions for slave ownership.

Studying the jurists not to understand the legal institution of slavery but the owner-slave relationship, and shifting of the locus of study to the mind, necessitates an examination of other sources that discuss the mind. This study of nonlegal sources is helpful for understanding how the jurists discuss the autonomy of the mind as these sources share a common vocabulary. The language of liberty and autonomy we find in Seneca and Epictetus is intrinsically a legal language. Seneca's discussion of mental autonomy in, for example, *On Benefits*, is particularly relevant for understanding the mind of the slave: He casts the question of the liberty of the slave's mind and the ownership of the slaveholder not only in legal language, but within the parameters of the law.[26] Similarly, as

25. This discussion relies on Kara W. Swanson's "Race and Selective Memory: Reflections on *Invention of a Slave*"; the quotation is found in Swanson 2020, 1087.

26. Sen. *Ben*. 3.19–21.

we just saw, Epictetus discusses volition (*prohairesis*) in terms of ownership and possession.[27] This book places juristic sources in conversation with the philosophical and literary in an effort to locate broader cultural sentiments and representations rather than genre-specific ones.

This comparative examination of texts discussing the mind of the slave is grounded in a study of language, which contributes to our understanding of the Latin language of the mind (*animus*, *mens*, and *ingenium*). This language encompasses the thinking, purposive, and emotional mind of a human being either free or enslaved. Before discussing our sources further, however, it is important to be cognizant of the role and limitations of language in our ancient texts, regardless of genre. While some of these sources draw on witnessing the experiences of the enslaved and their own interactions with them, they are not firsthand accounts of enslavement and are all largely approached from the subject position of the enslaver and the slaving class. Coming from this perspective, the jurists interpret the mind with generic biases and are purposefully working to enslave and dominate the slave in order to exploit them for the benefit of the owner. They consider the mind then in constrained ways and with express goals in play.

In light of these limitations, this project reads a range of pragmatic texts—legal documents, juristic writings, and agricultural handbooks—alongside contemporary philosophers, rhetoricians, and historiographers in order to learn about the Roman conceptions of knowledge and autonomy that bear upon the question of slavery. Concerned with upholding and interpreting Rome's civil law, the Roman jurists' judgment of slaves' actions at times diverges from the literary sources' treatment of similar scenarios. Jurists' and literary writers' diverse opinions about the double nature of slaves, and the relationship between those opinions and actual practice, provide inroads into the issues at the heart of understanding the character of slave ownership at Rome.

The rhetorical training and philosophical thought of the period are a fruitful place to consider this relationship. It is not a matter of how closely the "law" of literary works can be mapped onto the law of legal sources,[28] but rather a matter of studying the two together to gain a better understanding of the intellectual and social atmosphere that gave rise to the sort of law and legal thinking practiced in the first centuries of the Empire.[29] The education of the elite is

27. Epict. *Diss.*1.1.21–25, discussed above.
28. Bloomer 2011, 178–91 and Bloomer 2007, 304–5.
29. Montefusco 1996, 209–28, on the ties between rhetoric and jurisprudence, in particular, 210.

particularly important because it helps reinforce the idea of a cultural unity among the elite classes regardless of their later professions. While not a jurist, Aulus Gellius devotes several narratives to the discussion of legal language, such as the differing opinions of the jurists on the meaning of disease and defect. That he is a contemporary of the Antonine jurists and shared their cultural interests can be seen, for example, in his exploration of the term *humanitas*.[30] Gellius' work demonstrates how knowledge of Roman law was a part of Roman education and elite culture; he underscores the idea that there was a cultural understanding of law and that the questions of juristic interpretation went beyond the courts.[31]

Outside of legal works, the question of the nature of slaves and the relationship between the owner and slave is not solely taken up by pragmatic literary texts that openly and expressly reflect on ownership and slave management. In letters between friends and in poetry, we find discussions on whether slaves have an essential nature, the qualities that make a good slave, anxieties about how to determine if a slave has those qualities, and concerns about purchasing bad slaves. The philosophical texts concern themselves with the nature of slavery and freedom in order to understand human nature and liberty in the imperial period; the genres and ends of these literary works are at times vastly different. Yet these writers were all members of the elite classes and likely slave owners; they had both a personal and societal interest in understanding the nature of slavery and enslavement. There is, for example, an inherent difference in the purposes of texts by the contemporaries Columella and Seneca. Columella is concerned with the nature of slaves with respect to the practice of farming; he seeks to control his slaves and exploit their ability to work in order to gain maximum economic results. Seneca instead is concerned with the question of the nature of slaves with respect to understanding freedom under empire. Studying the two together in terms of understanding ownership in itself and in relation to other superiorities, however, can be fruitful and shows us that it was not only philosophers or jurists in their separate domains who were considering these questions. In almost every literary genre, we find accounts of slaves who behaved in a particularly good or bad manner or in a way deemed unsuitable for their status, as well as the ramifications for the relationship between owner and slave. These literary sources discussing slaves

30. Gell. *NA* 13.17. See Howley 2018.
31. See Howley 2013.

influenced one another and contributed to an understanding of the expected behavior and mentality of someone in a state of slavery.

While these questions regarding the nature of Roman slave ownership have existed in literary sources since at least the time of Plautus (c. 254–184 BCE), this book will focus on the literature of the first centuries of the Empire because our high imperial legal sources predominantly come from the second and third century CE. As much as possible, this book attempts to compare contemporary sources. While the majority of the jurists discussed belong to the Antonine (117–192 CE) and Severan (193–235 CE) periods, when possible an effort is made to take note of the first-century CE jurists. This allows us to not only study a potential shift in juristic thought but also to locate commentary contemporary with many nonlegal sources such as Seneca and Columella, who wrote in the mid-first century CE. Although Cicero is much earlier than many of the jurists studied, his writings are also examined due to Cicero's tendency toward both the legal and philosophical; here it is also possible to track any shifts in thinking that might have occurred between the Late Republic and the Empire. Apart from these earlier sources, the prominent role of the Antonine jurists in the council of the emperor (*consilium principis*) is important because it allows us to understand the jurists, in their roles as advisors to the *princeps*, as a part of the imperial court. As such, their interpretations of edicts are concerned with both the protections of the rights of the owner and the societal ramifications of the laws in question.[32]

This book is indebted to the long and rich history of the study of ancient slavery, the modern era of which is still responding to Moses Finley's division of "slave societies" and "societies with slaves."[33] In the last forty years, scholars studying ancient slavery have often followed Orlando Patterson's formulation of slavery, which provocatively did not include ownership; slavery is for Patterson "the permanent, violent domination of natally alienated and generally dishonored persons," or "social death."[34] Recently, John Bodel and Walter Scheidel's *On Human Bondage: After Slavery and Social Death* assessed the state of the field thirty-five years after the publication of *Slavery and Social Death*. In the volume, David Lewis offers a critique of Patterson's dismissal of property as

32. Ibbetson 2005, 184–85; Bauman 1989; Honoré 1981.
33. See Finley (1980) 1998, though he first used the division in 1968. See discussion of Lenski below, a critique of this approach.
34. Patterson 1982, 13. Ancient historians have adopted Patterson's model including Bradley 1994. See Vlassopoulos 2011 on the differing approaches.

fundamental to the definition of slavery, and many scholars of antiquity have followed suit.[35]

In a book such as this, which holds ownership to be foundational to understanding the owner-slave relationship both at its extremes and in the necessary day-to-day give and take on both sides, the property element must be considered. Building on the definitions of Patterson and that of the 1926 Slavery Convention, Noel Lenski recently put together a description of slavery that holds both social death and property together because, as he notes, "such a bipartite approach acknowledges the reality that slavery is fundamentally a dialectical relationship."[36] He offers the following:

> Slavery is the enduring, violent domination of natally alienated and inherently dishonored individuals (slaves) that are controlled by owners (masters) who are permitted in their social context to use and enjoy, sell and exchange, and abuse and destroy them as property.[37]

This approach stresses both "the benefits the slave offers to the master" via property rights and "the disadvantages imposed by the master on the person of the slave" via social death.[38] Pushing further, Kostas Vlassopoulos has argued for strategies of studying slavery that do away with static and essentializing histories. He emphasizes the importance of holding in mind the various contexts of slaving and the multiple forms of identity, at times generated from being human property and at other times despite it, that are possible for enslaved people.[39] This framework contains the flexibility needed to grapple with the Roman slaving system while not losing sight of the individuals involved. This approach has also been adopted by scholars of the early medieval period, as can be seen in Alice Rio's *Slavery after Rome, 500–1100*, which expertly showcases the elasticity needed in studying slavery across boundaries and time periods.

---

35. Lewis 2017 does this most explicitly, critiquing Patterson's understanding of ownership vis-à-vis Honoré 1961, but see also Lewis 2018, 25–56. Lewis does note that social death is a useful concept to think about the experience of the enslaved. On the adoption or critique of Patterson by ancient historians, see Bodel and Scheidel 2017 more generally.
36. Lenski 2018a, 50.
37. Lenski 2018a, 51, see 47–57 on the development and use of this model. Lenski's project here, along with his coeditor Catherine M. Cameron, is to critique Moses Finley's framework of slave societies in contrast to societies with slaves that has dominated the study of ancient slavery since the late 1960s. See, on the history of the concept, Lenski 2018b.
38. Lenski 2018a, 50–51.
39. Vlassopoulos 2021. This emphasis on keeping in mind various contexts of slaving is held also in Lewis 2018 about "Greek" slavery.

Turning from questions of systems, institutions, and definitions, scholars attend to the lived experience of enslaved people themselves. Much of the scholarship on the Roman owner-slave relationship centers the physical domination of the owner over his slave, and a standard work remains Keith Bradley's *Slaves and Masters in the Roman Empire: A Study in Social Control.* Edward Cohen's recent volume, *Ancient Inequalities: Affluent Slaves, Businesswomen, Legal Fictions*, draws needed attention to seeming status outliers such as, notably for this book, slaves in charge of accounts. Cohen emphasizes the vast sums that these enslaved accountants controlled in order to complicate the idea of status necessarily correlating to wealth. For Cohen, however, the enslaver—the legal owner both of the sums that the accountant controlled and of the accountant themself—is largely absent; the present volume looks instead to these same enslaved accountants to consider the negotiated and ever evolving relationship between slaves and their owners.[40]

To that end, I follow scholars who have built on the work of James C. Scott and greatly furthered our understanding of slavery on an interpersonal level. In *Domination and the Arts of Resistance: Hidden Transcripts*, Scott argues that the dominant discourse of society is a product of elite anxiety rather than acquiescence of those subject to the elite; there are "hidden transcripts," or instances of resistance, that materialize obliquely and particularly when the oppressed are speaking to one another rather than to their oppressors. Marshalling Scott, Amy Richlin has done much to illuminate the experience of enslaved people, freed people, and the broader Roman populace in *Slave Theater in the Roman Republic: Plautus and Popular Comedy*.[41] Along similar lines, the work of Sandra Joshel has fundamentally changed the way historians read resistance in Roman slavery.[42] The material of the jurists is veiled differently, and perhaps more heavily, than Plautus, but Scott's work on resistance can help critically situate the mind of the slave as constructed by Roman jurists and slave owners. Attending to moments where we can locate hidden transcripts can forestall sliding into the solipsism of the master narrative as truth.

"The mind of the slave," as we largely have it, is a construct of the Roman jurists and other thinkers. While we must approach ancient sources critically in

40. Cohen 2023.
41. Richlin 2017. Plautine studies have focused on the complex and diverse forms of owner-slave relations; see also K. McCarthy, *Slaves, Masters, and the Art of Authority in Plautine Comedy* (2000) and R. Stewart, *Plautus and Roman Slavery* (2012).
42. Joshel 2013 most explicitly but see also Joshel and Petersen 2014.

order not to conflate masterly ideals with the realities of enslavement, the construct is important for the intellectual history of slavery because it advanced the development of concepts essential to slaving, particularly ownership. It is equally important for the study of enslaved people in the Roman world because such concepts played a double role in both dictating the parameters within which enslaved people could live and reacting to the lives of enslaved people. This is the case even if the precise details of an enslaved person's life are lost to us. In some cases, the questions put forth in juristic literature were based on historical incidents with identifying details scrubbed out. In other cases, the questions raised by the jurists were academic—to understand where the boundaries of legal concepts lay. These two types of cases are revelatory of the experience of enslaved people because they represent, both in the everyday and in the extreme, the wider cultural context in which we might understand the actions of enslaved people. As scholars such as Marisa J. Fuentes, Saidiya Hartman, and Walter Johnson have argued, the context, that is to say, the conditions of their enslavement, deeply guided the actions of enslaved people. These scholars' purpose is to complicate the binary of resistance and compliance that often arises from studying slavery through the lens of agency.[43] Incorporating comparative histories of slavery and Black feminist theory, the work of Dan-el Padilla Peralta has brought attention to these difficulties in the study of enslavement in antiquity.[44] Most enslaved people did not live their lives within this binary as the situations dealt to them were rarely without complicating factors. What to do and how to act was not always clear; these moments of uncertainty are the object of study in this book.

On terminology and translation: All literary translations are my own unless otherwise specified. I have preserved the standard Watson edition translation of the *Digest of Justinian* except where I thought modification would help provide clarity especially to a nonspecialist audience. As noted just above, the jurists made a practice of removing the identifying details from their works for the sake of generalizing. On the other hand, at times it is unclear whether a writer like Seneca is discussing an actual enslaved individual or an archetype he has given a name. When discussing actual individuals in the historical record

---

43. Fuentes 2016, 1–12; Johnson 2003; Hartman 1997. See, for example, Hartman 1997, at 54: "The particular status of the slave as object and as subject requires a careful consideration of the notion of agency if one wants to do more than 'endow' the enslaved with agency as some sort of gift dispensed by historians and critics to the dispossessed."

44. See, for example, Padilla Peralta 2023, 2020, 2017.

or people at least presented as such, I will use the term enslaved person as much as possible with the hope of creating a less essentializing narrative.[45] However, I do not think it is useful to move away from the terminology of owner or slave entirely both because these are legal statuses and because I believe, as problematic as these terms are for a relationship between two human beings, they deserve more study not less.

Fault Lines

This book is organized around three crucial and uncertain stages of enslavement; these instances of uncertainty showcase fault lines in ownership: when to buy, when to trust, and when to free a slave. While these moments are instigated by the owner and begin from the owner's perspective, each one represents an instance of uncertainty as the owner must attempt to know the slave. *When to buy*: What is the value of a particular slave? What kind of slave are they? How does the owner decide they will be a good slave? What is a good slave? *When to trust*: Is the slave competent and loyal enough to make financial decisions on behalf of the owner? Do they have the moral fortitude to resist bribes or running away? *When to free*: What virtues has the slave displayed to show themself ready, in the eyes of the owner and the law, to be a Roman citizen? Are the qualities that make a slave a good slave the same as those that will make them a good citizen? These three moments (purchase, placement or loss of work position, and the end of the owner-slave relationship) reflect the constant evaluation of slaves that recurred throughout their lives and underscore that slave ownership was not static and unchanging. The answers to these questions of character and intention invariably and essentially affect the owner and the slave themself.

Chapters 1 and 2 study the difficulties inherent to selecting good slaves. Chapter 1 examines the process of evaluation: What qualities did owners seek in slaves and how did they go about determining whether a slave had those qualities? Columella, Seneca, and Pliny all discuss the appraisal of slaves for different purposes; their discussions reveal this process of appraisal as an attempt to understand not only the physical nature of a slave but also their character, tal-

45. See Foreman et al., "Writing About Slavery/Teaching About Slavery: This Might Help."

ents, and mental weaknesses.[46] The chapter focuses on the evaluative and examinatory process because it is the first act of domination over a slave and a first insight into the relationship between the mind of the slave and the ownership of the slaveholder. Through an examination of the terms *morbus* (disease) and *vitium* (defect) in the Edict of the Aediles[47] and Roman literature and philosophy,[48] this chapter shows the medicalization of unwanted servile behavior as moral defect. I focus on cases where slave behavior is wayward enough that the jurists deem the slaves "mentally defective." The slave who is found to have a mental defect is exhibiting a mentality that is not beneficial to the owner. I argue that the jurists emphasize the importance of slave speech because it was thought to reveal or lead to an understanding of a slave's character and intention; as such, speech determined whether the slave was mentally healthy and morally good. Examining this evaluative process at the slave market underscores that the value of the slave was in their utility, and part of this utility was the owner's ability to have a level of control over the mind of the slave.

Chapter 2 discusses the cases of the deranged slave (*servus furiosus*) and the runaway slave (*servus fugitivus*), two situations in which slaves have mental defects (*vitia animi*) so severe that, according to the Edict of the Aediles, they were allowed to be returned to the seller. The jurists discuss different forms of madness, including a *servus phrenētikos*, a *servus lunaticus*, and *servi melancholici*, but the category most distinct and most discussed by the jurists is the *servus furiosus*.[49] Both free and slave *furiosi* are equated with children (*impuberes*) by the jurists when considering delictual liability;[50] they lack many legal rights and are not able to be the object of legal responsibilities because of their insufficient reasoning capabilities. The *furiosus* is deemed not to have a will by both the jurist Pomponius[51] and Cicero.[52] As such, the slaveholder cannot hope to extend their ownership over the slave's mind to ensure that they act accord-

---

46. Columella *Rust.* 1.8.15–16; Sen. *Ep.* 47.15; Plin. *Ep.* 1.21.
47. D. 21.1, on definitions, see D. 21.1.1.7–8 Ulpian, *Curule Aediles' Edict*, book 1; D. 50.16.101.2 Modestinus, *Distinctions*, book 9; G. 3.214; Gell. *NA* 4.2.2–5.
48. Including Celsus *Med.* 3.5.5; Vitr. *De arch.* 2.8.12; Sen. *Ep.* 109.7; Cic. *Fin.* 5.35, *Tusc.* 4.
49. The *phrenētikos*: D. 21.1.1.9 Ulpian, *Curule Aediles' Edict*, book 1; *lunaticus*: D. 21.1.43.6 Paul, *Curule Aediles' Edict*, book 1; *melancholici*: D. 21.1.2, Paul, *Curule Aediles' Edict*, book 1; *furiosus*: D. 21.1.23.2, Ulpian, *Curule Aediles' Edict*, book 1, citing Pomponius, D. 21.1.43.6 Paul, *Curule Aediles' Edict*, book 1.
50. D. 9.2.5.2 Ulpian, *Edict*, book 18, citing Pegasus; D. 21.1.23.2 Ulpian, *Curule Aediles' Edict*, book 1, citing Pomponius; D.47.10.3.1 Ulpian, *Edict*, book 56; G. 3.106–109. See also D. 6.1.60 Pomponius, *Sabinus*, book 29; D. 48.8.12, Modestinus, *Rules*, book 8.
51. D. 50.17.40 Pomponius, *Sabinus*, book 34.
52. Cic. *Tusc.* 3.11, Cicero's understanding of the *furiosus* comes in part from the Twelve Tables.

ing to the owner's desires. The second half of the chapter focuses on the runaway and the related scenarios of the suicidal and wandering (*erro*) slave; jurists treated the slave's intention in each case as central to determining if the slave was a runaway. In contrast to the *furiosus*, the runaway possesses their full faculties, but the slave themself takes their mind (and usually, though not always, their person) away from their owner's property. Pulled together from different branches of literature and cultural knowledge, this constructed understanding of madness becomes the manner in which the Romans understood wayward slaves. Examining which mental ailments allow restitution shows which defects rendered a slave effectively unable to be owned by a slaveholder. The inability of the owner to predict that the slave they are purchasing will run away or become deranged comes to be explained by the fact that they have a mental defect (*vitium animi*). In this chapter, I argue that part of ownership must be understood to be not only the owner's ability to control their slave but also the slave's ability to be controlled. The *furiosus* and *fugitivus* show us a limit of ownership: These mental defects make the mind, essential to ownership, impermeable to the owner.

Chapters 3 and 4 reflect on the ownership of the slaveholder during the life of the slave and examine how the Romans balanced the financial and social need for competent and trusted slaves with the underlying anxieties of a slave society. Chapter 3 considers the necessary economic relationship between the ownership of the slaveholder and the agency and mental autonomy of the slave. Before turning to legal matters, the chapter begins with a consideration of Columella's idea of the *vilicus* or foreman. Columella fixates on the limitations of his foreman because of his servile nature (*ingenium servile*) and debates whether the foreman was nevertheless capable and trustworthy enough to perform high-level tasks responsibly.[53] The chapter then studies two legal situations: (1) slaves in charge of their owners' financial accounts and (2) indirect agency in commercial relations. The section on account management focuses on three passages that illustrate differing levels of autonomy of certain slave business agents.[54] Along a similar vein to Columella, the jurists discussing account management and indirect agency take note of a slave's capacity for responsibility and good faith. While the responsibility of anything gone awry in a business run by a slave would ultimately fall to their owner (they could surrender the

53. Columella *Rust.* 1.8.10.
54. D. 35.1.32 Africanus, *Questions*, book 9; D. 40.7.40pr Scaevola, *Digest*, book 24; D. 40.7.40.3 Scaevola, *Digest*, book 24.

slave or pay their debt), the introduction to the remedies on the *peculium* (an account managed by a slave) made an owner who claimed ignorance of their slave's actions less exposed.[55] In commercial relations, a slaveholder's ownership manifests in their accruement of property through the decisions and skills their slave uses; however, the owner does not know what the slave is specifically thinking and willing, and this mental autonomy is built into the law.

Chapter 4 instead examines instances when a slave's mental autonomy and agency are not in the service of their owner and are instead detrimental to them. The chapter considers the betrayal of the slave, their compulsion at the hands of a third party, and the implications for ownership through a reading of two legal scenarios: the action on corrupted slaves (*actio servi corrupti*) and noxal surrender. I argue that the juristic commentary on the *actio servi corrupti* removes the faculties that a slave has as a human being for independent thought and action; rather, the jurists emphasize the force and compulsion that a would-be corrupter must use to persuade a slave to betray their owner.[56] Ulpian's concern with the possible detrimental effects of tricksters on slaves illuminates Columella's counsel that slaves should be protected from life beyond the owner's house.[57] The chapter considers the failure of the owner in their role as protector of their slave and the condemnation of the free person who corrupts the slave as the corrupter of a household. Turning then to "guilty" slaves, where there is no free person to lay the blame on, I examine situations of noxal liability: An owner was accountable for their slaves even if they were unaware or not consenting of their actions. When a slave had committed an outrageous action, the owner could surrender the slave instead of paying damages.[58] This chapter studies the anxiety, found in both juristic and literary sources, between the need for highly talented and independent slaves and the concern about betrayal and moral corruption.

While the previous chapter looked at the effects that bad or insubordinate slaves had on ownership, the final section instead focuses on bad owners and virtuous slaves. Chapter 5 examines the end of the owner-slave relationship through two sets of restrictions: (1) the excessive cruelty on the part of the owner, which could lead to a forced sale of a slave; and (2) the Augustan legislation that put controls on manumission. Despite the oft-cited power of life and

55. D. 14.1.6 Paul, *Short Notes*, book 6pr.
56. Juristic discussion of the *actio servi corrupti* is largely found in D. 11.3.
57. D. 11.3.1.5 Ulpian, *Edict*, book 23; Columella *Rust.* 1.8.6–7.
58. D. 9.4.2 Ulpian, *Edict*, book 18.

death, there were some restrictions on what an owner could do with their slave (though enforcement is suspect), and literary authors tell moralizing stories of irrationally violent owners. I compare the infamous tale of the cruelty of Vedius Pollio and the clemency of the state, in the persona of the Emperor Augustus, with the rescript of Antoninus Pius that states that while the powers of owners should not be infringed upon, owners must justify severe violence toward their slaves or the state will intercede for the benefit of owners as a whole.[59] Making use of the juristic commentary on the *lex Aelia Sentia* and literary texts discussing virtuous slaves, I examine whether the status of slave precluded enslaved individuals from exhibiting the qualities and virtues of a good Roman citizen. In *On Benefits*, Seneca attempts to reconcile the capacity of slaves for natural goodness with their servile status;[60] Roman jurists show a similar preoccupation with slaves' actions when determining reasons to manumit. While the philosophers consider whether a slave can be a good person, the jurists measure the qualities of a good slave—one deserving of manumission—against what the Romans considered to be a good Roman; this section includes a study of trials of slaves who claimed to be free,[61] as well as philosophical discussions[62] of what made a person a slave. The book concludes with an epilogue reflecting on the implications of death as a form of loss and the importance of commemoration.

59. For the tale of Vedius Pollio, see Sen. *Ira* 3.40.1–3. Ulpian gives the rescript of Antoninus Pius, D. 1.6.2 Ulpian, *Duties of Proconsul*, book 8; cf. I. 1.8.1–2.
60. Sen. *Ben.* 3.
61. The *causa liberalis* is discussed in D. 40.12.
62. Primarily Dio Chrys. *Or.* 15.

PART ONE

New Slaves and New Owners

ONE
Evaluating Slaves

Listening

In a letter to his friend Plinius Paternus, Pliny the Younger discusses the importance of knowing the characters of his slaves and the best methods for discovering them at the slave market.

> Pliny sends his greetings to his friend Plinius Paternus
> I give as much credit to the judgment of your mind as to that of your eyes not because it is great (don't kid yourself), but because your taste is as good as mine, although that in and of itself is a lot. Joking aside, I think the slaves bought for me under your counsel are suitable. We'll see if they are worthy; in slaves we judge that sort of thing better by our ears than our eyes. Farewell.
>
> C. Plinius Plinio Paterno Suo S.
> Ut animi tui iudicio sic oculorum plurimum tribuo, non quia multum (ne tibi placeas) sed quia tantum quantum ego sapis; quamquam hoc quoque multum est. Omissis iocis credo decentes esse servos, qui sunt empti mihi ex consilio tuo. Superest ut frugi sint, quod de venalibus melius auribus quam oculis iudicatur. Vale.[1]

In this brief exchange, Pliny lays out his methodology for slave purchase and his anxieties about these transactions. Slave buying is a sensory experience: one

1. Plin. *Ep.* 1.21. On Pliny's life, see Gibson 2020. Sherwin-White 1966, 135, notes that the date of this letter is not known. He suggests that Plinius Paternus is the same addressee as of the Letters 4.14, 8.16 (on the illness of some slaves), and 9.27; and is possibly the man mentioned in Mart. 12.53.

may use their eyes, their ears, and Pliny even plays with the idea of taste with a pun on *sapio* (taste/understand) to get a read on slaves.[2] While Pliny softens any criticism of Paternus' skill at identifying enslaved people who merit purchase by equating it with his own, Paternus' skill is not enough to ensure that the enslaved people are worthy or honest (*frugi*). He sets up a distinction between how one can acquire knowledge via the senses. Both he and Paternus use sight and taste to appraise slaves, but this leads to the most subjective language (*credo*) in a letter rife with subjectivity (*animi tui iudicio, ex consilio tuo, iudicatur*); the result of Paternus' judgment is that Pliny thinks the enslaved people are suitable (*decentes*). The opening judgment of Paternus' mind and eyes and its result, *servi decentes*, is paralleled with the closing (yet to be realized) judgment of the ears over the eyes and its result, *servi frugi*. Pliny is bringing out the importance of the knowledge that will come from what is heard. *Decens*, suitable or proper, can be used to describe the external physical appearance of someone, meaning becoming or symmetrical. In contrast, *frugi*, worthy or honest, and often relating to slaves, pertains more to internal moral character.[3] While Paternus was not necessarily buying these enslaved people for their beauty (though people did do this), his selection was grounded in their appearance. In contrast, Pliny's concern with their character helps explain why he counseled appraisal based on listening rather than sight: only listening to slaves talk will in time reveal their character.

In general, the language that Pliny uses to describe Paternus' encounter draws attention to the subjective nature of assessing slaves and emphasizes the uncertainty that accompanies purchasing slaves. His letter speaks of the difficulty in knowing a potential slave's character and evidences that this was a consideration that the Roman slave-owning class took seriously. The understanding of a slave's character had important economic repercussions and was a fundamental part of running a successful and efficient house. An owner might also be embarrassed if their slaves constantly ran away, misbehaved, or challenged his authority.[4] In Pliny's teasing of Paternus, we observe that slave selec-

2. On the idea of feasting with your eyes at the slave market, see Mart. 9.59.1–6 (discussed below).
3. The term *frugi* (from *frux*, "fruit") ranges in meaning from useful and frugal to honest and virtuous (at times strengthened with *bonae*) and often serves as a catch-all for a range of desirable characteristics in slaves, see, for instance, Plaut. *Cas.* 255, 268; Hor. *Sat.* 2.7.1–4; Sen. *Controv.* 7.9; Ps.-Quint. *Dec.* 388.22; Gell. *NA* 2.23.18; Apul. *Met.* 8.24 (at the slave market).
4. Lendon 1997, 36, discusses honor from the procession of one's slaves. Kirschenbaum 1987, 31–32 and 36–37, discusses honor accrued from successful, well-behaved, and skilled slaves. See also Harper 2011, 201–348, in particular 326–48, on ties between honor and slaves.

tion was an undertaking based on skill and experience. The selection of slaves was not solely a rudimentary physical examination; the process was not taken lightly, and friends would counsel each other on how to make a successful purchase. A secure knowledge of the mind does not come easily and was a source of concern and debate: this first act of domination is difficult.

Scholars have taken this "listening" to mean hearsay or any sort of reputation a slave had accrued.[5] While this is certainly possible, in both legal and literary sources about the purchase and management of slaves, there is an emphasis placed on the speech of slaves themselves;[6] having a slave speak reveals information otherwise hidden. A prospective owner might consider the following: Do they speak Latin? Are they eloquent? Do they have difficulty speaking, which could, it was believed, be a sign of a greater mental impairment?[7] This chapter examines this process of evaluation: What qualities did potential owners seek in slaves and how did they go about determining whether a slave had those qualities? The process of appraisal at the slave market is an attempt to understand not only the physical nature of a slave, but their character, talents, and mental strengths and weaknesses. I focus on this evaluative and examinatory process because it is a first insight into the relationship between the mind of the slave and the ownership of the purchaser.[8] This evaluative process is significant because it occurs both at and beyond the slave market. The amount of ink spilled on the topic suggests the process was not foolproof: It was subjective, and the buyer might experience remorse. As slave owners remained concerned

5. See Hoffer 1999, 45–49, and Krenkel 1984, 358.
6. The references to slaves in these examples pertaining to speech are made exclusively in the masculine form of the Latin word for slave (*servus*); however, it seems likely that this is the generic use of the masculine form rather than these concerns being particular to male slaves.
7. On speech and its connection to concerns about mental fitness and madness, which will be discussed at length in the final section of this chapter, see D. 21.1.1.7 Ulpian, *Curule Aediles' Edict*, book 1, citing Sabinus on stammering (*balbus*); D. 21.1.1.9–10 *Curule Aediles' Edict*, book 1, citing Vivian on uttering ravings as a bacchant and sanity; D. 21.1.3 Gaius, *Curule Aediles' Edict*, book 1, on slaves who do not speak (*muti*); D. 21.1.8 Ulpian, *Curule Aediles' Edict*, book 1, citing Ofilius on whether a slave who has lost a tongue is considered healthy; D. 21.1.9 Ulpian, *Sabinus*, book 44, on slaves who do not speak (*muti*) in contrast to those who speak but whose meaning is elusive to varying degrees and for different reasons (*graviter, asaphōs, asēmōs*); D. 21.1.10.5 Ulpian, *Curule Aediles' Edict*, book 1, on slaves who have speech impairments of various kinds (*balbus, blaesus, atypus, tardius loquitur, varus, vatius*). See also D. 21.1.4.3 Ulpian, *Curule Aediles' Edict*, book 1, citing Pomponius on a babbling slave (*fatuus*), and D. 21.1.12.2 Ulpian, *Curule Aediles' Edict*, book 1, on a slave who by nature speaks gutturally (*gutturosus*). These passages will be discussed below.
8. For a discussion on the Roman law of ownership generally, see Giglio 2018; Capogrossi Colognesi 2016; du Plessis 2015; Diósdi 1970. For a discussion of ownership particularly relevant to this project, see Birks 1985 (and see discussion in introduction).

with the character and other mental attributes of their slaves well after purchase, they also looked for guidance in models of evaluation such as medical and philosophical discussions of mental illness and faults of character. The Roman jurists categorize undesirable mental characteristics of slaves generally as "mental defects" (*vitia animi*), which can be broken down into three types: faults of character, forms of madness (*insania*), and running away. This chapter considers these faults of character in the context of the slave market, first from a masterly and then from a juristic perspective. The present section suggests that listening to slave speech was a fundamental part of this ongoing evaluation of the mind.

Pliny is not alone in his concern with the internal workings of a slave's mind and the best methods for uncovering them. The agronomist Columella has a substantial discussion on slave management in his treatise *On Agriculture*.[9] Columella serves as a particularly informative source because while his work speaks to the larger project of elite Romans writing agricultural literature, he is also writing a work for Roman farm owners, instructing them on his idea of proper slave management. For example, he advises owners to spend time getting to know their enslaved country workers as he found it lightened their burdens. While Columella does not discuss the slave market, he does give advice as part of the introductory book of his treatise in which, among other things, he discusses choosing the right piece of land, the organization of different spaces, and tenant farmers. Following these topics, Columella turns to how to pick a slave foreman (*vilicus*, at 1.8.1–14, discussed in chapter 4) and what he calls "precepts to be upheld among other slaves" (*in ceteris servis haec fere praecepta servanda sunt*).[10] One bit of advice is listening to slaves to learn about them:

> Now I do this often, I consult with them about any new work as if they were more experienced and in this way I get to know the natural talent of each one, and in what way he is skilled. Then I see that they approach the work even more willingly because they think I consulted them and their own counsel was followed.

---

9. Columella synthesizes and elaborates on the discussion of slave management found in his predecessors Cato and Varro. On Columella, see Reitz 2013; Maestre Maestre, Charlo Brea, and Serrano Cueto 1997; Martin 1985; and Forster 1950. On Columella and slavery, see Diederich 2007b; Scheidel 1990; and Martin 1974. On the Roman agronomists more generally and Columella's place among them, see Thibodeau 2018; Diederich 2007a; Noè 2002; Martin 1971. On Roman farming and agriculture, see Hollander 2018; Thibodeau 2016; White 1970.
10. Seemingly a joke on the believed etymology of *servus* coming from *servare*.

> Iam illud saepe facio, ut quasi cum peritioribus de aliquibus operibus novis deliberem et per hoc cognoscam cuiusque ingenium, quale quamque sit prudens. Tum etiam libentius eos id opus adgredi video, de quo se cum deliberatum et consilium ipsorum susceptum putant.[11]

Amid other tenets of good slave management including jocularity and manipulation, Columella describes his method of evaluation. He compels his slaves to reveal themselves through speech and planning so that he might know them. While it is possible that the more experienced enslaved workers were wise to the true intention behind this masterly audience, the process of assessing a slave's abilities was meant to teach the owner about the slave's character.

The passage of Pliny echoes Columella's insistence on the importance of knowledge that comes from listening, that is to say, from the speech of a slave. As with Pliny, the focus is on the internal and unseeable attributes of the slave. Columella suggests an owner must study his slave's character and natural talent (*ingenium*); it is in his interest to know what the innate capabilities of his slaves are, and which ones possess greater skill sets (*prudens*). Deceptively, he seeks out advice and learns (*cognosco*) not about what his questions point to—advice on a new project—but about the slaves themselves. In taking the responses of enslaved workers at face value, Columella recognizes that slaves too can fall prey to the allure of ego: They will work harder on a project that they had a hand in planning. He shows that by asking slaves their opinions on a new project (and presumably permitting them to carry it out accordingly), Columella grants them control of the project, which in turn allows them to proceed more willingly (or more freely—*libentius*). There is a sense of economic instrumentalism in Columella's desire to know his slaves' minds: The performance of listening not only instructs the owner in his slaves' aptitudes but also had the additional benefit of getting workers more invested in their project. In both Pliny's letter on the purchase of new slaves and Columella's precepts in his handbook on agriculture, we see these two Roman slave owners evaluating their slaves and trying to perceive beyond physical capabilities and into the realm of a slave's morality and mental abilities (*frugi, ingenium, prudens*). Despite the legal ownership of slaves, learning about their minds poses a challenge.

---

11. Columella *Rust.* 1.8.15–16. See Bradley 1984, 21–24, 26–28, on Columella and slave control. See also Howley 2025.

In Seneca's well-known letter on owners and slaves (*Ep.* 47), the same methods of evaluation are deployed despite the letter's lack of concern with economic productivity.[12] The aim is one of Stoic education—in this case, to convince Lucilius and other slave-owning readers not to be prejudiced against someone because of their legal status or lowly situation in life, but to judge people on the merits of their character. A recurring theme in the letter is the contrast between the owner who banquets amid slaves quietly standing at the ready and the owner who enjoys friendly commensality with his slaves.[13] The letter emphasizes this contrast with the language of silence and speech. We are treated to a vivid description of the gluttonous, disgusting, prone slave owner who gorges himself while slaves stand silently by: their lips must not move to speak, cough, sneeze, or hiccup, let alone utter a peep without being beaten—they must stand there all night, hungry and quiet.[14]

There is a healthy dose of Roman pragmatism accompanying Seneca's moral point. This demand for silence is not beneficial to the owner; the slaves who do not talk in front of their owner do so to other people. It's clear from just this that beyond idle gossip, Seneca is referring to slaves remaining silent under judicial torture (and while everyone is innocent until proven guilty, there are no guarantees in Nero's Rome).[15] The rhetoric of feasting with silent slaves (47.6–8) and dining in conversation with slaves (47.13–16) continues throughout the letter. While Seneca's aim is not to learn the intellect and character of a slave to assess their economic value or even productivity, he suggests the same mechanism of evaluation—talking—for these would-be moral companions.

> "So, what? Should I seat all my slaves at my table?" No more than all freemen. You are wrong if you think that I would reject certain slaves because of their lowly work, for instance, the mule driver over there, or the ploughman. I will

---

12. On any ties Columella may have had to Seneca, see Griffin 1976, 89, 253, 290. Bradley 1984, 145, expresses skepticism about this view.
13. Edwards 2019, 182, notes a similar sentiment is expressed in *De Ira* 3.35 (where Seneca urges the slave owner to use their ears and eyes to hear and see their slaves). On Seneca's letters, see Edwards 2019 more generally. On Seneca, see Bartsch and Schiesaro 2015 and Griffin 1976 remains essential.
14. Sen. *Ep.* 47.3. See Edwards 2019 *ad loc.* who notes, "there is a strong contrast between the extreme control exercised over the slaves' bodily orifices . . . and the total license accorded to the master's."
15. Sen. *Ep.* 47.4 referring to slaves in the past who were able to talk to their owners, which made them more loyal: "They spoke during banquets, but were silent under torture" (*in conviviis loquebantur, sed in tormentis tacebant*). On slaves' "grumbling," or speech that was not for the ears of owners, see Richlin 2017, 332–33.

evaluate them not by their duties, but by their character; each person gives his character to himself, but chance assigns duties. Let some dine with you because they are worthy and others so that they become worthy; if there is in fact anything servile in them because of their lowly associations, it will be shaken off by interaction with more honorable men.

"Quid ergo? omnes servos admovebo mensae meae?" Non magis quam omnes liberos. Erras si existimas me quosdam quasi sordidioris operae reiecturum, ut puta illum mulionem et illum bubulcum. Non ministeriis illos aestimabo sed moribus: sibi quisque dat mores, ministeria casus adsignat. Quidam cenent tecum quia digni sunt, quidam ut sint; si quid enim in illis ex sordida conversatione servile est, honestiorum convictus excutiet.[16]

Talking to slaves does two things that benefit the owner. First, the slaves who are morally good (regardless of their position in the house) are morally good for the owner. And, second, the slaves who are not morally good but are able to change are improved by conversation, therefore making them better slaves.[17] As with Columella's slaves, conversation is meant to foster compliance and loyalty. In order to achieve this, Seneca instrumentalizes the moral virtue of these slaves in much the same way that he instrumentalizes other aspects of his slaves for his own purposes, such as when he treats the aging of an enslaved man as a timepiece of his own mortality (*Ep.* 12.3) or the work of enslaved men carrying his litter as his own vigorous exercise (*Ep.* 55.1).

This letter also brings up the idea of evaluation; a freeman judges another freeman (*existimare*) and an owner, like Seneca, evaluates his own slaves (*aestimare*). Seneca's interlocutor questions Seneca's idea that he should associate with his slaves. However, Seneca sets aside the question of legal status; he does not consider one slave worthier of a seat at his table because of their assigned duty (*ministerium*), but on account of their character (*mores*). Each slave's character is varied, changeable, and under his own control (*sibi quisque*); notably, however, his duty is due to fate (*casus*).[18] A man has the status of slave because

16. Sen. *Ep.* 47.15.
17. At 47.16 Seneca counsels Lucilius to not only look in the Senate house or forum, but that there is the raw material of friendship at home ("often good material goes unused for lack of a craftsman" [*Saepe bona materia cessat sine artifice*]). On the idea that slaves were moldable, see Sen. *Ep.* 27.6 (discussed in the introduction) and Hor. *Epist.* 2.2.2–19 (discussed below).
18. Seneca uses *casus* to talk about how a slave gets a particular position. This would be up to the slave's owner to decide (so in the context of Seneca's dinner table, Seneca himself), but from the

of happenstance, but he can control how he chooses to act. Just as Pliny considers whether potential slaves are honest, Seneca proposes to judge his slaves on their character rather than their duties. He suggests the following technique for searching for friends in all places,

> Just as someone is a fool if he buys a horse without inspecting the horse itself but only its saddle and bridle, so a person is a great fool if he evaluates a man from his clothes or status, which is just a cloak that covers us.
>
> Quemadmodum stultus est qui equum empturus non ipsum inspicit sed stratum eius ac frenos, sic stultissimus est qui hominem aut ex veste aut ex condicione, quae vestis modo nobis circumdata est, aestimat.[19]

While Seneca's humane ideas about who might be virtuous fall short of not relating people to horses, the language of inspection at the marketplace returns us to Pliny's worry that appearances may be deceiving.

The three texts discussed above have very different purposes: Pliny considers slave purchase, Columella slave management, and Seneca a reconsideration of the typical view of people based on status and position. Pliny concerns himself with honesty, Columella looks for innate aptitudes, and Seneca seeks good character. All three look for attributes beyond rudimentary physical ability or job performance and instead grapple with how they can understand the mind of a slave. Seneca and Pliny look explicitly at moral character (*mores*; whether the slaves are *frugi*). Seneca and Columella differ in their views on slave nature; Seneca proposes that anything servile (*servile*) about the slaves will be removed by placing them in more honorable association (*honestiorum convictus*). Columella instead converses with his slaves in order to understand their limitations and capabilities, and unlike Seneca does not believe that slaves can be elevated beyond the servile.[20] And while they have different answers, both Columella and Seneca consider the extent to which the status of slavery produces a servile character or mindset, and their preoccupations rest upon the same issues: Is there a true nature of a slave, can it be found, and can it be changed? This ques-

perspective of the enslaved person, this is a random decision and largely beyond their control.

19. Sen. *Ep.* 47.16.

20. For Columella, a foreman must have the ability to humor the good workers and show consideration to the lesser ones; however, the mind of the foreman could only hold these managerial virtues "as far as servile nature allows" (*quantum servile patitur ingenium*), *Rust.* 1.8.10. This passage is discussed in chapter 3.

tion of whether the capacity for change exists in slaves is central to a society that manumits slaves and grants them citizenship.[21]

This process of evaluation underscores a (potential) owner's inability to truly know their slave's nature. The attention to evaluation is also important because *aestimare*, to value, gives birth to the Roman concept of *existimatio*, the manner in which Roman elites measured their own abilities and selves.[22] The word *aestimare* is old and is tied in its etymology with commercial interests (*aes* being a word for money). It is perhaps not an accident then that in his letter (*Ep.* 47.15) Seneca uses *existimare* when a freeman is evaluating a fellow freeman and *aestimare* when a slave is under scrutiny. *Aestimare* recalls the marketability of the slave; the owner must evaluate the skills and nature of their slave versus their monetary price (*aes*) as a saleable good. *Aestimare* is not solely an economic word, however; a broader value judgment is taking place as well. This evaluation was constant and took many forms. In the slave market, each buyer made decisions primarily by looking at the slaves on a platform; this inherently created a standardized scene, or even model, of evaluation.[23] But scrutiny did not cease after purchase, since slaves were continually reevaluated—their value changed as they accrued more respect and trust (i.e., if they were foremen or managed their owners' accounts honestly) and diminished if they acted in ways deemed undesirable (i.e., ran away).

The language of slave evaluation spills over into situations beyond the marketplace. In a different letter (*Ep.* 80), Seneca counsels his reader to look past any furnishings that might distract from seeing the true person.[24] Before ending on his ultimate subject, the evaluation of oneself, Seneca moves quickly from the inspection of horses to the evaluation (*aestimare*) of slaves and sizing up foreign kings. As a negative example, Seneca discusses the deceit of slave-dealers (*mangones*) who would work to hide any underlying defects (*vitia corporis lateant*). And just like one would have a horse's blanket, a slave's clothes or

21. Seneca's conviction that slaves' characters could change fits well with Roman manumission practice, which at times was based on a slave's character or good deeds; this will be discussed in chapter 5.

22. For a larger discussion on *existimatio* in Roman literature and its tie etymologically to *aestimare*, see Habinek 1998, 45–59. Habinek 1998, 46, has shown that the verb forms an evaluative relationship between money (*aes*) and property. On the selection of slaves and the tie to reputation, "The buyer not only purchased his own idea of a workman, servant, or companion; in the slave or in the act of purchase he also got a certain image of himself," Joshel 2010, 106.

23. See Hughes 2006 on standardized artistic representations of the slaves on the platform. And on the use of platforms (*catastae*), see Fentress 2005. Habinek 1998, 185n44, shows that the grammarian Festus ties *aestimare* to *exemplum* (example).

24. Sen. *Ep.* 80.9–10.

adornments, or a king's crown removed for evaluation of the animal or person underneath, so he tells his reader to weigh themselves with their money and effects set aside with the verb *perpendere*, which evokes the scales of the marketplace.[25] The language of the marketplace and the evaluation of slaves is so ingrained into elite culture that it comes to serve as a way for elites to measure themselves.

In the process of purchasing a slave, the prospective buyer performs a masterly act that they will repeat time and again: the evaluation of the slave. They appraise who the slave is, where they are from, their strengths and capabilities, education and intellect, and moral character. This assessment of a slave is tied implicitly to the determination of their monetary value, their *aestimatio*. The prices of slaves varied depending on a number of factors and the calculus behind price at times seems to elude us, though Walter Scheidel has shown that age and to a lesser extent sex are the primary factors for price differences in Roman Egypt.[26] Most of the evidence we have on slave prices comes from Egypt, but scholars have argued that even the Egyptian data is not sufficient to put an average price on slaves. For example, Jean Straus presents the case of two enslaved people of the same sex and from the same place who were sold around the same time (18 March and 7 April 154 CE) and most likely in the same place (Alexandria). Despite their similarities, the two enslaved men have vastly different prices. We know that the more expensive enslaved man (2,800 drachmas) was around seventeen years old and was an *oikogenēs*, or homeborn, slave. The age and the birth status of the less expensive enslaved man (1,400 drachmas) is unknown. As to the cause of the price difference, Straus notes, "you can let your imagination run wild but you can't prove anything."[27] Setting aside a possible difference in age, the fact that the more expensive enslaved man was homeborn most likely explains the price discrepancy; with that said, any number of other undocumented attributes like language or appearance or possibly a particular skill set (though it seems likely this would be mentioned) could

25. *Pendo*, e.g., Ov. *Met.* 14.270; Suet. *Aug.* 12; Tac. *Ann.* 2.87.

26. Scheidel 2005a matches the prices of slaves to grain in order to get the relative cost of slaves in Athens and the Roman Empire and see Groen-Vallinga and Tacoma 2017 and Salway 2010 on the cost of labor in Diocletian's Price Edict. A working number of 2000 *sesterces* is offered by Scheidel 2005a, 6, as "arguably the most representative value . . . for a (presumably adult and not exceptionally skilled) slave that is attested both in the Digest and in an inscription from North Africa." But see Riggsby 2019, 83–129, on approximation and fairness in the marketplace. Koops 2020, 60–64, discusses the market value of slaves in the context of purchasing freedom.

27. Straus 2004, 300. See the charts of the sales of slaves in Straus 2004, 296–300, and see also Drexhage 1991, 249–79.

have made the difference.[28] A variety of unmentioned circumstantial factors such as any shortages in the slave supply or the skill of one slave-dealer in swindling his customers could also be at play. Moreover, as we saw from Pliny's letter, the purchasing of slaves was subjective and uncertain; the slave one person wanted, another did not—there was no accounting for taste. This first step into ownership emphasizes that the evaluation of enslaved people was by no means foolproof and, at least for those slaves prized for their moral character or intellect, listening to their speech was an important means of insight.

Slave Market

Slaves were sold throughout the Roman Empire.[29] While many of the pragmatic and historical details of slave sales elude us, such as the number of sales per year, we can reconstruct the following. There were continuous markets in large slave centers such as Alexandria, Ephesus, Delos, Puteoli, and Rome. There were also occasional markets that came to individual towns and cities on a fixed schedule. Markets could additionally be set up after large battles that yielded many captives. In these wartime markets, Roman commanders would decide either to sell the slaves at the site of battle or to take the prisoners to an established market, including to Rome. It generally fell to slave-dealers to negotiate and manage the movement or sale of the newly enslaved captives.[30]

Outside the theater of war, a slave could be sold from their current owner to another in a large market via auction or in a relatively small setting where seller, purchaser, and slave might know each other. While it seems that some material imprint would remain, especially from larger markets where slaves were held, washed and prepared for sale, and finally displayed on platforms (*catastae*), it

28. On homeborn slaves generally, see Herrmann-Otto 1994, and on slave-breeding and the slave supply, see Bradley 1987a.

29. See Scheidel 2011, 288–92, on the population of slaves in Roman Italy (1–1.5 million) and in the Roman Empire (5–8 million). He calculates that about 250,000–400,000 people needed to be added each year in order for the slave population to be maintained at this level. This addition of people was due to both warfare and breeding (see Bradley 1987a), but Scheidel notes that after the main influxes of people into the Italian slave population during the Republic, reproduction must have been the main form of maintaining the slave population.

30. On the sale of prisoners of war and conquered peoples called *sub corona vendere*, see Gell. *NA* 6.4.2–3; Scheidel 2011, 294–97; Volkmann 1990, 106–9; Welwei 2000. And most recently on prisoners of war in the Republic and slave status, see Huemoeller 2021. On slave-dealers, see Bodel 2005.

has been difficult to locate slave markets in the archaeological record.[31] Known sites for slave markets are few and far between, with the odd exception: Seneca tells us that a market for slaves (whom he deemed worthless) existed near the Temple of Castor in the Forum;[32] Martial notes the beautiful boys for sale in the luxury markets of the Saepta Julia,[33] the sale of a woman, Leda, on the Via Sacra,[34] and makes reference to the purchase of enslaved people in the Subura, an area associated with sex workers.[35] The archive of the Sulpicii mentions enslaved people being sold at auction at the *chalcidicum Caesonianum* at Puteoli;[36] and Plutarch laments that some people would frequent what he calls a "monster market" (ἡ τῶν τεράτων ἀγορά) at Rome.[37] To this list, Elizabeth Fentress argues that we should suspect that buildings that have *chalcidica*, such as the Eumachia building in Pompeii, were likely sites of slave auctions.[38] There is also an ongoing scholarly debate about whether the Agora of the Italians on Delos was a slave market.[39]

There were, in other words, many ways to buy a slave, and the marketplace was set up to play to the desires of the purchaser. While it was possible for a prospective buyer to browse without an idea in mind, it seems likely that a combination of personal and general desires governed the potential slave own-

31. See Trümper 2009 and Fentress 2005 on the difficulties of situating slave markets in the archaeological record. On slave markets in Louisiana, see Johnson 1999 to which many of our reconstructions are indebted; and for slave markets in fifteenth-century Valencia, which had ties to Roman slave laws, see Blumenthal 2009, 46–79.
32. Sen. *Constant.* 13.4.
33. Mart. 9.59.1–6.
34. Mart. 2.63.
35. Mart. 6.66.
36. *TPSulp* 85.
37. Plut. *Curiositate* 10 520C, discussed below.
38. What specifically makes a *chalcidicum* a *chalcidicum* is subject to debate; see Fentress 2005, 223, on the *chalcidicum* as two platforms or portico. Fentress 2005, 232, argues, correctly in my view, that the hesitation to attribute slave auctions to some of these *chalcidica* based on their location near the monumental centers of cities is based on "only our modern perception of slave sales." Leanne Bablitz *per litteras*/Zoom approaches the tie between slave auctions and *chalcidica* as a tie between raised platforms and legal activity. Fentress, along with Braconi and Coarelli (and Bodel, though he is preoccupied with the traders rather than the buildings, and Pucci, who looks at representations of slave sales), argue in a 2005 set of papers in *JRA*, "Selling People: Five Papers on Roman Slave-Traders and the Buildings They Used," that the Agora of the Italians at Delos, the Eumachia Building at Pompeii, the Crypta Balbi in Rome, the Tempio Rotondo in Ostia, the Basilica in Herculaneum, the Chalcidicum in Lepcis Magna, the Prytaneion in Magnesia on the Maeander, and the Serapeum in Ephesus were slave markets. Trümper 2009 disputes that these buildings were used specifically for slave markets, though the majority of the aforementioned scholars agree that the buildings were multiuse.
39. Strabo 14.5.2 tells us that up to ten thousand slaves a day were sold on Delos; however, whether this occurred in the Agora of the Italians is unclear. See Trümper 2009 and 2008; Coarelli 2005 and 1982; Bruneau 1975; and Cocco 1970.

er's purchase as they examined the people on the block. Following the text of a document from the archive of the Sulpicii (*TPSulp* 85), Elizabeth Fentress notes that while the sale of slaves was on the podium at the *chalcidicum Caesonianum* in Puteoli, the actual purchase would have taken place at street level in front of the podium.[40] This is perhaps where a purchaser could examine a potential slave more closely. We see this close inspection in Seneca's *Letter* 80 (discussed above) where he juxtaposes the inspection of horses with the purchase of slaves.[41] Health is one of the primary concerns for a potential buyer. This was assessed in the market by having the slaves move and jump around; slaves could be stripped, poked, and physically inspected. The acknowledgment of the health of the slave is seen in contracts of sale.[42] We also find several accounts in literary sources on how to prepare slaves so that they looked healthier or fit for work. We hear tell of mixing the bulbs of hyacinth with sweet wine to keep slaves looking prepubescent; rubbing resin over the bodies of enslaved people to make them appear well-fed; the depilatory properties of the tuna fish, and more generally on different dyes and fats slave-dealers used to alter the appearance of slaves at market.[43]

While we cannot speak with absolute certainty, it seems reasonable to infer that there was a sliding scale of individualized desired characteristics that corresponded to how close in proximity the enslaved person was to their owner. For those enslaved people bound for basic agricultural labor, general health and good character as it applies to work and productivity would seem sufficient. The evidence of sale can also tell us about masterly concerns with internal attri-

---

40. Fentress 2005, 224–25, bases this on the wording of *TPSulp* 85, which states slave sales were "before (*ante*) the Chalcidicum Caesonianum."

41. Our evidence suggests that a comparison of human and animal sales is worth considering; literary writers like Seneca conflate the sale of horses and slaves (*Ep.* 80), and legal material such as the regulations on the slave market additionally regulate the sales of beasts of burden (D. 21.1) as well as the Zarai tariff of 202 CE in which slaves are grouped with animals (*CIL* 8.4508). If this is the case, we might look to texts like the opening of Xenophon's *On Horsemanship* where he notes that the first topic will be how to best avoid being cheated in the purchase of a horse. Notably, as will be discussed below, the Roman jurist Ulpian (D. 21.1.1.2) tells us that the regulations on the slave market are developed in order to curb the trickery of slave-dealers.

42. On the importance of health, see, for example, *FIRA* 3.132, a contract of sale from 166 CE for a boy of about seven, which records that the buyer stipulated that the enslaved boy must be healthy in accord with the Edict of the Aediles (discussed below), and the seller swore to this. See Tomlin 2003 for a more detailed discussion of a guarantee of health, which also notes that origin, and not being a runaway or a wanderer, were common in sale contracts.

43. Mart. 4.42 and 10.98 on slave appearance and Mart. 6.66 on the humiliations to which an enslaved person could be subjected. On how to prepare slaves for sale, see, e.g., Plin. *HN* 21.170 (on hyacinth mixed with sweet wine), 24.35 (on resin), 32.135 (on tuna); and Quint. *Inst.* 2.15.25 (on the dye and fat for the marketplace).

butes; for enslaved people who were to do more skilled labor, some ability or potential would presumably be required as well, and if the labor was sensitive or involved a large amount of capital, some idea of trust would surely be wanted. Particularly in the domestic sphere, these generalized requirements of health, good character, and productivity would combine with additional personal desires: gender, appearance, a specific skill set (e.g., a knowledge of a specialty cuisine or particular language), or ethnicity. And while slaves were expensive, Roman households of more moderate means would have one or two slaves who took on many roles.[44] Romans had stereotypes about which origins predisposed slaves to particular functions.[45] The census required the origin (*natio*), age, duties, and skills to be listed for each slave.[46] The names of slaves (e.g., Eros or Fides) were often representative of what the owner was looking for, although Varro acknowledges that the name of a slave could be misleading.[47]

It is clear that owners preferred to purchase either those whose slave status was recent or a *verna* (the Latin term for a homeborn slave) who likely had never before been sold and presumably had an understanding of enslavement, Roman society, and Latin.[48] The homeborn slave also plays into the ideal of the owner as father and the enslaved as part of the *familia*; this might make the potential owner believe the enslaved person would be easier to control and manipulate. The newly enslaved, meanwhile, often had their feet chalked white to indicate their new status.[49] Plutarch tells us in his biography of Cato the

---

44. Scheidel 2005b, 66–67, draws on Roman Egyptian evidence, where 20 percent of households owned slaves—most of them just one or two individuals—to hypothesize sub-elite slave-owning in Roman Italy.

45. D. 21.1.31.21 Ulpian, *Curule Aediles' Edict*, book 1: "Those selling slaves should declare their origin when making the sale; for the slave's origin may often induce or deter a purchaser; therefore, we have an interest in knowing the origin; for there is a presumption that some slaves are good, coming from a people without a bad reputation, while others are thought bad, since they come from a people with a worse reputation" (*Qui mancipia vendunt, nationem cuiusque in venditione pronuntiare debent: plerumque enim natio servi aut provocat aut deterret emptorem: idcirco interest nostra scire nationem: praesumptum etenim est quosdam servos bonos esse, quia natione sunt non infamata, quosdam malos videri, quia ea natione sunt, quae magis infamis est*).

Varro *Rust.* 2.10.4–7, discusses suitable occupations for slaves of different origins and in 4.42 Martial wants an Egyptian boy, though more for his beauty than his labor.

See also Straus 2004, 276–82 and 1971; Tomlin 2003, 47–48; Joshel 1992, 40–41, 194n52, 196n65.

46. D.50.15.4.5 Ulpian, *Censuses*, book 3, with Wiedemann 1981, 103. See also D. 21.1.31.21 Ulpian, *Curule Aediles' Edict*, book 1, on selling and declaring the origin of slaves. For a more comprehensive view on the *natio* of a slave, see Isaac 2004, 170–207. For a more detailed discussion of the sources of slaves in the Empire, see Gonzalès 2002.

47. Joshel 2010, 95: "Names like *Eros* (love), *Fides* (trust, good faith), *Hilarus* (cheerful), or *Felix* (lucky) imprinted the owner's hopes or fantasies on the slave." See also Varro *Ling.* 8.21.

48. The contrast to this is the oft-sold slave, the *palimpratos*; see Scheidel 2011, 306.

49. Prop. 4.5.51–52.

Elder that the statesman preferred new slaves because they were easier to train, and it seems that new slaves began learning Latin in the slave market.[50] This is echoed by the legal sources and literary writers.[51] Horace uses a fictional sales pitch for a homeborn slave as an analogy for his friend Florus when he complains that Horace never writes to him, even though Horace told him of this particular character flaw. Here we get a picture of the idealized slave for sale:

> Perhaps someone wanted to sell you a boy born at Tibur or Gabii and he said this: "He is fair and beautiful from the top of his head to the tips of his toes. He will be yours for 8,000 *sesterces*. This homeborn slave is trained to do his duties at the nod of his owner's head. He knows some Greek and is fit for whatever task is pleasing to you. With this wet clay you can model him after whomever you please. He can sing even, untrained, but sweet to listen to when drinking. Many promises lower a buyer's confidence, i.e., when a seller praises more than is fitting a slave he wants to get rid of. Nothing compels me. I am not wealthy, but I am not broke. None of the slave-dealers would do this for you; a random stranger would not get the same from me. As it happens, he strayed once, but fearing the hanging whip, he just hid under the stairs. Give me the payment, if the one exceptional flight mentioned is not a bother for you." I am sure he would get the price without fear of penalty. You bought him aware of his defects—you know the law. Will you harass him and detain him with an unjust suit?
>
> Si quis forte velit puerum tibi vendere natum
> Tibure vel Gabiis et tecum sic agat: "hic et
> candidus et talos a vertice pulcher ad imos
> fiet eritque tuus nummorum milibus octo,
> verna ministeriis ad nutus aptus erilis,
> litterulis Graecis imbutus, idoneus arti
> cuilibet; argilla quidvis imitaberis uda;
> quin etiam canet, indoctum sed dulce bibenti.
> multa fidem promissa levant, ubi plenius aequo

50. Plutarch records that Cato the Elder (*Vit. Cat. Mai.* 21.1) wanted young war captives, because they were more easily trained than other slaves. On learning Latin in the slave market, see Gell. *NA* 4.1.6, and upon enslavement, Varro *Ling.* 8.6.

51. D. 21.1.37 Ulpian, *Curule Aediles' Edict*, book 1, on the desire for a new slave because they are more malleable and on not passing off a long-standing slave as a newly enslaved person. See also D. 21.1.65.2 Venuleius, *Actions*, book 5, on new versus experienced slaves.

laudat venalis qui volt extrudere merces.
res urget me nulla; meo sum pauper in aere.
nemo hoc mangonum faceret tibi; non temere a me
quivis ferret idem. semel hic cessavit et, ut fit,
in scalis latuit metuens pendentis habenae.
des nummos, excepta nihil te si fuga laedit,"
ille ferat pretium poenae securus, opinor.
prudens emisti vitiosum, dicta tibi est lex:
insequeris tamen hunc et lite moraris iniqua?[52]

Although imagined, the pitch shows what an owner could look for in a new slave: not only their price, their appearance, and their health, but also their character, intellect, skills, and talents. Horace stops listing the slave's qualities because he acknowledges that too many promises make the buyer skeptical and question why this ideal slave is for sale. He then reveals that the slave ran away once and hid under the stairs. The admission of the slave's relatively minor bad behavior and the fact that the slave remains controllable because he fears punishment more than he desires freedom makes the slave all the more appealing, and the slave-dealer more trustworthy. This admission plays directly into a masterly fantasy of the mind of the slave: fearful and pliable, but also able to entertain. Notably, Horace incorporates language that, as we will see, comes to define marketplace restrictions on the sales of slaves in his fictional pitch (e.g., *vitium, fuga, lex*).

Particular desires were especially catered to at the specialty markets. Evidence about certain kinds of specialty markets, such as those for slaves with certain physical features, is more readily available and can help inform us about markets that catered to masterly desires directed toward the mind of the enslaved. As noted above, Plutarch, in stating the problems of being a busybody (*polupragmōn*), references people who instead of fixating on the beauty of the boys and women for sale go browse the so-called monster market (*hē tōn teratōn agora*).[53] This impulse goes as high as the imperial court, as often in the emperor's retinue there were dwarf people, eunuchs, and others with physical disabilities.[54] Along similar lines, Quintilian, in lamenting that people do not

52. Horace *Ep.* 2.2.2–19. Morris 1968, 164, suggests the date of this letter is 20–18 BCE.
53. Plut. *Curiositate* 10 520C. See Husquin 2022 on "atypical" bodies.
54. On this, see Trentin 2011, which shows how Suetonius and the *SHA* document this phenomenon

recognize the effort that goes into preparing straightforward and natural speech, notes that people consider deviations (*deflexa*) to be more sophisticated (*exquisitiora*) than the norm. His example for this is people who put a higher price on bodies that are "disfigured and in some way monstrous" (*distortis et quocumque modo prodigiosis corporibus*) or those who consider cosmetic appearance more attractive than the beauty of uncorrupted nature.[55]

The desire for slaves who might be found at the "monster market" goes hand in hand with the desire for those who were made up to be appealing as sex workers. The best evidence, at least in the literary record, of the specialty markets is for these enslaved sex workers. These markets were varied, some more exclusive than others: Martial tells us of Mamurra, who feasted on some boys with his eyes (*oculisque comedit*) without any hope of acquiring them. We get a further detail about these boys; they were not the enslaved people on offer in the stalls out front, but were rather kept in a private showroom beyond the reach of the average shopper.[56] This closed, private inspection would likely assist a potential buyer in not being swindled by a slave-dealer, or perhaps the very opposite: The secluded nature of the setting might awe the potential buyer into a purchase.

There were other specialty markets, but their records are harder to reconstruct. For example, locating skilled labor at the slave market is largely reliant on comparative data. We have an abundance of evidence for the procedures that enslaved sex workers endured in preparation for sale.[57] In the case of disabled slaves, we have one gruesome account of enslaved people being caged to stunt growth and a considerable amount of juristic discussion about castrated men; the literary sources also mention Domitian's ineffective ban on castra-

---

in particular with the "bad emperors"; "good emperors" like Augustus, at least according to Suetonius, wanted to stay away from dwarfs (*pumili*) and "disfigured" people (*distorti*) (Suet. *Aug.* 83). On disability in the ancient world, see Laes 2022a and 2018; Laes, Goodey, and Rose 2013; Garland 1995 (2010).

In Letter 50, Seneca complains of having to take care of Harpasté, the slave of his wife, who is described as a "fool" (*fatua*) and a "monster" (*prodigium*) (*Ep.* 50.2). Pliny the Elder records that Andromeda, the freedwoman of Julia Augusta, was the woman of shortest stature, and that Conopas was the shortest man (Plin. *HN* 7.75).

55. Quint. *Inst.* 2.5.11.

56. Mart. 9.59.1–6. On this passage and the exclusivity of certain slaves (*pueri*), see Huemoeller 2016, 236–39, and Fentress 2005, 220–21. On the sale of slaves and sex work, see Huemoeller 2016, 219–83; on sex workers more generally, see McGinn 2011, 2004, 1998 and Levin-Richardson 2019, 2013, 2011 (in particular for a material culture approach).

57. See note 43 above. See also Huemoeller 2016, 220–21, on the alterations to the body that slave-dealers and others like the midwife Salpe performed to prepare sex workers for sale, and especially Huemoeller's compelling interpretation of *pueros mangonicavit* (Plin. *HN* 32.47), understanding *mango* not only as slave-dealer but "slave-maker," Huemoeller 2016, 221.

tion.[58] In thinking about the specialty market for skilled slaves (already a broad category), we might consider our sources' rhetoric about slaves being like clay or moldable. Seneca, for example, tells the story of Calvisius Sabinus, who wanted enslaved people that could recite specific poems; if he could not find people who could do this, he had them made to order (*non invenerat, faciendos locavit*). The jurist Modestinus also refers to a possessor making a slave into a craftsman (*artificem fecerit*).[59] Slaves could be generically trained in the same way that slave-dealers prepared sex workers for the market, at least for discrete skill sets.[60] There would presumably be some performative aspect of evaluation where the enslaved person was made to exhibit their skill or trade.[61] The legal sources make it clear that if a person is selling a slave as a cook, this slave needs to know how to cook but does not need to be a gourmet chef. A buyer would also have to rely on the reputation of the slave-dealer: Is this the place to get a good copyist or scribe?[62] We have some evidence that people bought slaves (or they were born into their house) and sent them to be apprenticed in a particular skill. For example, one Panechotes writes to apprentice his slave Chaerammon to Apollonius, a writer of shorthand, for two years. Panechotes will pay in installments as Chaerammon progresses through his studies, and Apollonius can make use of Chaerammon's labor as he teaches him.[63] This form of purchasing or apprenticeship would seem to be adequate for slaves who had, or were to learn, a discrete skill set such as scribal work; but roles like being the

58. See, e.g., Suet. *Dom.* 7.1 and D. 48.8.3–6.
59. This passage of Seneca is *Ep.* 27.6 (discussed in detail in the introduction) and of Modestinus, D. 6.1.32 Modestinus, *Differences*, book 8. See also, in Horace, *Ep.* 2.2 above, "With this wet clay you can model him after whomever you please" (*argilla quidvis imitaberis uda*).
60. A succinct account of this can be found in Bodel 2011, 330–34.
61. In Lucian's *Philosophies for Sale*, the philosophers are made to explain what they have to offer a potential buyer (as well as putting themselves forth for physical inspection—their potential use as skilled slaves does not save them from physical humiliation). On this, see Stewart 2012, 26, and Bradley 1991, 126–27. More pragmatically on apprenticeship contracts, see Bergamasco 1995.
62. On the gourmet chef, see D. 21.1.18.1 Gaius, *Curule Aediles' Edict*, book 1, where Gaius does explain that if the slave-dealer did claim him to be an excellent cook (*optimus cocus*) the slave should be excellent in that craft (*optimum in eo artificio praestare debet*), but if he just says a cook, he does not need to be a good cook (*etiamsi mediocrem cocum*). It does seem clear that slave-dealers were selling skilled slaves at large markets; see, for example, D. 18.1.43pr Florentinus, *Institutes*, book 8, who says that a vendor can say what he wants about obvious things (like if a house is well constructed or a slave is beautiful) without incurring liability, but if he says a slave is educated (*litteratus*) or a craftsmen (*artifex*), the slave must be these things as the vendor can ask for a higher price as a result. Similarly, as discussed below, a vendor need not provide a wise slave (*sapiens*) but the slave cannot be so unintelligent that he cannot function (D. 21.1.4.3 Ulpian, *Curule Aediles' Edict*, book 1). Notably, Gaius, in the same fragment as the one about the cook, discusses even more intangible things like loyalty and being hardworking (D. 21.1.18pr).
63. *P.Oxy.* 724. 155 CE.

foreman (*vilicus*) of an estate, which require executive function and trust, seem unlikely to fit here. Skilled slaves might also have been more likely to be sold between private individuals; we might wonder if Cicero's friend Atticus, who trained even his footmen (*pedisequi*) to be skilled readers (*anagnostae*) and copyists (*librarii*), ever sold or gifted these educated slaves to acquaintances.[64]

While being fooled was always a possibility when purchasing any slave, the higher financial stakes in the specialty markets made this prospect loom large in the minds of prospective buyers. Pliny the Elder tells the story of Marc Antony being swindled by a slave-dealer for an astonishing amount of money. The slave-dealer, Toranius, sold Marc Antony two handsome enslaved boys (*pueri*) whom, on account of their similar appearance, the slave-dealer claimed were twins. They were not twins—one was from across the Alps and the other from Asia—and Marc Antony discovered this shortly after the sale because of their speech. The *pueri* might well have been in on the trick, incentivized to appear as twins particularly if they wanted to stay together. Antony returned to the slave-dealer to protest the deceit, in particular because he had paid 200,000 *sesterces* for the twins. Toranius convinced Marc Antony that they were so expensive precisely because they were not twins.[65] The story involves the crucial aspects of Roman slave-buying culture discussed previously in this chapter: the reasons why one buys a particular slave, the variability of price, the different origins of slaves, the deceitfulness of slave-dealers, and especially, the importance of listening to the speech of slaves. This sort of trickery brought about stricter regulations on the sale of slaves.

Disease and Defect

The first half of this chapter was preoccupied with masterly desires; what slave owners wanted and wished for in their slaves. From here we turn to Roman law, which was more directly focused on implementing this desire and protecting slave owners through legislation and the work of the jurists. This allows us to see what traits and qualities in enslaved people were prized and which ones caused the most anxiety. Regulations on the sale of slaves created a legal language and framework for buyers to better evaluate the character and qualities of their poten-

64. Nep. *Att.* 13. Plutarch also reports that Crassus trained and taught his slaves, Plut. *Crass.* 2.5–6.
65. Plin. *HN* 7.56. For more on slave-dealers and what they legally must reveal, see Bodel 2005; Harrill 1999; and Watson 1987b.

tial slaves. The Twelve Tables (451–450 BCE), according to Cicero, stipulated that if a vendor made a formal oral declaration that was not true, he was liable to a double penalty.[66] Protections for the buyer were further intensified under the action on purchase (*actio empti*). Sales had to be made "in good faith" (*bona fides*); the buyer would have an action if the seller purposefully did not disclose a reason why the value of the property bought would diminish. For the buyer to be recompensed, they had to show that the seller was aware of the defect.[67]

Under these protections, the curule aediles, the magistrates in charge of the marketplace, introduced regulations specifically for the purchase of slaves and draft animals that gave the buyer even more security.[68] The jurist Ulpian quotes the portion of the edict that refers to the redhibition or rescission of slave sales (*actio redhibitoria*) by which a buyer could return a slave to the seller under certain circumstances:

> The aediles say: "Those who sell slaves are to apprise purchasers of any disease or defect in their wares and whether a given slave is a runaway, a wanderer, or still subject to noxal liability; all these matters they must proclaim in due manner when the slaves are sold. If a slave be sold without compliance with this regulation or contrary to what has been said of or promised about him at the time of his sale, it is for us to declare what is due with respect to him; we will grant to the purchaser and to all other interested parties an action for rescission in respect of the slave. The purchaser, however, will have to make good on all of the following cases: any deterioration in the slave after the sale and purchase which is attributable to the purchaser himself, his household, or his manager (*procurator*); anything born of or acquired through the slave since the sale; and anything else which accedes to the slave consequent upon the sale or any profits which the purchaser acquires through him. Equally, there will be due to the vendor any accessories which he himself may have provided. Again, vendors must declare at the time of the sale all that follows: any capital offense committed by the slave; an attempt which he has made upon his own life; and whether

66. Cic. *Off.* 3.65.
67. On the *actio empti*, see Stein 1958, 5–27; Jolowicz and Nicholas 1972, 279–304 on contract and 292–97 on the *actio empti* specifically; generally, on the law of sale, see Zimmerman 1996, 230–337.
68. On the *actio redhibitoria*, see Ortu 2008; Cloud 2007; Donadio 2004a; Garofalo 2000; Jakab 1997; Manna 1994; Watson 1987a, 47–52; and Impallomeni 1955. On the aediles, see Daguet-Gagey 2015. See Frier and Kehoe 2007, 120–21, on why the aediles intervened in the slave (and livestock) market and not elsewhere.

he has been sent into the arena to fight wild animals. On these grounds also we will give the action. In addition, we will grant the action if it be alleged that a slave has been sold, with deliberate wrongful intent, in contravention of our provisions."

Aiunt aediles: "Qui mancipia vendunt certiores faciant emptores, quid morbi vitiive cuique sit, quis fugitivus errove sit noxave solutus non sit: eademque omnia, cum ea mancipia venibunt, palam recte pronuntianto. Quodsi mancipium adversus ea venisset, sive adversus quod dictum promissumve fuerit cum veniret, fuisset, quod eius praestari oportere dicetur: emptori omnibusque ad quos ea res pertinet iudicium dabimus, ut id mancipium redhibeatur. Si quid autem post venditionem traditionemque deterius emptoris opera familiae procuratorisve eius factum erit, sive quid ex eo post venditionem natum adquisitum fuerit, et si quid aliud in venditione ei accesserit, sive quid ex ea re fructus pervenerit ad emptorem, ut ea omnia restituat. Item si quas accessiones ipse praestiterit, ut recipiat. Item si quod mancipium capitalem fraudem admiserit, mortis consciscendae sibi causa quid fecerit, inve harenam depugnandi causa ad bestias intromissus fuerit, ea omnia in venditione pronuntianto: ex his enim causis iudicium dabimus. Hoc amplius si quis adversus ea sciens dolo malo vendidisse dicetur, iudicium dabimus."[69]

If the slave-dealer failed to announce any of this then the aediles will grant an action for rescission within six months of purchase and for a reduction in price within one year (*actio quanti minoris*). Differently than the general rules of sale guided by *bona fides*, the slave-dealer was now liable for defects even if they were latent or he was unaware of them. The aediles justify the provisions in this part of the edict as a means of warding off and protecting against the deceit of slave-dealers.[70] While the precise date of the Edict of the Aediles is unclear, most scholars consider a version of the edict to be in place by the early second century BCE and it certainly was in effect by the first century BCE, as Cicero notes the differences between the Aedilician regulations and the regular accommodations for sale.[71]

69. D. 21.1.1.1 Ulpian, *Curule Aediles' Edict*, book 1.
70. D. 21.1.1.2, 6 Ulpian, *Curule Aediles' Edict*, book 1.
71. Cic. *Off.* 3.71. On the turn of the second-century BCE date, see Cloud 2007, 68; Jakab 1997, 128–29; Manna 1994, 11–32; Cloud 2007, 68. Manna argues that this is due to the influx of slaves following the wars with Carthage, Macedonia, and the Seleucids in the early second century BCE. This date is supported by Plautus' use of legal language for the return of slaves; see, e.g., *Capt.* 803–825; *Merc.* 416–419;

My interest here is not in the protections the edict afforded a buyer, but in the juristic interpretations regarding potential diseases and defects that were attributed to enslaved people. As we will see, while the jurists turn to wider cultural debates about diseases and defects of the mind, this history of defect is profoundly grounded in centuries of experimentation around the pervasiveness and realities of slavery. The amount of detail about the specific diseases and defects of slaves that constitute a possible redhibitory action is not surprising given the high price of slaves and the many roles they played in Roman society. Certain aspects of this medicalization of the behaviors and attributes of enslaved people had to be created by the jurists for this redhibitory purpose. It is for this reason that the juristic discussion of disease and defect in their commentary on the Edict of the Aediles is one of the foremost treatments on the topic in antiquity.[72] In the literary sources discussed earlier in this chapter, Roman writers consider methods of evaluating not only the physical capabilities of slaves but also their mental qualities and character. Here the jurists discuss a variety of perceived physical and mental ailments and deficiencies, then catalog them into corporeal or mental diseases (*morbi*) or defects (*vitia*). This process, particularly the scrutiny given to mental ailments, explicitly draws attention to the slave as *persona*.[73] As these actions are for the return of or financial compensation for a "defective slave," they bring to the fore the owner's inability to know the slave over whom they have taken ownership.

The juristic engagement with medical language to describe the potential maladies of slaves is not our only evidence that potential Roman slave purchasers were interested in a medical approach.[74] We can also detect this interest

Mostell. 795–800; *Mil.* 725–730. See Manna 1994, 23, on the relationship between Plautine comedy and the edict. On Plautus and Roman law, see Bartholomä 2019, and on Plautus and Roman slavery, see Richlin 2017 and 2014 and Stewart 2012. Others suggest the first half of the second century BCE because of the reference in D. 21.1.10.1 Ulpian, Curule *Aediles' Edict*, book 1 to Cato's discussion of *morbus*, see Daube 1956, 91–97. Daube based his dating on the use of future imperatives, suggesting the late third century BCE to early second century BCE and goes as far as to suggest that the edict was created at the urging of Cato. See Watson 1971, 134–35, on this date but he dismisses the idea about Cato's role and see also Manna 1994, 26. Aulus Gellius quotes a seemingly earlier version of the edict than the one preserved in *Digest* 21.1, which was standardized by the jurist Julian along with the Praetorian Edict during the reign of Hadrian (after 132 CE) at *NA* 4.2.1. See also Gellius *NA* 17.6.2–3 on the *servus recepticius*, the slave returned on account of defects. See Manna 1994, 4, and DeZulueta 1945, 50, on this being an earlier form of the edict, *contra* Impallomeni 1955.

72. On the Latin terminology of disability and the prominence of this juristic discussion of disease and defect, see, for example, Laes 2022b, 5–9.
73. On *persona*, see Mantovani 2010.
74. See, for example, D. 21.1.5 Paul, *Sabinus*, book 11, "And just as there is a distinction between those defects which the Greeks describe as a bad disposition and those which they categorize as affliction, disease, or weakness, so there is a distinction between these faults and a disease whereby the

from the lost treatise of the physician Rufus of Ephesus, *On Buying Slaves*, which Simon Swain conjectures was about physiognomic indicators.[75] In *La Maladie de l'Âme*, Jackie Pigeaud questions the role of medicine in law and shows that of the three great traditions of madness (i.e., tragic, medical, and philosophical), the vocabulary of the law is drawn from the philosophical tradition. He argues that the third book of Cicero's *Tusculan Disputations* gave birth to the philosophical-juridical tradition of the study of madness.[76] The jurists discussing potential mental ailments of slaves quickly dispense with disease (*morbus*) and discuss these problems as defects of mind (*vitia animi*).[77] Mental defects fall largely into three kinds: faults of character, forms of madness, and being a runaway (the discussion of madness and being a runaway will take place in chapter 2).

The jurists carefully cataloged the diseases and defects of slaves; contextualizing the meaning of disease and defect more broadly will help us understand how the jurists and other Roman writers characterized, evaluated, and sorted the bodies and minds of both free people and slaves. This, in turn, will help us determine whether Romans perceived any fundamental medical differences between legal statuses, especially given the role that the history of slavery played in this process. Following his quotation of the edict, Ulpian states his understanding of *morbus* and *vitium* in which he medicalizes utility. Ulpian's interpretation is not focused on the nature of disease or defect, or even what the difference between the two might be. Rather, he concentrates on any condition (*morbus* or *vitium*) that might impede a slave's ability to perform their assigned use or duty (*usus ministeriumque*), and whether this is grounds for rescission.[78] For Ulpian then, the slave begins and ends with their *usus* and *ministerium*; he also considers the question of disease and defect not through a physical or cor-

usability of a slave is reduced" (*Et quantum interest inter haec vitia quae Graeci* κακοήθειαν *dicunt, interque* πάθος *aut* νόσον *aut* ἀρρωστίαν, *tantum inter talia vitia et eum morbum, ex quo quis minus aptus usui sit, differt*). See also D. 21.1.10.4 Ulpian, *Curule Aediles' Edict*, book 1.

75. Swain 2008, 121, bases this argument on the prevalence of physiognomy in relevant (medical, ethical) Muslim texts that drew heavily from Rufus. On buyers of slaves potentially having access to the ongoing discussion of madness, see Nutton 2008, 153–55, who shows that some awareness of the medicine of the day was a part of cultural knowledge from dinner banquets to doctor-patient relationships. Toohey 2013 and Trenchard-Smith 2010 argue instead that the work on madness by the jurists is separate from the medical and philosophical tradition. On madness and the law, see Diliberto 1984 and Nardi 1983.

76. Pigeaud 1989, 250. On the connection between law and philosophy with respect to the treatment of slaves in particular, see Knoch 2005, 45–122.

77. On *vitia animi*, see Aubert 2011; Cocatre-Zilgien 2008; Parlamento 2001.

78. D. 21.1.1.7–8 Ulpian, *Curule Aediles' Edict*, book 1. See Ortu 2008, 161, discussing Ulpian's ultimate indifference on *morbus* and *vitium*.

poreal schema, but in terms of usefulness to the owner. Although Ulpian suggests that the aediles use both *morbus* and *vitium* to cast a wider net over potential ailments rather than to dissect their semantic difference, the distinction between *morbus* and *vitium* was not ignored. He provides this distinction as understood in the work of the jurist Caelius Sabinus,[79] which is preserved in more detail in Aulus Gellius' *Attic Nights*:

> So the earlier jurists investigated what is properly said to be a "diseased slave" and a "defective" one and how much a "disease" differs from a "defect." Caelius Sabinus, in the book which he wrote, *On the Edict of the Curule Aediles*, quotes Labeo, who defines "disease" with these words: "Disease is a condition of the body contrary to nature, which diminishes its utility." But he says a "disease" sometimes affects the entire body and sometimes a part of it only. A "disease" of the whole body is, for example, consumption or fever, but of a part of the body would be blindness or a weakness of the foot. He adds, "while a person who stammers or speaks inarticulately is defective more than diseased and a horse which bites or kicks is defective not diseased, a person who is diseased is at the same time defective. But the opposite is not always the case: for it is possible someone is defective and not diseased. So when considering a diseased man," he said, "it is fair to say 'how much less the price will be on account of this defect.'"

> Propterea quaesierunt iure consulti veteres, quod "mancipium morbosum" quodve "vitiosum" recte diceretur quantumque "morbus" a "vitio" differret. Caelius Sabinus in libro, quem *De Edicto Aedilium Curulium* composuit, Labeonem refert quid esset "morbus" hisce verbis definisse: "Morbus est habitus cuiusque corporis contra naturam, qui usum eius facit deteriorem." Sed "morbum" alias in toto corpore accidere dicit, alias in parte corporis. Totius corporis "morbum" esse, veluti sit phthisis aut febris, partis autem, veluti sit caecitas aut pedis debilitas. "Balbus autem," inquit, "et atypus vitiosi magis quam morbosi sunt, et equus mordax aut calcitro vitiosus, non morbosus est. Sed cui morbus est, idem etiam vitiosus est. Neque id tamen contra fit; potest enim qui vitiosus est non morbosus esse. Quamobrem, cum de homine morboso agetur, aeque," inquit, "ita dicetur: 'quanto ob id vitium minoris erit.'"[80]

79. D. 21.1.1.7 Ulpian, *Curule Aediles' Edict*, book 1.
80. Gell. *NA* 4.2.2–5. On this passage, see Ortu 2008, 93–143; Manna 1994, 34–39; Impallomeni 1955, 39–43, 94–99.

Gellius notes that the discussion of the difference between *morbus* and *vitium* is an old one, referencing the "old jurists" (*iurisconsulti veteres*), and that Caelius Sabinus is actually giving the definition of *morbus* according to Labeo, a jurist of the Augustan period. Like Ulpian nearly two hundred years later, Labeo's interpretation of *morbus* and *vitium* is, in the end, one of economic expediency. While he does consider the differences and relationship between the terms, they are not always mutually exclusive: The person who stammers (*balbus*) or speaks inarticulately (*atypus*) is more (*magis quam*) defective than diseased, rather than only one or the other.[81]

Labeo understands disease to be more encompassing than defect; a diseased man is also defective, but the defective man is not necessarily diseased. *Morbus* is "a state contrary to nature" (*habitus contra naturam*). *Vitium* is not described as a state (*habitus*), and the discussion refers more to the defective (*vitiosus*) than the defect (*vitium*). A *morbus* can affect the whole or a part of the body, but it is unclear whether a *vitium* can affect the whole body. However, a worker's loss in value is due to *vitium* rather than *morbus*. For Labeo, it seems that the defect is the manifestation of the ailment; the defective part of the disease is that which deteriorates the utility of the diseased man (*qui usum eius facit deteriorem*). This would seem to fit with his understanding that a horse that kicks or bites is defective rather than diseased (though the internal logic of these distinctions is not entirely clear).

Ulpian's rendering of Caelius Sabinus' distinction between *morbus* and *vitium* tells us that *vitium* is very different than *morbus* (*vitiumque a morbo multum differre*); but he too preserves the *magis quam* clause, that one who stammers is more defective than diseased, which suggests that the line is not entirely unambiguous for Ulpian either.[82] The jurist Modestinus instead offers a different approach toward the distinction between *morbus* and *vitium*.[83] In a work discussing differences in terminology, Modestinus makes the distinction between *morbus* and *vitium* a temporal one; a permanent ailment is a *vitium*, a recoverable one a *morbus*. While controversy and debate are not surprising

81. The contrast with the straightforward "(the horse) is not diseased" (*non morbosus est*) seems to support the translation of *magis quam* as "more than" here.

82. D. 21.1.1.7 Ulpian, *Curule Aediles' Edict*, book 1.

83. D. 50.16.101.2 Modestinus, *Distinctions*, book 9, "It is right that 'disease' is a temporary weakness of the body, 'defect,' however, is a permanent flaw in the body, as, for instance, if someone has broken his ankle; for someone one-eyed is also defective" (*Verum est 'morbum' esse temporalem corporis inbecillitatem, 'vitium' vero perpetuum corporis impedimentum, veluti si talum excussit: nam et luscus utique vitiosus est.*). On this passage, see Ortu 2008, 102; Manna 1994, 36.

among the jurists, we might still wonder why the juristic debate on the exact difference between the two terms and the scope of each was so extensive. I would suggest that the acute interest in the *morbi* and *vitia* of slaves in the juristic works is indicative of a wider cultural interest in the health of slaves. So while marketplace pragmatism guides the legal result—loss of utility is what matters in terms of return or compensation for a diseased or defective slave—the discussion has the auxiliary effect of addressing the need in Roman slave-owning society to understand slave health. It is important then not to view this discourse as merely a puzzle or academic exercise of the jurists without any real-world application. It is tied to a wider discussion on mental ailments and value—but social, cultural, and philosophical value rather than that of the marketplace. In their work on the Edict of the Aediles, the jurists generally import two existing technologies of diagnosis by equating the physical disability of slaves with that of free people and at times that of animals, as well as by drawing upon philosophical writings to examine mental afflictions. However, as we will see, for unwanted attributes that are exclusive to the enslaved population, the jurists must develop their own methods of diagnosis.[84]

A wider cultural discussion on mental ailments and value that reflects upon the differences between *morbi* and *vitia* can be seen not long before Labeo's day; Cicero considers the matter in the *Tusculan Disputations* of 45 BCE.[85] Cicero contrasts the *morbi, aegrotationes* (sicknesses), and *vitia* of the body with those of the mind and explains that a *morbus* is a *corruptio* (a corruption, spoiling) of the whole body; an *aegrotatio* is a *morbus* with *imbecillitas* (weakness), and a *vitium* a *corruptio* leading to an asymmetry in body parts. Cicero goes on to say that a *vitium* is a *pravitas, distortio,* or *deformitas* of a limb or body part. While there are differences between Cicero's and Labeo's conception of these terms, they have similar concerns about whether the terms relate to the whole or part of the body; they also agree that *vitia* seems to generally come in a secondary capacity.[86] Cicero's choice of language brings an element of morality into his

84. On equating the physical ailments of slaves with animals, see, for example, D. 21.1.4.3 Ulpian, *Curule Aediles' Edict*, book 1, on restitution not being available to beasts of burden (*iumenta*) for mental defects; D. 21.1.8 Ulpian *Curule Aediles' Edict*, book 1, on the loss of a tongue in a horse and in an enslaved person; and D. 21.1.38 Ulpian *Curule Aediles' Edict*, book 2, on the applicability generally of the edict and juristic commentary on beasts of burden.

85. Cic. *Tusc.* 4.28–29. See Pigeaud 1989, 250, and Graver 2002, 148–60.

86. On Cicero and his reception among the early imperial jurists, see Wibier 2016. While Cicero discussed the differences between mental and physical disease and defect in several places, he does not directly reference any of the jurists who investigate the issue and at times differs from their understandings. Cicero was a friend of the Republican jurists Ofilius and Trebatius Testa, both of whom are quoted in the juristic commentaries of the Edict of the Aediles.

discussion of *morbus, aegrotatio,* and *vitium. Corruptio* can be used to mean a bodily condition, highlighting an aspect of degradation; however, *corruptio* is rarely used without a moralizing tone.[87] The tie of these physical ailments to *corruptio,* of *aegrotatio* to *imbecillitas,*[88] and of *vitium* to *pravitas, distortio,* and *deformitas* suggest that to have an ailment of the body negatively impacts the goodness of the person.[89] The term *pravitas,* when referring to the body, concerns a physical crookedness;[90] but the word also carries strong ties to the morally debased.[91] *Deformitas* too contains both physical and moral aspects: physical difference along with the idea of disgrace.[92]

Cicero then turns directly to the distinction between *morbus, aegrotatio,* and *vitiositas* (defectiveness) in the mind (*animus*).[93] For Cicero, the difference between a *morbus* and an *aegrotatio* of the mind is only theoretical. He describes *vitiositas* of the mind as a permanent state or manner that is out of sorts and inconsistent with itself. Cicero's description of defectiveness (*vitiositas*) of the mind is similar to Labeo's understanding of disease (*morbus*). While Labeo considers a *morbus* to be a state against nature (*habitus contra naturam*), Cicero here regards the defectiveness of the mind as a state or manner (*habitus aut adfectio*) that is in disagreement with itself (*a se ipsa dissentiens*). Cicero's discussion of *morbus* and *vitium* differs from that of the jurists in technical terminology; however, it is clear that he, like the jurists, uses the language of morality to discuss physical and mental ailments. The morality evidenced in Cicero is consistent with wider Roman ideas about disability and illness as well as with the jurists who consider *vitia animi* as problems of character intrinsically linked to morality. More surprisingly, this moralizing frame remains the same across the status lines of freedom and enslavement.

At times, Roman authors of different genres use the terms *morbus* and *vitium* together to mean "the defect of disease;" we see the phrase *vitium morbi* used in the medical writings of the encyclopedist Celsus.[94] Vitruvius uses the term to discuss a disease that people thought could be contracted at the Fountain of Salmacis. He refers to the disease as venereal (*venerius morbus*), but the condition is not what we would immediately associate with a medical ailment.

---

87. Cic. *Verr.* 1.5–6; Tac. *Ann.* 2.55.5, 11.2.1, 12.46.3.
88. *Imbecillitas* refers to a feebleness or helplessness: D. 16.1.2.2 Ulpian, *Edict*, book 29; D. 46.3.68 Marcellus, *Digest*, book 16; Cic. *Ad Brut.* 1.10.4, *Fam.* 1.4.3 (SB 14), *Off.* 2.75; Sen. *Ben.* 7.27.3.
89. Garland 1995, 73–86, on the derision of disabled people.
90. Cic. *De or.* 2.91 (a distortion of the mouth when speaking), *Leg.* 1.51; Columella *Rust.* 4.20.1.
91. Sen. *NQ* 3.5; Quint. *Inst.* 1.1.37, 2.15.2; Tac. *Ann.* 3.16, 3.34, 14.38.
92. Cic. *Fam.* 10.6 (SB 360); Sen. *Ben.* 1.10.2, *Ep.* 83.27; Tac. *Ann.* 11.32; Gell. *NA* 3.3.6.
93. Graver 2002, 158, notes that *vitiositas* is created by Cicero.
94. Celsus, *Med.* 3.5.5, regarding common fevers.

Using this language of "the defect of the disease," Vitruvius gives us what is, in a sense, a symptomatology of the disease: a man is too effeminate or soft (*mollis*) and too impudent or wanton (*impudicus*).[95] While the medicalization of concerns about manliness and personality may at times operate as a metaphor, it is clear from these technical writers that the Roman cultural and linguistic understanding of disease incorporated precisely these sorts of concerns about character. Seneca uses the image of men so afflicted "by a defect of a disease" (*vitio morbi*) that they cannot taste the sweetness of honey to suggest that the wise should only consort with other men of sound body and mind (i.e., those who can taste the sweetness of honey).[96] Seneca here deploys the language of disease and defect to discuss the philosophical good and bad man; medical terminology is adopted to discuss matters of character (as seen in the man made effeminate) and morality (the good of avoiding bad people). Virtuvius and Celsus were writing at nearly the same time as Labeo, and Seneca shortly after. Their use of *vitium morbi* to mean "the defect of the disease" does not stray too far from Labeo's understanding that a man with a disease is defective. For these authors, the disease is the original problem and the defect is the manifestation: The symptoms are the defects of the disease. The passages of Vitruvius and Seneca highlight how medical terminology found its way into a variety of different genres. The prevalence of medical imagery and metaphor across genres, including juristic literature, allows us to create a broader picture of how sanity of the mind and body was viewed and how it valued or devalued people.

The jurists use the above language to discuss forms of disability, difference, and physical illnesses and injuries that may allow for the rescission of a slave sale. Notably, and seemingly beyond the scope of interest for the practically minded classical jurists (and compilers of the *Digest of Justinian*), the defect's or disease's end result is not always the determining factor in the granting of rescission. For example, when the jurists consider which ailments would render a female slave defective, pregnant women are considered healthy, but the question of infertility is raised. The jurist Trebatius Testa, cited by Caelius Sabinus

95. Vitr. *De arch.* 2.8.12. In *De Finibus*, written in 45 BCE, Cicero discusses the contrary-to-nature movements of a man, citing a man who is too effeminate. He argues that even if it is caused by a mental defect it leads to a physical problem (Cic. *Fin.* 5.35). Cicero's conception tracks well with the juristic idea of mental defects becoming a problem when they affect the body; see Donadio 2004a, 125, on the jurist Vivian discussing the *vitium corporis* that goes even to the mind (*usque ad animum penetrat*, D. 21.1.4.1 Ulpian, *Curule Aediles' Edict*, book 1).

96. Sen. *Ep.* 109.7.

and then Ulpian, says that women who were naturally infertile were healthy, but if the infertility was due to a physical defect (*vitium corporis*) then the woman was defective.[97] Regardless of whether the infertility was congenital, infertility does affect the use of this slave, though only the purchaser of a slave with noncongenital infertility could return the slave (there are practical and even more gruesome issues as well: How might this be determined, and if uncertain, which form of infertility was assumed?). For free Roman women, infertility (congenital or not) was grounds for divorce.[98] The freewoman's *vitium corporis* has a slave counterpart: the free woman is divorced, the enslaved woman is devalued and returned.

Physical injury, by definition congenital, was also discussed: The loss of a limb or body part was not always grounds for rescission. The jurists seem to disagree, for example, about whether a castrated enslaved person was diseased.[99] This is likely because castrated slaves were desired by a subset of the population and young castrated slaves would command higher prices.[100] Loss of fingers and toes largely depended on whether the injury was accompanied by a loss of utility for the slave owner and, similarly, congenital disabilities like conjoined fingers also were measured by loss of utility.[101] While utility as a met-

97. D. 21.1.14.1 Ulpian, *Curule Aediles' Edict*, book 1, on pregnancy. D. 21.1.14.3 Ulpian, *Curule Aediles' Edict*, book 1, on naturally infertile rather than due to bodily defect, "Where an infertile woman is concerned, Caelius says that Trebatius took a distinction: If she be naturally infertile, she is healthy, but not if her infertility be due to some bodily defect" (*De sterili Caelius distinguere Trebatium dicit, ut, si natura sterilis sit, sana est, si vitio corporis, contra*). See, on this same passage, Gell. *NA* 4.2.8–10. See Ortu 2008, 144–50, discussing the relevance, or Donadio 2004a, 101–2, on the difference between Trebatius and Labeo.

98. Dalla 1978, 246–50, discusses the role of infertility in divorce. See also Treggiari 1991, 442, 462, 465, on infertility as grounds for divorce. Bonner 1949, 122–24, on the trope of divorcing a wife after five years if no child was born. See Evans Grubbs 2002 on children being the purpose of marriage: 81, 83, 122, 171–73. In the legal sources, see D. 24.1.60.1 Hermogenian, *Epitome of Law*, book 2. See also D. 21.1.14.7 Ulpian, *Curule Aediles' Edict*, book 1, with Ortu 2008, 179, and Donadio 2004a, 101–2.

99. D. 21.1.7 Paul, *Sabinus*, book 11, argues that if the castrated enslaved person lacks a necessary body part he is diseased; D. 21.1.6.2 Ulpian, *Curule Aediles' Edict*, book 1, suggests that a castrated man is not diseased any more than a person missing one testicle (and thus can still procreate); D. 21.1.38.7 Ulpian, *Curule Aediles' Edict*, book 2, in a discussion on differences between diseases in animals and humans, Ulpian cites Caelius writing that not all castrated animals were defective (he gives the example of the mule who has not been made weaker by castration). Caelius (within the citation of Ulpian) cites Ofilius who says a gelding is healthy as is a castrated slave, but if the buyer did not know, an action on purchase (*actio empti*) would be given (Ulpian agrees with Ofilius).

100. On castrated people at the slave market, see Huemoeller 2016, 229–32, and Tougher 2013, 48–72.

101. D. 21.1.10pr-2 Ulpian, *Curule Aediles' Edict*, book 1, reports that Cato called a slave who lost a finger or a toe diseased (*morbosus*). This is one of the fragments that is used to date the edict, though Cato could be speaking of defective slaves before the edict came about; on this, see Ortu 2008, 107–17. D. 21.1.1.10pr Ulpian, *Curule Aedlies' Edict*, book 1, citing Ofilius on the importance

ric rather than the particular number of fingers or toes is consistent with the jurists' application of the redhibitory action more generally, the juristic discussion of the loss of fingers and the loss of ability resonates with the importance of hands to Roman power relations. As Erik Gunderson has argued in his study of declamation, "the loss of hands is always ready to be confused with a loss of authority" and, as he notes, *manus* is the method by which one takes possession (*manum inicere*), gives a daughter away to a husband in an archaic form of marriage (*cum manu*), and frees a slave (*manu mittere*).[102] Slaves lack authority and are always the object of *manus* relationships, but the loss of hands affects the primary criterion that gives them value in Roman society: their ability to be used. The juristic interpretation of the Aediles' Edict on the sale of slaves is drawn from developed branches of knowledge about medicine and the mind, as well as the jurists' own construction of slave medicine based on masterly understandings of the qualities and characteristics desired from the enslaved population. The jurists' study of disease and defect reveals masterly concerns about the slave, especially regarding their mind. Evaluation is already difficult, and especially so when it regards internal attributes—this difficulty itself accounts for the breadth of medical juristic discussions about slaves, as well as the emphasis on slave speech as a guide.

Talking Tool

In his introductory comments on the Edict of the Aediles, Ulpian notes that if a disease or defect can be seen (*intellego*), then the edict has no grounds as its purpose is to ensure the buyer not be misled. The jurist explains that defects are often revealed by their symptoms (*signa*), and perhaps this tie between obvious physical loss and some greater internal issue is one reason that leads the jurists to discuss visible injuries and disabilities.[103] The shift away from the loss of util-

---

of utility loss when it comes to limb loss; D. 21.1.10.2 Ulpian, *Curule Aediles' Edict*, book 1, on having more fingers or toes, and again only allowing rescission if there is loss of utility.

D. 21.1.14.6 Ulpian, *Curule Aediles' Edict*, book 1, where much of Ulpian's discussion relates to diseases and defects from birth, the jurist considers also the man born with conjoined fingers not healthy (*non sanum*), but only if his utility is diminished. For more discussion, see Ortu 2008, 176–77.

102. For tying the loss of hands to a loss of authority and power in declamation, see Gunderson 2003, 59–89, quote at 60. In this vein, see D. 1.1.4 Ulpian, *Institutes*, book 1, on the juristic discussion of the etymology of manumission.

103. D. 21.1.1.6 Ulpian, *Curule Aediles' Edict*, book 1.

ity (seemingly the point of the edict) to more minor physical afflictions like loss of fingers or issues of speech, as will be discussed below, underscores the symptomatology that the jurists and other Romans engaged in.[104] This close attention to symptoms reflects Pliny the Younger's idea that to understand what a slave is really like, one must pay attention and listen to them. In the juristic discussion of a different law, the *lex Aquilia* on wrongful damage to property, a case involving a talented enslaved painter who lost a thumb shows how physical loss and impairment indicates the loss of an internal characteristic. The case is as follows: Sometime in the year before his death, an enslaved painter lost his thumb at the hands of a third party. The person who killed this slave must pay the painter's owner his highest value in the last year which, according to Julian in this case, would be before he lost his skill (*ars*) along with his thumb.[105] If this situation were transposed to the slave market, the loss of the thumb would signify the loss of the slave's skill and thus trade, lowering his market value not to the amount of a thumb, but to the amount of his lost skill.

A similar line of judgment pertains to the tongue, speech, and intellect if we return to the Edict of the Aediles. There is discussion among the jurists about whether a slave who does not speak or speak clearly is healthy. Some of the jurists' opinions are determined physically: Ofilius says a horse whose tongue has been cut out is not healthy; Ulpian cites this to indicate a slave would not be either.[106] Issues with speech too serve as a symptom or malady in their own right; Ulpian reports in his commentary on the works of Massurius Sabinus, "Sabinus says that a nonspeaking slave (*mutus*) is diseased; for it is clear that to be without a voice is a disease; whereas someone who speaks with difficulty (*graviter*) or unclearly (*asaphōs*) is not diseased; obviously, the slave whose speech is unintelligible (*asēmōs*) is diseased to that extent" (*Mutum morbosum esse Sabinus ait: morbum enim esse sine voce esse apparet. Sed qui graviter loquitur, morbosus non est, nec qui* ἀσαφῶς: *plane qui* ἀσήμως *loquitur, hic utique*

104. It is not my intention to give a full account of the maladies the jurists discuss, for example, problems with vision and the eyes are also mentioned often.

105. D. 9.2.23.3 Ulpian, *Edict*, book 18, "Julian also writes that the valuation of the dead slave is made as at that time in the preceding year when he was worth most; and accordingly, if the thumb of a most valuable painter had been cut off beforehand and within a year of its loss he is killed, the Aquilian action lies and he must be valued at his price before he lost his skill together with his thumb" (*Idem Iulianus scribit aestimationem hominis occisi ad id tempus referri, quo plurimi in eo anno fuit: et ideo et si pretioso pictori pollex fuerit praecisus et intra annum, quo praecideretur, fuerit occisus, posse eum Aquilia agere pretioque eo aestimandum, quanti fuit priusquam artem cum pollice amisisset*).

106. D. 21.1.8 Ulpian, *Curule Aediles' Edict*, book 1.

morbosus est).[107] The distinctions provided by Sabinus reveal how slave speech was valued as a sign of underlying rationality: The slaves who speak with some difficulty (*graviter, asaphōs*) are trying to communicate rational thoughts but with trouble; meanwhile, the slave whose speech is unintelligible or nonexistent (*asēmōs, mutus*) cannot verbalize rational thoughts. This can be understood more clearly when we keep in mind that *asaphōs* is common terminology for something obscure, while *asēmōs* is a more technical term used to refer to unstamped metal or coin: there is nothing there.[108]

The importance of slave speech invites us to revisit Varro's infamous definition of a slave as a "talking tool" (*instrumentum vocale*) in contrast to an "inarticulate" (*semivocale*)—that is, cattle (*boves*)—or "nonspeaking" (*mutum*) one—that is, wagons (*plaustra*).[109] While it can be difficult to see beyond the brutish inhumanity of equating humans with cows and carts, it is worth bearing in mind the importance Varro attributes to speech as his criterion of distinction between the three. Varro does not call slaves "animate tools" or "tools with minds," but we might think that is precisely what he means. As Varro's later counterpart Columella counseled, the emphasis on the speaking slave might point to an underlying attitude akin to "these tools talk, and it is worth listening to what they have to say." As we have seen, listening to slave speech was a fundamental part of the masterly evaluation process of the skills, abilities, and character of slaves. Lack of speech, on the other hand, is a profoundly striking manner of describing a wagon or other farming equipment. The nonspeaking cart is not a cart that does not talk but a thing without a mind. Following this logic, then, a slave who is nonspeaking would be deemed "inanimate," and without a mind, this person could not work. But while nonspeaking slaves are not included in Varro's tripartite division of tools, they are found in the legal sources.

Nonspeaking slaves (*muti*) are mentioned again by Gaius in his commentary on the Edict of the Aediles. Ulpian mentions a *balbus* slave twice: once when citing Sabinus on the definition of *vitiosus* in contrast to *morbosus*, and again when posing the question of whether the *balbus*, *blaesus*, and *atypus* slave, or those slaves who speak *tardius*, *varus*, or *vatius*, were healthy (he

107. D. 21.1.9 Ulpian, *Sabinus*, book 44. Dalla 1989 on deafness and muteness. Ortu 2008, 169; Donadio 2004a, 113–19, on *servus mutus*. See Donadio 2004a, 105–13, on *balbus* and *atypus* as a *vitium corporis*.

108. On *asēmōs* see, e.g., Hdt. 9.41.

109. Varro *Rust.* 1.17. On the importance of slave speech, especially in Plautus, with comparative analysis from the United States, see Stewart 2012, 156–89.

believes they are). There is also a question of whether the slave who by nature speaks gutturally (*quis natura gutturosus*) is healthy (they are).[110] The precise distinctions between these different speech impairments are at times unclear.[111] *Balbus*, stammering, *blaesus*, lisping or potentially slurring speech when drinking, and *tardius*, speaking slowly, appear straightforward.[112] It is also clear why Ulpian regards a slave with any of these speech impairments as healthy; these kinds of impairment are not presented as symptoms of a wider medical problem. Less clear is the *atypus* slave and those who speak *varus* or *vatius. Atypus* can be classed as stammering or speaking inarticulately, but how it differs from *balbus* is unclear. Similarly, *varus* and *vatius* seem typically to refer to a physical disability, the bending outward of the legs, so this could analogously refer to a distortion of speech or some physical difference, perhaps around the mouth, which affects speech.[113] Ulpian also regards these slaves as healthy, however. Similarly, the slave who speaks *natura gutturosus* can still communicate (and there is a stress with *natura* on this being a congenital issue; perhaps one who comes to speak gutturally would be considered defective). These speech impairments are important then not because the owner would have grounds for an action on rescission, but because slave speech is revelatory. As we saw from a masterly perspective with Pliny wanting to listen to slaves at the slave market, Columella questioning slaves in order to better allocate jobs, and Seneca conversing with slaves at his dinner table, Roman owners used slaves' speech to gain a better understanding of their character and intellectual abilities. Roman free people were put under the care of a tutor if they were nonspeaking and lost their ability to make decisions on their own. Speech was an index to understand

---

110. *Mutus*: D. 21.1.9 Ulpian, *Sabinus*, book 44; D. 21.1.3 Gaius, *Curule Aediles' Edict*, book 1. *Balbus*: D. 21.1.1.7 Ulpian, *Curule Aediles' Edict*, book 1, citing Sabinus; D. 21.1.10.5 Ulpian, *Curule Aediles' Edict*, book 1. *Blaesus*: D. 21.1.10.5 Ulpian, *Curule Aediles' Edict*, book 1. *Atypus*: D. 21.1.10.5 Ulpian, *Curule Aediles' Edict*, book 1. *Loquitur Tardius*: D. 21.1.10.5 Ulpian, *Curule Aediles' Edict*, book 1. *Varus*: D. 21.1.10.5 Ulpian, *Curule Aediles' Edict*, book 1. *Vatius*: D. 21.1.10.5 Ulpian, *Curule Aediles' Edict*, book 1. *Gutturosus*: D. 21.1.12.2 Ulpian, *Curule Aediles' Edict*, book 1. And see also (discussed below) *fatuus*: D. 21.1.4.3 Ulpian, *Curule Aediles' Edict*, book 1.

111. On the language of speech impairment in antiquity, see Laes 2013, especially 150–52. On speech more generally in classical antiquity, in particular tied to social class, see Kruschwitz and Cousins 2022.

112. These kinds of speech impairments were noticed and noted upon, as is seen in what seems to be a posted advertisement for a runaway slave, *P.Oxy.* 3616 (third century CE), where a boy of fourteen is described as, among other things, "faltering in speech" in some way (*psellos*) but a word that is distinguished by Aristotle (*Hist. an.* 492b32, *Pr.* 902b22) from lisping (*traulos*). See also *P.Oxy.* 3617, another runaway notice from the third century CE in which a slave is described, again among other things, as not knowing Greek and speaking with a "piercing voice" (*oxeiai phōnēi*).

113. On *varus* and *vatius*, see, e.g., Hor. *Sat.* 1.3.47; Varr. *Rust.* 2.9.4; Mart. 12.70.1.

the mind; and, as will be discussed below, at the extreme, there is a close tie between madness and unclear speech or lack of speech.[114]

Many of the remaining "defects of the mind" (*vitia animi*) that are discussed by the jurists but do not lead to rescission are behaviors that slave owners would find undesirable or problematic in their recently purchased slaves. Like Vitruvius's and Seneca's use of the term "defect of the disease" (*vitium morbi*), these are generally considered faults of character. However, when ascribed to slaves, these *vitia animi* look more like what could be considered the day-to-day resistance that enslaved people performed against their owners and enslavement.[115] The jurist Vivian (cited by Ulpian) gives us a few examples: the frivolous (*levis*), superstitious (*superstitiosus*), religiously fanatic (*fanaticus*), quick to anger (*iracundus*), or insolent (*contumax*) slave. These are all "defects of the mind," but too minor to bring about any sort of recompense.[116] As noted, the jurists were primarily concerned with the owner getting use (*usus*) out of their slave; Vivian does not believe these mental defects will impair the slave's ability to work. On the other hand, Vivian argues that owners who realized that their slaves were too timorous (*timidi*), desirous (*cupidi*), greedy (*avari*), or quick to anger (*iracundi* again) could bring an action on purchase (*actio empti*), just as with a slave who is too extravagant (*luxuria*).[117] These faults of character were severe enough that the owner could seek some damages, but not full restitution. The jurist

---

114. The relationship is most clearly noted here: D. 21.1.4.1 Ulpian, *Curule Aediles' Edict*, book 1, "But if a physical affliction should have mental consequences, say that the slave raves in consequence of his fever or wanders through the city quarters, talking nonsense in the manner of the insane, there is, in such cases, a mental defect flowing from a physical one, and consequently, rescission will be possible" (*Sed si vitium corporis usque ad animum penetrat, forte si propter febrem loquantur aliena vel qui per vicos more insanorum deridenda loquantur, in quos id animi vitium ex corporis vitio accidit, redhiberi posse*). While a speech impairment did not necessarily indicate madness, the terms are often presented in close proximity to each other, see, for example, D. 29.5.3.8–11 Ulpian, *Curule Aediles' Edict*, book 50, on exceptions to the *Senatus Consultum Silanianum*, the law that dictated that when a slave owner was murdered in his house, the slaves "under the same roof" were to be put to death, and Aulus Gellius, *NA* 4.2.15, in his discussion of the terms of the Edict of the Aediles.

115. On day-to-day resistance, see Camp 2004, but specific to Greece and Rome, see Hunt 2016, McKeown 2016, and Bradley 2011.

116. D. 21.1.1.9 Ulpian, *Curule Aediles' Edict*, book 1.

117. D. 21.1.4pr Ulpian, *Curule Aediles' Edict*, book 1, "For all these defects, for which he says that rescission is not applicable, Vivian would give the action on purchase" (*ob quae vitia negat redhibitionem esse, ex empto dat actionem*). While this holds true with the examples just above, given the manner in which the compilers of the *Digest* put this section on *vitia animi* together we must be cautious to necessarily apply the *actio empti* to the *vitia animi* discussed in D. 21.1.1.9 Ulpian, *Curule Aediles' Edict*, book 1. Donadio 2004a, 126, notes that D. 21.1.2 Paul, *Curule Aediles' Edict*, book 1, and D. 21.1.3 Gaius, *Curule Aediles' Edict*, book 1, are both incomplete and must have been cut down by the compilers of the *Digest*.

Pomponius (cited by Ulpian) does not believe that the Edict of the Aediles applies to gamblers (*aleatores*), wine drinkers (*vinarii*), gluttons (*gulosi*), imposters (*impostores*), liars (*mendaces*), or the belligerent (*litigiosi*). Additional mental defects mentioned by the jurists include someone who is melancholic (*melancholicus*), too forward (*protervus*), or watches the games or studies paintings too much.[118] The Roman jurists are not alone in medicalizing behaviors that resist enslavement or are otherwise undesirable to the owner; a nineteenth-century American physician who engaged in pseudoscientific medicine termed similar behaviors in enslaved people "dysaesthesia aethiopica."[119]

While these mental ailments were not exclusive to the slave population or solely a topic of discussion for Roman jurists, the jurists classified them as problematic behaviors for slaves and made some of them actionable. The jurists are responding to the same societal norms as medical writers and philosophers when they consider ailments of the mind. For example, Cicero, in the first book of *On the Ends of Good and Evil*, discusses the Epicurean ideal of living without pain.[120] He views the charms (*iucunditates*) of life as being impeded by diseases of the body and the mind (*morbi corporis* and *morbi animi*). Some of the mental diseases that he describes match well with the jurists' ideas: Cicero's "boundless and vain desires for riches" (*cupiditates inmensae et inanes divitiarum*) fits with the jurists' concerns about luxury (*luxuria*).[121] His "excessive desire for sexual pleasures" (*libidinosae voluptates*) agrees with the jurists' determination of impudence (*protervus*)[122] and desire (*cupidus*) as *vitia animi*.[123] Cicero's "troublesomeness" (*molestia*) has a similar meaning to being irascible (*iracundus*);[124] and "grief" (*aegritudo*) and "sorrow" (*maeror*) are similar concerns to those the jurists have about the melancholic (*melancholicus*).[125] The language that the

118. D. 21.1.2 Paul, *Curule Aediles' Edict*, book 1; D. 21.1.3 Gaius, *Curule Aediles' Edict*, book 1; D. 21.1.65 Venuleius, *Actions*, book 5.

119. Samuel Cartwright is perhaps better known for "drapetomania," a supposed mental illness that caused enslaved people to run away.

120. Cic. *Fin.* 1.59.

121. D. 21.1.1.9–10 Ulpian, *Curule Aediles' Edict*, book 1, citing Vivian.

122. D. 21.1.3 Gaius, *Curule Aediles' Edict*, book 1.

123. D. 21.1.1.11 Ulpian, *Curule Aediles' Edict*, book 1, citing Vivian.

124. D. 21.1.1.9, 11 Ulpian, *Curule Aediles' Edict*, book 1, citing Vivian.

125. D. 21.1.2 Paul, *Curule Aediles' Edict*, book 1.

Cicero also mentions *aegrotationes animi* that have some relation to the *vitium animi* the jurists discuss, *Tusc.* 4.26: *avaritia, ambitio, mulierositas, pervicacia, ligurratio, vinulentia, cuppedia, "et qua similia."* Compare the *servus cupidus* or *avarus* (D. 21.1.1.11 Ulpian, *Curule Aediles' Edict*, book 1, citing Vivian) or the *servus gulosus* or *vinarius* (D. 21.1.4.2 Ulpian, *Curule Aediles' Edict*, book 1, citing Pomponius). See Graver 2002, 150, on the Greek terms for the *aegrotationes* Cicero lists.

jurists and Cicero employ to discuss ailments of the mind are not the same, but their conceptions of what constitutes a mental ailment share similar overtones. While Cicero focuses on the *animus* of the free and the jurists the slave, both engage the language of medicine to discuss moral problems of character. These parallels reflect how the jurists absorbed categories and distinctions developed in other fields of knowledge in order to solve masterly problems inherent to the daily experience of enslavement.

Beyond Cicero, we find Roman literary sources using *vitium* when the defect is one of character and can be translated as "vice." *Vitium* is often discussed in terms of virtue and vice or accompanied by moralizing terminology such as *peccare* (to mistake, err, transgress).[126] Seneca employs the term *vitium animi* several times in his philosophical works.[127] In the preface to the *Natural Questions*, Seneca tells Lucilius that he has broken free of the defects of the mind (*effugisti vitia animi*) and proceeds to outline what some of these defects are: dishonesty (*non est tibi frons ficta*), sycophancy (*nec in alienam voluntatem sermo compositus*), greediness (*avaritia*), extravagance (*luxuria*), and ambition (*ambitio*). Seneca follows Lucilius' freedom from (*effugere*) *vitium* with his search for virtue (*virtutem affectare*).[128] Seneca's rendering of the defects of the mind fits well with the jurists' version. Where Seneca says dishonesty (*non est tibi frons ficta*), Pomponius describes a liar (*mendax*);[129] Seneca describes not following others but speaking his own mind (*nec in alienam voluntatem sermo compositus*), while Vivian calls the superstitious and religious fanatics (*superstitiosus, fanaticus*) mentally defective.[130] Vivian too describes the greedy (*avarus*) and the slave affected by excess (*luxuria*) as having a mental defect.[131] However, Seneca is describing a self-evaluative process—he himself is determining whether he is honest or generous. In contrast, jurists are making use of broader contemporary understandings of mental defects in their commentaries; they

---

126. See, for example, on jealousy, Hor. *Sat.* 2.3; on cruelty, Cic. *Clu.* 199; on desire, Cic. *De or.* 2.339; *Off.* 3.26; Quint. *Inst.* 6.2.30, 12.9.9; Plin. *HN* 30.14; on virtue and vice, Vitr. *De arch* 3.pr; on *peccare*, see Cic. *Tusc. Disp.* 3.4, 5.5; Sen. *Ep.* 97.10; 108.23; Juv. 8.140–41. Gell. *NA* 13.21.15–20 (on *peccatus*).

127. In *De Clementia* 2.4.3 he calls *misericordia* (pity) a *vitium animi*. In *De Ira* 2.15.3 he describes the more minor faults of some gentler minds: *misericordia, amor,* and *verecundia* (pity, love, and shame). See also *De Ira* 2.2.2.

128. Sen. *NQ* 1.pr.6.

129. D. 21.1.4.2 Ulpian, *Curule Aediles' Edict*, book 1, citing Pomponius.

130. D. 21.1.1.9 Ulpian, *Curule Aediles' Edict*, book 1, citing Vivian. In *Ep.* 123.16, Seneca refers to the superstition (*superstitio*) as an *error insanus*.

131. D. 21.1.1.11 Ulpian, *Curule Aediles' Edict*, book 1, citing Vivian; D. 21.1.1.10 Ulpian, *Curule Aediles' Edict*, book 1, citing Vivian.

turn this self-evaluative process into an evaluation of others: slaves. And a person like Pliny, in the market for slaves, would be trying to assess precisely these qualities of mind.

The use of the medical language of disease and defect permeates philosophical texts.[132] The double use of *vitium* as vice and defect helps establish the medical aspects of philosophical questions. Catharine Edwards notes that Seneca uses descriptions of physical disease and defect as an allegory for problems of the mind.[133] We have seen that the jurists similarly use the language of disease and defect to discuss the character faults of slaves. By using such language, the Roman jurists are both participating in a larger societal conversation about mental defect and adapting that conversation for the slave market.

In trying to explain the applicability of the redhibitory action, Pomponius provides us with extremes: The slave-dealer does not need to sell a wise slave (*sapiens*), but if he sells a slave who is too silly or such a fool (*fatuus vel morio*) that he cannot perform his work (*usus*), they will be considered defective.[134] It is worth pausing on *fatuus* and *morio*, which bring out relevant characteristics of the slave market. While *fatuus* can generally mean silly, it is etymologically tied to the god Faunus who told the future, and *fatuus* was connected by Romans with the speaking word *fari*. The *fatuus* slave then is a slave who speaks in such a way that he is understood to be silly or without sense (in contrast to the *sapiens*), so we might think of this like babbling.[135] The babbling speech of a slave indicates not a speech impairment, but a problem with the mind: there is "no utility in that slave" (*usus nullus in eo*). *Morio* on the other hand can mean fool (especially in contrast to *sapiens*), but Martial also uses this word to describe a physically disabled person; this might suggest that the slave has some

132. In *De Ira* (1.16.4), Seneca describes seeing many different kinds of mental defects and invokes the practice of medicine to cure these defects (even though these are character-based rather than physical). Also see *De Vita Beata* 26.5.

133. See, for example, *Tranqu.* 2.11–12, *Ep.* 8.2, 53.5–9, 68.8–9, 75.7. Edwards 1993, 20–22, looks at the tradition in the Roman world of the link between the philosophical and the medical, and emphasizes that this is found most in Stoic texts. See also Edwards 1993, 63–97, and Edwards 2023.

134. D. 21.1.4.3 Ulpian, *Curule Aediles' Edict*, book 1, citing Pomponius, "Pomponius, again, says that although a vendor is not required to produce a slave of full intellect, still if he sells one so silly or such a fool that he is useless, there is a defect under the edict. Generally, the rule which we appear to observe is that the expression 'defect and disease' applies only in respect of physical defects; a vendor is liable in respect of a defect of mind, only if he undertake liability for it; otherwise, not" (*Idem Pomponius ait, quamvis non valide sapientem servum venditor praestare debeat, tamen si ita fatuum vel morionem vendiderit, ut in eo usus nullus sit, videri vitium. et videmur hoc iure uti, ut vitii morbique appellatio non videatur pertinere nisi ad corpora: animi autem vitium ita demum praestabit, si minus, non*).

135. See, e.g., Serv. *Ad Aen.* 7.37. Michael Weiss *per litteras*.

physical impairment as well, and brings us back to Plutarch's description of the specialty market for slaves with disabilities.[136]

The majority of ailments or complaints in the juristic discussion of undesirable mental characteristics are a single word or a short phrase without much description. The case of the bacchant slave and whether they are healthy, however, gives us a more detailed picture:

> The question is raised in the work of Vivian whether a slave, who from time-to-time associates with religious fanatics and tosses his head back to join in their utterances, is, nonetheless, to be regarded as healthy. Vivian says that he is, for he says that we should still regard as sane those with minor mental defects; otherwise, he says, the position would be reached that on this sort of ground, we would deny that slaves are healthy without limit, for example, because he is frivolous, superstitious, quick-tempered, obstinate, or has some other mental defect. . . . Vivian says further that although, at some time in the past, a slave participated in Bacchanalian revels around the temples and joined in with the Bacchic utterances, if he no longer does this, there is no defect in him and there is no more liability with respect to him than if he once had a fever. But if he persists with this defect, cavorting around the shrines and joining in Bacchic utterances as if out of his mind, even though this be the consequence of excess and thus a defect, it is still a mental, not a physical, defect and so constitutes no ground for return.

> Apud Vivianum quaeritur, si servus inter fanaticos non semper caput iactaret et aliqua profatus esset, an nihilo minus sanus videretur. Et ait Vivianus nihilo minus hunc sanum esse: neque enim nos, inquit, minus animi vitiis aliquos sanos esse intellegere debere: alioquin, inquit, futurum, ut in infinito hac ratione multos sanos esse negaremus ut puta levem superstitiosum iracundum contumacem et si qua similia sunt animi vitia . . . Idem Vivianus ait, quamvis aliquando quis circa fana bacchatus sit et responsa reddiderit, tamen, si nunc hoc non faciat, nullum vitium esse: neque eo nomine, quod aliquando id fecit, actio est, sicuti si aliquando febrem habuit: ceterum si nihilo minus permaneret in eo vitio, ut circa fana bacchari soleret et quasi demens responsa daret, etiamsi per luxuriam id factum est, vitium tamen esse, sed vitium animi, non corporis, ideoque redhiberi non posse.[137]

136. Mart. 6.39.17. Seneca also makes this connection between mental impairment and physical difference in *Ep.* 50.2.

137. D. 21.1.1.9–10 Ulpian, *Curule Aediles' Edict*, book 1. On slave religiosity, see Padilla Peralta 2017,

Bacchic revelry is considered a mental defect and therefore not grounds for restitution; but the *actio empti* may apply. Vivian presents two scenarios. The first involves a slave who at one point celebrated Bacchic rites, running riot around the temples. If the slave no longer does this, he is deemed cured and healthy; action here guides the question of mental health. In the second scenario, the slave continues to engage in Bacchic revels and shouting as if out of his mind (*demens*). In this scenario, Vivian holds that the slave has a defect, but it is a mental one, and therefore the slave is not restitutable.

The defect, Vivian tells us, comes from extravagance (*luxuria*). Here the *vitium animi* of the slave originates as a character flaw, which leads to the slave behaving as if they were out of their mind. Those who participated in Bacchic rites were generally considered to be in a state of frenzy. When Vivian first posited the question of slaves joining in religious rites, he considered the participants *fanatici*, which can mean someone inspired by a divinity, but also comes to mean mad. While the supposition that a slave might participate in Bacchic rites may seem idiosyncratic at first, two matters must be considered. A slave who is running around temples and engaging in Bacchic rites has left their owner's house, presumably without their owner's permission. This slave is then either heedless of their owner's commands or has been given a great deal of license to move around the city, which might be a way to understand why Vivian bases the slave's mental defect on *luxuria*. Notably, this slave is never discussed as a possible runaway.

Where did a slave who suffers from *luxuria* contract such a *vitium animi*? It is possible the slave is newly enslaved and was a bacchant before his enslavement. It is also possible that the slave's owner prior to sale did not exert enough control over the slave to curb such impulses; perhaps they were even permissive of this sort of behavior. In either case, the bacchant slave emphasizes the morality intrinsic to the juristic interpretation of *vitia animi* not solely because of his conduct during the revels, but because a slave with *luxuria* is a slave who is not behaving in an appropriate manner for a slave. While long ago, this slave would evoke the *Senatus consultum de Bacchanalibus* of 186 BCE passed to curb Bacchant behavior.[138] While it is impossible to know for certain why this is the one anecdote our sources (either Ulpian or the compilers of the *Digest*) have kept, I suggest that the nature of the bacchant's defect comes closest to the two kinds of mental defects that allow rescission and thus is worth Vivian's and Ulpian's

which is focused on the Middle Republic but discusses this case in interesting comparative ways.

138. On slavery and the *senatus consultum de Bacchanalibus*, see Padilla Peralta 2017, especially 339.

longer reflection. While the bacchant's actions are not depicted as resistance to enslavement, this case presents a problem because a slave who is a bacchant is a slave serving another master even if in a temporary, and as such controlled, form of madness and flight. This slave comes right up to the line of being able to be returned until he stops shouting (thus revealing he is not mad) and running (thus revealing he is not in flight).

The commentaries on the Edict of the Aediles were pragmatic documents; the jurists are primarily concerned with ensuring that a new owner is able to make use of their slave as they wish. The very fact that "faults of character" did not generally comprise restitutable defects underscores the idea that the value of the slave was primarily in the body and specifically in a slave's ability to carry out their job. The slave's ability to do physical work would have been of primary importance for owners. Yet the Roman jurists also acknowledged the importance of the mind of the slave in determining their usefulness to the owner. The juristic discussion of the *vitia animi* came about because slaves were not behaving as society expected or wanted from them; they were, in a sense, bad slaves. The need for evaluation, both at market and after purchase, arises from this very practical realization that slaves could fail to come completely under the ownership of their new masters. The construction of a medicine of the slave market worked to shore up masterly concerns whether they be of the body, mind, or, as we will see particularly in the next chapter, unique to the condition of enslavement. The presence of this extensive juristic discussion alone reveals the sheer difficulty of evaluation, which in turn reveals the fragile fault lines (or even impossibilities) of ownership over the mind.

TWO

Sanity and the Slave Market

I didn't wait until he gave his permission: I ran, out of my mind.
(*non expectavi dum iste permitteret: amens cucurri*)

—Seneca Rhet. *Controv.* 2.4.1

In the previous chapter, I suggested that the attention given to the sometimes bacchant slave by the jurists Vivian and Ulpian was because he exhibited characteristics that when left unchecked could lead to a successful action for rescission (*áctio redhibitoria*) for the purchaser.[1] The symptoms that this slave presents—running around temples, joining in Bacchic utterances as if out of his mind—are considered temporary as the slave will eventually stop celebrating these rites. They are also attributed to a mental defect (*vitium animi*)—excess (*luxuria*); as such, restitution is not granted. *Luxuria* is one of the many *vitia animi* that can be categorized as behaviors or personality traits that were undesirable to the slave owner and which might be considered faults of character.[2] This chapter instead turns to two remaining categories of *vitia animi* that the jurists discuss: forms of madness and forms of flight. Medical writers or encyclopedists like Celsus did not seem to have much of an interest in the difference between slave and free when it came to medical matters. However, the legal outcomes for a free person with, for example, *furor* ("derangement"), or an

1. The redhibitory action (*actio redhibitoria*) allowed for the rescission of the sale of a slave (or animal) and left the buyer "restored" to his circumstance prior to the sale (i.e., restitution). The text of the action in the Edict of the Aediles is quoted and discussed in chapter 1 as is the passage about the bacchant slave (D. 21.1.1.9–10 Ulpian, *Curule Aediles' Edict*, book 1).

2. These types of *vitia animi* roughly correspond to what are often discussed by philosophers as "ethical" problems of the soul in contrast to medical ones; on this, see Thumiger and Singer 2018b, 21–22. While most of this behavior is normatively undesirable in both the free and enslaved populations, as discussed in the previous chapter, in the case of slaves, much of this behavior can be read as resistance to enslavement.

enslaved person with *furor* are different. Flight, in contrast, is a *vitium animi* that only pertains to slaves.

In both situations, the jurists consider the essential features of madness and flight to determine in which cases restitution should be allowed. While the jurists do not group the different types of madness (*phrenitis*, *melancholia*, *furor*, and a *servus lunaticus*) mentioned in the Edict of the Aediles under a category more specific than *vitia animi*, these types of mental illness were classified together in medical texts by the first century CE as different types of *insania*.[3] I argue that the jurists are interested in parsing these mental illnesses because some of these illnesses, in particular *furor*, allow for the action for rescission. A similar parsing occurs in determining what constitutes flight or makes one a *fugitivus* (runaway slave), another *vitium animi* that allows for restitution. The reason for this careful deliberation is that in both situations an essential part of the slave, the mind, is inaccessible to the purchaser; thus, the new owner cannot exert their control over the slave, rendering their ownership largely meaningless. However, the jurists treat these two mental ailments very differently. While attempting to diagnose a slave as *furiosus* ("deranged"), the jurists rely on medical knowledge and cultural understandings of mental illness, then adapt this information for the slave market. The situation of the *fugitivus* is different because the question of whether a person is a runaway is not a part of the human condition but the constructed slave one. As such, the jurists must create their own pathology of the *fugitivus*.

Insania: *Mental Illness*

The jurists discuss different forms of madness, including a frenzied slave (*servus phrenētikos*), a lunatic slave (*servus lunaticus*), melancholic slaves (*servi melancholici*), and the deranged slave (*servus furiosus*) twice.[4] A *phrenētikos* or person

3. Thumiger and Singer 2018b, 7–8, in the introduction to their volume on mental illness discuss Celsus as the "starting point" of the study of mental illness in the postclassical period (after the 5th and 4th centuries BCE) as his work incorporates now largely lost Hellenistic advancements as well as because the taxonomy or "nosological category" of mental illness (*insania*) he introduces only becomes more complex as we move further into the imperial period (see Celsus *Med.* 3.18). Celsus is the first to put three of these—*phrenitis*, *melancholia*, and *furor* (as *mania*)—together; Thumiger and Singer 2018b, 8–9, with discussion of the three afflictions at 10–15. This becomes the canonical formulation of the different types of mental illness with some variations, including epilepsy, introduced by other writers, see Thumiger and Singer 2018b, 22–23.

4. The *phrenētikos*: D. 21.1.1.9 Ulpian, *Curule Aediles' Edict*, book 1; *lunaticus*: D. 21.1.43.6 Paul,

with *phrenitis* had "acute delirium with acute fever."[5] If the frenzied slave did not recover their previous mental state after the fever, and the slave-dealer did not reveal the mental defect even though they knew about it, the new owner could bring an action on the purchase (*actio empti*), but not an action for rescission.[6] The jurists (Ulpian citing Vivian) note that the mental disorder of the frenzied slave is not purely a mental defect; it comes from a physical root, a fever, and therefore gives the jurists a more tangible cause on which to exercise judgment.[7] In what appears to be a more severe form of *phrenitis*, Ulpian then goes further and says that rescission would be allowed if a physical cause like a fever affected the mind to such a degree that the slave was made to talk in tongues or wander through neighborhoods babbling in the manner of the insane.[8]

The other three forms of mental illness discussed do not originate in a manifest physical cause like a fever. The melancholic slave (*servus melancholicus*) is considered to have a truly mental defect, but not one so severe that the slave can be returned: The sixth-century CE compilers of the *Digest of Justinian* place the mention of the melancholic slave in the midst of other jurists discussing non-restitutable mental defects. The sole mention in our legal sources of the lunatic slave (*servus lunaticus*) comes from the jurist Paul. He mentions the lunatic slave alongside the deranged slave (*servus furiosus*), stating that if the slave is so worthless that an owner has no want for him, the judge can actually allow an action for rescission.[9] The legal outcomes, then, for a lunatic or deranged slave

---

Curule Aediles' Edict, book 1; *melancholici*: D. 21.1.2 Paul, *Curule Aediles' Edict*, book 1; *furiosus*: D. 21.1.23.2 Ulpian, *Curule Aediles' Edict*, book 1, citing Pomponius and D. 21.1.43.6 Paul, *Curule Aediles' Edict*, book 1.

On the *servus melancholicus*, see Parlamento 2001. On the *servus furiosus*, see Ortu 2008, 238–55.

5. This is taken from Wright 2020, 533, who cites the definition of Byzantine encyclopedist Paul of Nicaea in her article on Augustine's use of *phrenitis* to make sin both a medical and ethical problem. On *phrenitis* more generally, see McDonald 2009.

6. The *actio empti* was not limited to slaves and livestock; it allowed a purchaser to sue the seller for damages if the slave, in this case, had some issue the seller did not disclose. See chapter 1 for further discussion.

7. See Cloud 2007 for an argument on Vivian's desire to only apply the *actio redhibitoria* to physical defects.

8. D. 21.1.4.1 Ulpian, *Curule Aediles' Edict*, book 1, "But if a physical affliction should have mental consequences, say that the slave raves in consequences of his fever or wanders through the city quarters, talking nonsense in the manner of the insane, there is, in such cases, a mental defect flowing from a physical one, and consequently, rescission will be possible" (*Sed si vitium corporis usque ad animum penetrat, forte si propter febrem loquantur aliena vel qui per vicos more insanorum deridenda loquantur, in quos id animi vitium ex corporis vitio accidit, redhiberi posse*). The introductory *sed* seems to suggest that Ulpian thinks there is a limit to when the *actio empti* should apply for situations like this.

9. D. 21.1.43.6 Paul, *Curule Aediles' Edict*, book 1.

and a melancholic slave are different. The melancholic slave is discussed in terms of potential problems that may occur with a slave, but the jurists hold the lunatic or deranged slave as far more problematic than the melancholic. Following Paul then, there is a division between these forms of madness; the melancholic slave can still serve their purpose (*usus*), while a lunatic or deranged slave cannot.

The melancholic had a long history in the ancient world, the term being derived from the Hippocratic theory of the humors, which held that black bile was the cause of its condition.[10] *Melancholia* also seemed more curable than *furor*; Celsus gives us some remedies. He refers to a type of madness (*genus insaniae*) that is a depression (*tristitia*) caused by black bile. He suggests that a patient suffering from melancholy should engage in lighthearted entertainment that healthy (*sanus*) people would not normally be interested in, namely storytelling and games.[11] The games are notable because attending too many games was considered a defect of slaves as well; however, while the jurists deem this slave to be mentally defective, it was not considered such a problem that a buyer could bring a case for restitution.[12]

The *lunaticus* and the *furiosus* then are more problematic for an owner than the slaves with *phrenitis* or *melancholia*. As noted, the *lunaticus* is mentioned by Paul alongside the *furiosus* as a slave who is allowed to be returned. The jurists do not return to the *lunaticus* again; however, the term seems, as does its Greek counterpart *selēniakos*, to relate to epilepsy.[13] Epilepsy would affect the ability of an owner to make use of their slave[14] and is one of the few specific diseases

10. For a detailed discussion of *melancholia* in antiquity, see Rufus of Ephesus' treatise *On Melancholy* in Pormann's 2008 edition, which contains contextualizing essays. More generally, see Thumiger 2017; Pigeaud 1989, 122–38.
11. Celsus *Med.* 3.18.17–18.
12. D. 21.1.65pr Venuleius, *Actions*, book 5.
13. See Metzger 2018, 84–89, on the connection between being moonstruck (*lunaticus, selēniakos*) and epilepsy. Matthew 17.14–18 tells the story of a boy who has moon sickness (*selēniazomai*; *lunaticus* Vulg. Matt. 17.15) who is cured by Jesus; Origen, who is roughly contemporary with the jurist Paul, then explains that this is the affliction of *epilēpsia* in his commentary on the passage (Orig. *In Mt.* 8.4). See Metzger 2018 more generally on the causes of mental illness, in particular epilepsy, being "naturalistic" or "demonological" in the early Christian period; in particular at 79 she notes that Origen argues that the disease was a form of possession. The argument whether epilepsy was of naturalistic or divine origin has a long history and is found in the Hippocratic text *On the Sacred Disease*. Owsei Temkin, in his book, *The Falling Sickness: A History of Epilepsy from the Greeks to the Beginnings of Modern Neurology*, uses the term "falling sickness" to cover *epilēpsia*, being "moonstruck," and possession; see Metzger 2018, 83n20. On moon sickness, see Wohlers 1999.
14. Javolenus, in *From the Works of the Posthumous Labeo*, book 1 (D. 21.1.53), includes epilepsy (*morbus comitialis*) in a discussion of people who are not considered healthy (*sani*) even when the

we find guarantees against in sale contracts.[15] On a more basic level, epilepsy may be a problem for successful slave ownership because of the understanding that epilepsy is a disease in which otherworldly agents (be it the sacred disease that the Hippocratic Corpus argues against, the possession of early Christians, or the moon) take control of a body that is meant to be under the control of the slave owner.

The category of madness most discussed by the jurists is the deranged slave (*servus furiosus*); the juristic treatment of derangement shows why this particular form of madness was problematic to the point of allowing restitution. The second mention of the deranged slave in the juristic commentary of the Edict of the Aediles tells us that they, like a child (*impubes*), are considered unable to commit a capital crime. Ulpian prefaces the fact that a deranged slave or a child cannot commit a capital crime by calling for an examination of intention and motive: "We believe that a capital offense is committed through malice and wickedness" (*Capitalem fraudem admisisse accipiemus dolo malo et per nequitiam*).[16] The jurists recognize that a person rendered deranged is incapable of having the intention (the *dolus malus* and *nequitia*) to commit the crime.

The equating of a deranged person with a child, therefore without many legal rights and responsibilities, is not exclusive to slaves who are deranged or to the commentary on the Edict of the Aediles. The tie between the child and the deranged person is due to their lack of proper reasoning capabilities, the first on account of age and the second because of their condition. Discussing business transactions, the jurist Gaius explains that an infant or one near in age to an infant is not very different from a deranged person because the infant has no understanding (*nullus intellectus*) while the deranged person does not understand what they are doing (*non intellegit quid agat*).[17] Considering lack of liability in cases of outrage (*iniuria*), Ulpian notes that a child or

---

affliction is not presently occurring. He holds the same for tertian or quartian fever (*tertiana aut quartana febris*) or gout (*podagra*). This fragment is not obviously about enslaved people or the regulations on the slave market. Lenel (fr. 161) places it in a section on wills in book 1, but this also seems quite speculative.

15. See, for example, *T.Dacia* 7 from 146 CE, a contract in which the vendor swears that the enslaved boy Apalaustus was, among other things, healthy (*sanus*) and not a wanderer, runaway, or epileptic (*erro, fugitivus,* or *caducus*). See discussion in Arzt-Grabner 2010, especially on this contract, 26–27.

16. D. 21.1.23.2 Ulpian, *Curule Aediles' Edict*, book 1, Ulpian continues, "Pomponius, accordingly, says that neither a child (*impubes*) nor a deranged slave (*furiosus*) can be thought capable of a capital offense" (*Unde Pomponius ait neque impuberem neque furiosum capitalem fraudem videri admisisse*).

17. G. 3.106–109.

deranged person cannot be considered guilty because they are not capable of (bad) intention (*doli capax non est*).[18] The deranged person, being compared to an infant, livestock, or a chance accident, is not liable under the *lex Aquilia* (on damage to another's property) because as the jurist Pegasus notes there cannot be fault (*culpa*) where there is no mental capacity (*mens*).[19] The jurist Pomponius notes that someone who has no will (*voluntas*) is deranged (*furiosus*) and is unable to have control of their property.[20] The very fact that the deranged slave (*servus furiosus*) is not able to be held accountable makes them subject to an action for rescission. Examining the juristic commentary on free deranged people alongside that on deranged slaves reveals not only the mental quality that made a slave unable to perform their allotted tasks, but also the quality that was needed for an owner to make use of their slave and have effective ownership over them. According to juristic understanding, a slave has a mind (*mens*) and a will (*voluntas*), and in order for a slave to be functional, they must be in possession of these faculties. A deranged slave is a slave who fails to play their part (as a slave) in the owner-slave relationship. We see most clearly in the case of the deranged slave—a slave so mentally defective they can be returned—that there is an intrinsic tie between the mind of the slave and the ownership of the slaveholder. The understanding, then, of ownership and of slaves as property extends to the mind, and the deranged slave presents a serious complication for ownership.

As noted above, in their commentaries on the Edict of the Aediles, the jurists do not make explicit distinctions on the differences between the types of madness. Given that these different forms of madness had different legal ramifications for owner and slave we must understand that this silence is not an oversight on the part of the jurists, but rather that these distinctions were known in a broader cultural context. In the *Tusculan Disputations*, Cicero distinguishes between derangement (*furor*) and other types of madness (*insania*).[21] Cicero is drawing from two older sources in his discussion of derangement. The primary one is the Greek tradition; according to Cicero, the Greek equivalent

18. D. 47.10.3.1 Ulpian, *Edict*, book 56.
19. D. 9.2.5.2 Ulpian, *Edict*, book 18, citing Pegasus.
20. D. 50.17.40 Pomponius, *Sabinus*, book 34, "There is no will in a deranged person or someone who does not have control over his property" (*Furiosi vel eius, cui bonis interdictum sit, nulla voluntas est*).

 See also on property, D. 6.1.60 Pomponius, *Sabinus*, book 29, and on the *lex Cornelia* on murder and poisoners, D. 48.8.12, Modestinus, *Rules*, book 8.
21. *Insania* here as with the Celsus fragment seems to function as a larger category of madness. See Cic. *Tusc*. 3.8–10.

to *furor* is *melancholia*, but he seems unsatisfied with the term because he does not think that someone becomes deranged solely from black bile (*atra bilis*). He suggests that often for the mind (*mens*) to become deranged deep wrath, fear, or pain were at play.[22]

The second place Cicero turns to for the distinction between madness (*insania*) and derangement (*furor*) is the Twelve Tables, the archaic law code of Rome (451–450 BCE). He recalls that the Twelve Tables did not allow someone (a free person) deemed deranged to have control of their property.[23] Cicero notes a distinction between types of madness, "and so it is not written, 'if mentally unsound,' but 'if he is deranged'" (*itaque non est scriptum, si insanus, sed si furiosus escit*). Cicero draws a definition of sorts from this distinction in the Twelve Tables, "but they considered derangement to be a blindness of the mind to everything" (*furorem autem esse rati sunt mentis ad omnia caecitatem*).[24] People with other sorts of madness (*insania*) could still function and perform their day-to-day tasks (*mediocritas officiorum*). Cicero's description of derangement as blindness of the mind suggests that the state is all encompassing and not recoverable. Margaret Graver proposes that mind (*mens*) here is the *hegemonikon* or the "directive faculty," that is, the *rational* mind.[25] A deranged person then cannot function according to reason or with intention.[26]

According to the Twelve Tables, Cicero, and Pomponius, a free deranged person will lose control of his property; he will not be able to be an owner (*dominus*) and will be under the power (*potestas*) of his family. The slave who becomes deranged does not have power over others or material goods. They are able to be returned solely for an internal problem: they have lost their will or mind (*voluntas, mens*). The free deranged person has lost control over his worldly possessions and himself; in the case of the deranged slave, this is inverted: the owner has lost control of his slave. A free deranged person, having no mind, loses one of the constituent elements of citizenship, the ability to con-

22. Cic. *Tusc.* 3.11.

23. Cic. *Tusc.* 3.11.

24. Cic. *Tusc.* 3.11. The Twelve Tables continue: "if he is deranged, then let his family members and relatives have power over him and his property" (*si furiosus escit adgnatum gentiliumque in eo pecuniaque eius potestas esto*, 5.7). Warmington 3.450–52. On this passage, see Graver 2002, 80–81. Cicero gives examples of derangement: Athamas, Alcmaeon, Ajax, and Orestes. See also Sen. *Ira* 2.4–5.

25. Graver 2002, 82. Pigeaud 1989, 258–59, argues that Cicero and Ulpian have the same "nosographic" table two centuries apart and that Ulpian's discussion of *furor* is a return to Cicero.

26. In the *Rhetorica ad Herennium* (2.24), written in the 90s BCE, the author tells us it is mental defect (*vitium animi*) that takes away reason.

trol his property; a deranged slave, having no mind, loses one of the constituent elements of enslavement, being subject to and successfully owned by another.

The deranged slave falls under the purview of the action for rescission while the melancholic slave does not for a second reason as well. A slave without a will is not a functional slave; they are not able to carry out even the most basic tasks. Additionally, it is more likely that the melancholic, like the frenzied (*phrenētikos*) slave or a slave who while participating in Bacchic rites seems as if he has lost his mind (*servus quasi demens*), could be cured or stopped.[27] The Bacchic slave is only discussed as if he had lost his mind when he participates in the rites; when he stops shouting, he ceases to be considered out of his mind.[28] The jurists' attention to the different types of mad slaves highlights the level of attention that goes into understanding the mentalities of slaves. The mention of four different kinds of mad slaves (*phrenētikos, melancholicus, lunaticus, furiosus*) suggests that the jurists were not only aware of the ongoing conversation about madness that was occurring in philosophical texts (as they are not simply using a generic term like "madness," *insania*), but were invested in the differences between them. There are discrepancies between how Cicero and the jurists conceive of the defects of the mind, as there were among more medically inclined sources, yet when they speak of the kinds of mental defects that affect slaves and free people, Cicero and the jurists' discussions converge; they share a philosophical approach. The same morality that exists in Cicero's discussion of the defective mind of a free person exists in the jurists' discussion of the mind of the slave. The mental defects of the slave, like the free person's, can be seen to be a problem of character or mentality. The jurists' discussion of the defects of the slave brings the medical discussion of maladies of the mind into the slave market in order to broach this problem in slave ownership.

Peter King, in his dissertation "The *Cognitio* into Insanity," considers the idea that there was not a legal definition for madness and discusses the investigations (*cognitiones*) that went on to determine if someone was to be rendered legally insane. King highlights several physical characteristics that indicate madness, including blanching and stillness, blazing, twisted eyes, and fierce-

---

27. On the *quasi demens* slave (discussed in chapter 1), see D. 21.1.1.10 Ulpian, *Curule Aediles' Edict*, book 1. Celsus (3.18) says that *phrenitis* really begins when a person who has a fever can no longer tell the imagined from reality. He continues to discuss therapies for *phrenitis*; see Thumiger and Singer 2018b, 11, on therapies.

28. See Graver 2002, 6, on *demens* as "being out of one's mind" (in contrast to *amens* "losing one's mind") in Cic. *Tusc.* 3.10.

ness. He shows that flight is an indicator of madness in Roman literature.[29] Flight or wandering as an indicator of madness is particularly noteworthy because the jurists classify these actions as mental defects (*vitia animi*). Pulled together from different branches of literature and cultural knowledge, these methods of determining madness become the manner in which the Romans understood wayward slaves; it is a masterly diagnosis rather than a medical one.

The inability of the owner to predict that the slave they are purchasing will run away or become deranged comes to be explained by the fact that the slave has a mental defect. Part of ownership must be understood to be not only the owner's ability to control their slave but also the slave's ability to be controlled. These slaves have a defect so severe that they are unable to come under effective ownership of their new owners and are therefore able to be returned. These diagnoses also have the effect of condensing the behavior of enslaved individuals into these categories of mental illness that obfuscate their experiences. As will be seen in the following section on the fugitive slave, the jurists must artificially create this category of defect from the various experiences of slaves; as such, we have a small window into some of the experiences and scenarios that lead to being labeled a runaway slave.

The Fugitive Slave

In this section I will focus on the runaway and the related scenarios of the suicidal and wandering slave. The question of the runaway slave is largely examined by Ulpian, who cites many other jurists. What becomes clear is that the intention behind the flight serves as the guiding marker in their opinions. Similarly to the deranged slave, who cannot be held accountable for their actions by their owner because they lack will (*voluntas*), here the determination of whether a slave was a fugitive is connected directly to the intention of the slave. The language of intentionality and thought plays a central role in the jurists' discussion of the runaway slave. This includes a group of words that have different meanings but revolve around the question of will (e.g., *causa*, *mens*, *consilium*, *propositum*, *animus*, *voluntas*, and *invitus*). As the jurists must develop their own pathology in the case of the runaway, this scenario best exemplifies the

29. King 2000, 18–23. See also Rosen 1968, 98 and Bonner 1949, 93–94.

jurists' foray into "slave medicine." Their discussion can be divided into the following subcategories: the slave both in and out of the home; the wandering slave (*erro*); the suicidal slave and the self-preserving slave; and the unwilling, the unaware, and the liberated slave. The study of the runaway is important because the runaway has a mental defect so severe that restitution is allowed; this is a slave who cannot be controlled by their owner and whose mind fails to come under their owner's power.

The focus of the juristic interpretation of the fugitive slave passage (D. 21.1.17) is whether the slave had a good or bad reason (*bona* or *mala causa*—from the owner's perspective) to run away or, put another way, whether the act was deceitful (*dolus*), which, to be ascertained, required the intention of the slave to be known. The following passages consider the specific purpose (*causa*) guiding the slave's actions. The question here is not whether the slave has a will, but whether it is a good one or a bad one. Good intention must be in accordance with their status as a slave and the preservation of that status; bad intention is indicated by their escape from their status as a slave.

The action of leaving an owner's property of one's own volition is not an offense in and of itself. The state of the fugitive exists from a development in the mind; slaves in Rome had a certain amount of freedom of movement depending on their tasks and owners. However, the vast majority of slaves found off their owner's property without authorization (that is to say, of their own volition) were most likely attempting to flee rather than escaping a burning building, taking refuge at the statue of the emperor, running to their mother for help, or away from an abusive trainer.[30] Why did the jurists take the time to theorize the intellect and intention of potential fugitive slaves? The clearest answer is that vendors and buyers needed access to a formal understanding of what made someone legally classifiable as a runaway so as to limit liability under the Edict of the Aediles. Vendors were legally compelled to state physical defects and diseases that were not readily apparent, and the most common form of slave tattoo found was the tattoo marking a slave as a habitual runaway.[31] We see a similar preoccupation with why slaves ran away in literary sources.[32]

The runaway slave is considered to have stolen themselves (*furtum sui*); in

30. On these situations, see D. 21.1.17.3 Ulpian, *Curule Aediles' Edict*, book 1; D. 21.1.17.5 Ulpian, *Curule Aediles' Edict*, book 1; D. 21.1.17.12 Ulpian, *Curule Aediles' Edict*, book 1.

31. See Jones 1987; Thurmond 1994; Rivière 2002, 115–96; Kamen 2010; Fuhrmann 2012, 21–43. On what vendors needed to do, see Jakab 1997.

32. On runaway slaves in Roman literature, see, for example, Plaut. *Men.* 79–80; Dio Chrys. *Or.* 10.6–7, 31.42, 66.3; *Sen. Rhet. Controv.* 7.6.22–24.

a striking passage—and one of the few in which a female fugitive slave is explicitly mentioned—a woman is considered to commit theft of herself and her offspring.[33] Explaining that the vendors were generally liable only for physical defects and diseases, Ulpian notes that the Aediles specifically refer to the runaway and the wanderer because they are mental defects, but still grounds for restitution.[34] In an exploration of different scenarios, the jurists examine the physical manifestations of the slave outside of his owner's house in order to construct the parameters of this mental defect.

The Slave in and out of the Home

Ulpian begins his long discussion of the runaway with a citation from the jurist Ofilius. Ofilius' definition of a fugitive is based on the purpose behind the slave's actions. Ulpian quotes Ofilius, "a runaway is someone who stays away from his owner's house for the purpose of flight, in order to hide himself from his owner" (*fugitivus est, qui extra domini domum fugae causa, quo se a domino celaret, mansit*).[35] The status of *fugitivus* is determined not by the slave remaining out of his owner's house, but by his intention to do so for the purpose of flight (*causa fugae*). Ofilius describes his reasoning with the word *causa*, a word that can have many meanings, but which can be analogous to the purpose or intention of an action.[36]

Other jurists provide more detailed scenarios to define the runaway. In the subsequent case, the jurist Sabinus Caelius expands the definition of a fugitive slave who runs away for the purpose of flight (*causa fugae*) to contain a certain finality. While a slave's actions may be reversible, once the decision to run away is made their status as a fugitive is not erasable or redeemable. Ulpian quotes Caelius, "he, too, is a fugitive who leaves with a mind not to return to his owner,

33. D. 47.2.61 Africanus, *Questions*, book 7, "Just as a runaway slave-woman is regarded as stealing herself, so she makes her child a stolen thing" (*Ancilla fugitiva quemadmodum sui furtum facere intellegitur, ita partum quoque contrectando furtivum facit*). Lenel places this passage in the title *de possessione et usucapione*, Lenel fr. 74. Cf. D. 47.2.66 Ulpian, *Curule Aediles' Edict*, book 1, which has a palingenetic link to D. 21.1.17.1 on once a thief always a thief, and see also D. 21.1.31.1–2 Ulpian, *Curule Aediles' Edict*, book 1, on the vendor promising that a slave is not a thief and that if a slave woman who is returned under the *actio redhibitoria* has any offspring following her sale, they must be returned as well.

34. D. 21.1.4.3 Ulpian, *Curule Aediles' Edict*, book 1, "Hence, the express reservation of the wandering or runaway slave; for their defects are of the mind, not physical" (*et ideo nominatim de errone et fugitivo excipitur: hoc enim animi vitium est, non corporis*).

35. D. 21.1.17pr Ulpian, *Curule Aediles' Edict*, book 1.

36. On the legal uses of *causa*, see Hellegouarc'h 1963, 417.

but, with a changed plan, returns; [Caelius] says no one purges his offense by remorse" (*qui ea mente discedat, ne ad dominum redeat, tametsi mutato consilio ad eum revertatur: nemo enim tali peccato, inquit, paenitentia sua nocens esse desinit*).[37] Caelius' complication of the idea of who is a fugitive is grounded upon the original motivation of the slave; regardless of what the slave decides and does later, they remain a fugitive. Unlike the melancholic slave, this is not a curable mental defect and so restitution is allowed. The reconsidered action of the slave to return to their owner does not nullify the charge of fugitive as returns or compensation payments did in Roman commercial law.[38] It is the original intent here that matters.[39] Through a study of a slave's actions we see how the jurists are concerned with a precise understanding of the slave's mind in order to deem one a runaway: what they thought first and what followed.

Caelius presents various scenarios in which the jurists declare a slave a runaway while still on their owner's property. The first case considers a slave who hid—with the intention to escape overnight—outside a locked house that was on the property of their owner's own former owner. The freedman owner of this potential runaway continued to live on the estate of his former owner. Caelius deems them a fugitive, but his assessment would change if the house were one that was not locked up in that manner (a tacit grant that the slave was allowed to leave the house).[40] A slave that is not in a locked house has the opportunity to escape; yet if they do not, their inaction reveals their intention. The slave still on the estate, but outside the locked house, is a fugitive because they should be

37. D. 21.1.17.1 Ulpian, *Curule Aediles' Edict*, book 1. In this passage *mens* and *consilium* both have the meaning of intention or plan but *consilium* is more deliberative.

38. D. 21.1.17.2 Ulpian, *Curule Aediles' Edict*, book 1: the jurist Cassius has a similar definition of a fugitive, he writes of a *certum propositum* of the slave. Ulpian quotes, "a fugitive slave is one who with deliberate plan leaves his owner" (*fugitivum esse, qui certo proposito dominum relinquat*).

In the definitions of Caelius and Cassius, three words have appeared that reveal the intent of the slave: *mens*, *consilium*, and *propositum*. *Propositum* is more similar to *consilium* than *mens* specifically in terms of its lack of physicality; this is the only use of *propositum* in this section (D. 21.1.17) of the *Digest*.

39. On understanding intention through action, see Moatti 2016.

40. D.21.1.17.15 Ulpian, *Curule Aediles' Edict*, book 1, "A freedman was living with his patron in such circumstances that the whole premises were locked with one key. A slave of the freedman was beyond the latter's quarters with a mind of not returning to him (although still within the patron's establishment) and concealed himself for the whole night. Caelius says that he should be deemed a fugitive. Of course, says Caelius, if the establishment was not of the type above indicated and the freedman dwelt in a room to which there was common and general access to and from several rooms, the answer would be different; Labeo takes the same view" (*liberti apud patronum habitantis sic, ut sub una clave tota eius habitatio esset, servus ea mente, ne rediret ad eum, extra habitationem liberti fuit, sed intra aedes patroni, et tota nocte oblituit: videri esse fugitivum Caelius ait. plane si talem custodiam ea habitatio non habuit et in ea cella libertus habitavit, cui commune et promiscuum plurium cellarum iter est, contra placere debere Caelius ait et Labeo probat*).

inside the house. The location of the slave relative to their owner has no bearing upon the question of the fugitive slave; it is always the intention of the slave that is being judged.

A second case is about a slave on a country estate: "If a slave on a country estate leaves the house with the mindset (*mens*) of running away but is caught by someone before he has left the confines of the estate, he is a fugitive; for his mind (*animus*) makes him so" (*si servus, cum in fundo esset, exisset de villa ea mente, ut profugeret et quis eum, priusquam ex fundo tuo exisset comprehendisset, fugitivum videri: animum enim fugitivum facere*).[41] Caelius continues noting that even a step or two in flight will mark the slave as a fugitive. The flight of the slave comes from a particular mindset (*mens*) or decision to flee. This mindset permeates their entire *animus*; it is the *animus* that makes them a fugitive and is rendered defective. Both *mens* ("mindset") and *animus* ("mind") are at times contrasted with body (*corpus*) in the juristic discussion leading up to the runaway slave, though *animus*, not *mens*, is used exclusively to discuss mental defects (*vitia animi*). *Mens* is used here to highlight the active decision-making process that occurs when a slave decides to run away, while the *animus* is a larger construct of the mind. This difference between *mens* and *animus* in the jurists' discussion fits with other accounts. Cicero describes the *mens* as the governor of the whole *animus* in his discussion of diseases of the mind (*morbi animi*) in the third book of the *Tusculan Disputations*.[42] In this section on the fugitive slave we see a shift from the discussion about mental defects (*vitia animi*) as particular internal conditions or faults to a discussion about the external action or inaction that reveals a mental process—the decision to escape or return, or, as we will see, to wander off. The status of the slave as fugitive is a product of intention; the juristic discussion on the runaway slave highlights the evaluative process that Romans engaged in to understand the mind of their slaves.

The jurists are additionally concerned with determining why a slave is off their owner's grounds: in other words, whether the runaway had a good reason to be away from the house, such as if the slave ran away on account of some-

41. D. 21.1.17.8 Ulpian, *Curule Aediles' Edict*, book 1, as Caelius continues to explain at 9, "A slave who takes a step or two in flight or, indeed, begins to run but cannot escape his owner who is in pursuit is a fugitive" (*nec eum, qui ad fugam gradum unum alterumve promovit vel etiam currere coepit, si dominum sequentem non potest evadere, non esse fugitivum*).

42. Cic. *Tusc.* 3.11. Cicero makes a similar assertion in *Fin.* 5.34, where he describes the *animus* as the seat of the *mens*. This difference between the *mens* and *animus* diverges from the Stoic *mens-animus* distinction as represented in Aulus Gellius *NA* 19.1.17–18 (from the fifth book of Epictetus' *Discourses*).

thing like self-preservation, which might be considered in their owner's interest (discussed below).[43] As is shown in the above definitions of the runaway slave, the focus is on the intention of the slave; what begins to emerge from this concentration on the mind is the recognition of a slave's agency as separate from their owner's awareness. There is a space of autonomy from the slaveholder's ownership where the slave can choose to behave as they wish. In some cases, the slave can act autonomously, but still benefiting their owner. The self-preserving slave, for example, is seen to not be a fugitive, to not have a mental defect, because they behave as Roman owners expected and wanted from their slaves. They do not use their independent thought or agency to escape their status of slavery, but to preserve it.

The Wanderer

The jurists discuss various types of slaves that remove themselves from their owners: the wanderer (*erro*), the runaway (*fugitivus*), the suicidal slave, the slave who fears their owner and for their own health. The wanderer is dealt with only briefly, but they are far less troubling than the runaway—though they do abandon their post, they unfailingly return to their servitude. The suicidal slave, in essence, takes themself away from their owner, but their purpose is death not freedom. The wanderer and the suicidal slave do not dispute their statuses. The runaway, on the other hand, challenges their status as a slave. There is an inherent legal distinction between the wanderer, the suicidal slave, and the runaway slave, and the core of this distinction lies in the mental realm of thinking and willing. Ulpian cites Labeo discussing the wandering slave:

> Labeo defines a wanderer as a smalltime fugitive and, conversely, a fugitive as a bigtime wanderer. However, if we wish to be accurate, we define a wanderer as one who does not indeed run away but frequently indulges in aimless roaming and, after wasting time on trivialities, returns home rather late.
>
> Erronem ita definit Labeo pusillum fugitivum esse, et ex diverso fugitivum magnum erronem esse. Sed proprie erronem sic definimus: qui non quidem

43. Situations of escape for the sake of self-preservation: see especially D. 21.1.17.3–5, 12 Ulpian, *Curule Aediles' Edict*, book 1. In a similar situation, Pliny counsels his friend to forgive an erring freedman who seeks out Pliny's help in getting a pardon from his patron, *Ep.* 9.21, 24.

> fugit, sed frequenter sine causa vagatur et temporibus in res nugatorias consumptis serius domum redit.[44]

The definition of the wanderer as one who roams without purpose (*sine causa*) echoes the indicators of madness: flight, roving, and wandering. But this lack of purpose is one, it seems, entirely contrived from the jurist's perspective (with the interest of the slave owner in mind). This enslaved person does naturally have a purpose—what these "trivialities" (*res nugatorias*) are exactly has been scrubbed from our record, but it is easy enough to imagine an enslaved person visiting a loved one, having a meal, or making money on the side among countless other things. These actions are without purpose or deemed as worthless wandering only because they do not benefit the owner; with the construction of the category of *erro* as a person with a *vitium animi*, the jurists have begun to carve out ailments that are particular to slaves.

Discussing military affairs, the jurist Arrius Menander compares the wanderer (*erro*) and runaway (*fugitivus*) with their military counterparts, the AWOL (absent without leave) soldier (*emansor*) and deserter (*desertor*).[45] The AWOL soldier is similar to the wanderer; as Catherine Wolff explains, the length of time a soldier was gone mattered, but also his intention to return.[46] The discussions in the *Digest* of the AWOL soldier do not directly speak to the difference in mentality between an AWOL soldier and a deserter; however, the jurist Modestinus provides us with the difference: an AWOL soldier returns (*regreditur*) to camp while a deserter is brought back (*reducitur*).[47] The difference between the wanderer and the runaway is similar in the sense that the wanderer always intends to return, while a runaway returns if they are captured. The primary reason a soldier deserted was fear of death in battle, which is not generally applicable to slaves. However, other reasons for escaping slav-

---

44. D. 21.1.17.14 Ulpian, *Curule Aediles' Edict*, book 1. See also D. 21.1.64.2 Pomponius, *Letters*, book 17, in which Labeo says livestock (*iumenta*) are not wanderers or runaways when they wander or run.

45. D. 49.16.4.14 Arrius Menander, *Military Law*, book 1, "So the crime of absence without leave is treated more leniently, as is truancy among slaves, and that of desertion more seriously, as in the case of runaway [slaves]" (*Levius itaque delictum emansionis habetur, ut erronis in servis, desertionis gravius, ut in fugitivis*).

    On the *erro*, see Gamauf 2014, 269–87, and on the difference between the *erro* and the *fugitivus*, see Reduzzi Merola 2007 and Donadio 2004b, 137–77.

46. Wolff 2009, xv.

47. D. 49.16.3.2–3 Modestinus, *Punishments*, book 4. See also D. 48.19.16.5 Claudius Saturninus, *Penalties of Civilians*, sole book, "Time distinguishes someone who absents himself without leave from a deserter" (*Tempus discernit emansorem a fugitivo*).

ery, such as fear of harsh owners, living conditions, and punishments, fit well with the fears of soldiers that may make them desert.[48] The wanderer is a defective slave; however, their inevitable return can be read, at least by the jurists and their owner, as an acceptance of their owned status.

The Suicidal Slave and the Self-Preserving Slave

While a wanderer might become a fugitive if they never came back, the fugitive in general remains an exclusive category. As we will see, even though the jurists continue to pathologize the potential runaway slave, they make a distinction between a slave who attempted to die by suicide and one who ran away despite the grim reality that the results were not so different in the eyes of the owner.[49] If a slave tried but failed to run away or to kill themself, a vendor had to disclose these indiscretions to a potential buyer. As will become apparent, this is a highly idiosyncratic pathology of the enslaved psyche derived from imperatives of domination and legal ownership. The suicidal slave and the self-preserving slave, that is a slave who runs to get out of harm's way, are paired together here as they are discussed in somewhat similar affective modes as well as the fact that in the jurists' construction and understanding of these categories neither one intends to escape their status as a slave.

Ulpian again cites Caelius to show the precise line between the runaway and the suicidal slave:

> If you buy a slave who throws himself into the Tiber, he will not be a fugitive so long as his only plan (*consilium*) was to end his life; but if he first planned (*prius consilium*) to run away and then, with a changed intent (*voluntas mutata*), flung himself into the Tiber, he would be a fugitive; he says the same of a slave who throws himself from a bridge.
>
> Si servum emeris, qui se in Tiberim deiecit, si moriendi dumtaxat consilio suscepto a domino discessisset, non esse fugitivum, sed si fugae prius consilium

48. Wolff 2009, 67, discusses the fear of death in terms of a moral failure due to cowardice (*la lâcheté*); at 69, examining the bad conduct of those in charge, she mentions a story from Livy (23.26.4–5) where Hasdrubal's ship commanders betray him after he had blamed them rather harshly; at 70, the harsh conditions of military life and the poor material conditions led some to desert. She, at 85, argues that fear is the main cause of desertion and the generals in charge tried to change their soldiers' fear of death in battle to a fear of punishment for running away. See 264–87 more generally on psychological reasons for desertion.

49. D. 21.1.1.1 Ulpian, *Curule Aediles' Edict*, book 1. Manna 1994, 40, suggests that the suicidal slave is a part of a newer edict.

habuit, deinde mutata voluntate in Tiberim se deiecit, manere fugitivum. Eadem probat et de eo, qui de ponte se praecipitavit.[50]

The will to die rather than to escape enslavement must guide the slave. The nuance of the jurist shows the level of interest in parsing the precise thought process of the slave: Was this slave trying to flee his owner, or did he have a plan to die (*consilium moriendi*)? Even in death, the status of the runaway is irredeemable. As we saw with the fugitive who had a change of heart and returned home, Caelius here gives primacy to the slave's first decision (*prius consilium*). We might view this extreme example of judging the slave a fugitive from their first intention as a means to understand more fully when a slave is a fugitive. The jurist Proculus, again through Ulpian, provides a more generalized scenario of a slave leaping to their death that similarly emphasizes original intention via words of willing such as the verb *volo*.[51]

This case of the suicidal slave shows that the desire to run away was of greater concern to the jurists than the enslaved person intending to end their life. There is something more essentially troubling to the jurists about the runaway than the suicidal slave or the wanderer. As noted above, the wanderer, because their inevitable return is fundamental to their condition, does not challenge their status as a slave or the ownership of the slaveholder. In the case of the suicidal slave, because their purpose is death, they too do not challenge their enslavement or the ownership of the slaveholder as even in death the slave remains the property of the owner. The fugitive slave, on the other hand, is expressly invested in leaving the ownership of the slaveholder. In the cases regarding suicidal slaves, the jurists' concentration on the mindset of the slave and the language of mentality reveals that the financial ramifications of losing a slave were not the sole force behind the determination of these forms of mental defect. The suicidal slave was economically problematic, but not socially subversive.

A second reason for this legal hairsplitting between the fugitive and the suicidal slave may be found in the comments of Ulpian's contemporary, the jurist Paul: "A slave commits suicide when he seeks death out of wickedness or evil behavior or because of some shameful act committed, but not because he cannot endure physical pain" (*Mortis consciscendae causa sibi facit, qui propter*

---

50. D. 21.1.17.6 Ulpian, *Curule Aediles' Edict*, book 1. Both Proculus and Caelius use forms of will to describe the desire to die: Proculus uses the verb *volo*, Caelius the noun *voluntas*.

51. D. 21.1.17.4 Ulpian, *Curule Aediles' Edict*, book 1 (this passage is discussed at the end of this section).

nequitiam malosque mores flagitiumve aliquod admissum mortem sibi consciscere voluit, non si dolorem corporis non sustinendo id fecerit).[52] This explanation, like the description of the wanderer as roaming without cause, is from the perspective of the jurist. There is no reason to think this is what led an enslaved individual to die by suicide. They might, arguably, be exercising the very autonomy the jurist and the slave owner sought to deny them in death.

The reasons Paul emphasizes are worth pausing on, however: a slave ends their life over the morality of particular actions as morality is essential in the terms *nequitia* (wickedness), *mali mores* (evil behavior), and *flagitium* (a shameful act). This can be further supported by the second part of Paul's reasoning, that a slave does not kill themself because of their inability to endure bodily pain. The bodily pain may come from an abusive owner or from the duties of being a slave; however, in the mind of the jurist, the decision to die by suicide is not a question of physicality, but mentality. Is it the slave's own actions that drive them to death, and if so, were they voluntary, something the slave did on their own account, or were they ordered? Was the slave simply party to the actions or aware of them, or were they actions of their owner that they assisted with? Is it, then, out of the slave's own sense of shame that they kill themself? As the jurists approach these questions of unwanted behavior on the part of the slave entirely from the perspective of the owner, we might consider that Paul is thinking about the slave being ashamed about some ordered behavior rather than something the slave did of their own volition. A slave who kills themself because of shame over their actions robs their owner of their property, and their actions would suggest that a slave who is trying to live a more virtuous life is not necessarily a benefit for an owner.

If we consider the popularity of suicide as a literary trope and tool for political action in the Empire, the tie between the suicides of slaves and morality is perhaps not as surprising as it would seem.[53] Suicide at the time of Proculus and Caelius was often viewed as a noble and even rational exit for a person of principle.[54] Outside of the Aedilician Edict, jurists discuss the consequences of

52. D. 21.1.43.4 Paul, *Curule Aediles' Edict*, book 1.

53. See Hill 2004; Bellocci 1997; Plass 1995; Van Hooff 1990; Griffin 1986a, 1986b; Grisé 1982; and Veyne 1981, which outline and discuss the role of suicide in Rome, with particular emphasis on the first century CE. Griffin (1986a, 68) describes the Rome of Seneca as partaking in "the Stoic cult of suicide."

54. Proculus and Caelius were prominent jurists of the first century CE and leaders of the Proculian and Sabinian schools of jurists; see Leesen 2010, among many others, on the schools. Regarding the view of suicide at their time, we need only think of the depiction of the death of Thrasea Paetus in book 16 of Tacitus' *Annales* and Livy's presentation of the death of Lucretia (Livy 1.57–60).

a suicide or a suicide attempt in terms of the motivation behind the action. The Severan jurist Arrius Menander gives a rescript of the Emperor Hadrian in which he allows a soldier who attempted to take his own life to be dishonorably discharged rather than executed if he did so for the following reasons: the inability to endure pain (*impatientia doloris*), weariness of life (*taedium vitae*), disease (*morbus*), madness (*furor*), or shame (*pudor*).[55] Considering whether a person who dies by suicide can have an heir, the jurist Marcian cites a rescript of Antoninus Pius that allows for an heir if the person died because of the inability to endure pain (*impatientia doloris*), weariness of life (*taedium vitae*), or some other reason (*alius modus*); and Marcian likewise cites a rescript of Hadrian about a father who kills himself because of the pain (*dolor*) of having killed his son—he will keep his property.[56]

The rescript of Hadrian reported by Arrius Menander says that capital punishment should be left to those who have misbehaved due to drink or debauch-

---

55. D. 49.16.6.7 Arrius Menander, *Military Law*, book 3, "If a soldier has wounded himself or has attempted suicide in some other way, the Emperor Hadrian wrote in a rescript that the circumstances of the matter should be established, so that, if he had preferred to die out of inability to bear pain, or *taedium vitae*, or disease, or madness, or shame, the death penalty should not be inflicted on him, but he should receive a dishonorable discharge; but if he could put forward no such excuse he should suffer capital punishment. The capital penalty should be remitted to those whose misconduct was due to drink or jest, and change of service imposed" (*Qui se vulneravit vel alias mortem sibi conscivit, imperator Hadrianus rescripsit, ut modus eius rei statutus sit, ut, si impatientia doloris aut taedio vitae aut morbo aut furore aut pudore mori maluit, non animadvertatur in eum, sed ignominia mittatur, si nihil tale praetendat, capite puniatur. per vinum aut lasciviam lapsis capitalis poena remittenda est et militiae mutatio irroganda*).

56. D. 48.21.3.4–6 Marcian, *Accusers*, sole book, "However, the deified Antoninus wrote in a rescript that if someone puts an end to his life through *taedium vitae* or unendurable pain of some kind, or otherwise, he has a successor. The deified Hadrian wrote in a rescript that it appeared that a father, who had laid hands on himself because he was said to have killed his son, had primarily killed himself for grief at losing his son, and that, therefore, his property should not be confiscated. But this distinction is made, that a person's motive deciding on death is relevant, as when the question is raised of whether a soldier who has attempted suicide but has not carried it through should be punished, as if he carried out sentence on himself. For he should by all means be punished unless he was compelled to do so by *taedium vitae* or unendurable pain of some kind. And it is right that he should be punished if he has laid hands on himself without good cause; for he who has not been merciful to himself will much less be merciful to another" (*Si quis autem taedio vitae vel inpatientia doloris alicuius vel alio modo vitam finierit, successorem habere divus Antoninus rescripsit. Videri autem et patrem, qui sibi manus intulisset, quod diceretur filium suum occidisse, magis dolore filii amissi mortem sibi irrogasse et ideo bona eius non esse publicanda divus Hadrianus rescripsit. Sic autem hoc distinguitur, interesse qua ex causa quis sibi mortem conscivit: sicuti cum quaeritur, an is, qui sibi manus intulit et non perpetravit, debeat puniri, quasi de se sententiam tulit. nam omnimodo puniendus est, nisi taedio vitae vel inpatientia alicuius doloris coactus est hoc facere. et merito, si sine causa sibi manus intulit, puniendus est: qui enim sibi non pepercit, multo minus alii parcet*). A similar case is seen in Ulpian (quoting the jurist Neratius) where he discusses when a woman may remarry following the death of her husband. Neratius says that if the husband killed himself not on account of weariness of life (*taedium vitae*) but for a guilty conscience (*mala conscientia*), his wife will be dishonored (*infamia*) should she remarry, D. 3.2.11.3 Ulpian, *Edict*, book 6.

ery (*vinum aut lascivia*). In his discussion of the rescripts of Hadrian and Antoninus Pius, Marcian notes both that "a person's motive for deciding on death is relevant" (*interesse qua ex causa quis sibi mortem conscivit*) and that a soldier who tries to kill himself "without reason" (*sine causa*) ought to be punished (and he reiterates that pain and weariness of life are justifiable reasons).[57] The jurists and emperors gave consideration to the idea of the freeman, and, importantly, the enlisted man who suffers from weariness of life. The motivation for the suicide of free people was important and the jurists were sympathetic to reasons that were rooted in an intellectual, emotional, or moral dissatisfaction with life, even if it meant leaving one's post.

The jurists also allow that unbearable pain is a reason for a free person to take their own life, but notably Paul makes the claim that physical pain is not why a slave kills themself. The causes for slave suicide all derive from the mental realm. If Paul's rationale for slave suicide can be read in this same spirit of moral dissatisfaction, it fits with Seneca's Stoic view that when a person is presented with no options to live a virtuous life, it is right to end their life.[58] Philosophical discontentment plays a role in the jurists' discussion of suicide more generally and, perhaps not as explicitly, it does so in Paul's rendition of the motives for a slave to kill themself.[59] Seneca too does not prescribe suicide for

57. Notably, the reason Marcian gives for punishing the soldier who dies without a "good cause" is that one who is not merciful (*parcere*) with themselves will not be with others; see note 56 above, D. 48.21.3.4–6 Marcian, *Accusers*, sole book. Compare with D. 21.1.23.3 Ulpian, *Curule Aediles' Edict*, book 1, discussing cases in which rescission has taken place and everything must be restored to the state before the sale. An exception is a slave who has committed a capital offense and a slave who has attempted to take his own life. Here Ulpian says that a suicidal slave is a bad slave (*malus servus*)—the only negative language as far as I know in the discussion of suicidal slaves—because "it is as though there is nothing that he would not venture against others, who dares to do it against himself" (*tamquam non nihil in alium ausurus, qui hoc adversus se ausus est*). Where the suicidal soldier fails to be merciful with himself or others, there is nothing the suicidal slave won't dare to do.

58. Sen. *Ep.* 77, especially at 15, where Seneca likens a man unwilling to take his own life when he has no other option to someone in a state of slavery (*Nam vita, si moriendi virtus abest, servitus est*).

59. D. 28.3.6.7 Ulpian, *Sabinus*, book 10, "Therefore, the testament of such a person will not be made ineffectual before the emperor has replied that he should be executed; and, hence, if he has died before this, his testament will certainly be valid, unless he died by suicide. For *constitutiones* make ineffectual the wills of those who have chosen to die rather than be condemned, on account of their consciousness of having committed a crime, although they die still citizens; but if someone [chooses to die] because of *taedium vitae* or inability to bear ill-health or as a gesture, like some philosophers, their situation is such that their wills are valid" (*nec huius igitur testamentum irritum fiet, priusquam princeps de eo supplicium sumendum rescripserit: proinde si ante decesserit, utique testamentum eius valebit, nisi mortem sibi conscivit. nam eorum, qui mori magis quam damnari maluerint ob conscientiam criminis, testamenta irrita constitutiones faciunt, licet in civitate decedant: quod si quis taedio vitae vel valetudinis adversae inpatientia vel iactationis, ut quidam philosophi, in ea causa sunt, ut testamenta eorum valeant*).

those wishing to escape their status, but rather to escape an unvirtuous life.[60] The discussion of slave suicide is particularly interesting because so often in Roman literature the suicide of a slave is portrayed as an expression of loyalty to their owner, but in the context of the Edict of the Aediles it is being discussed as a potential defect of the slave. This must be read against the common literary trope of the faithful slave who takes their owner's place in death or kills themself when their owner dies.[61]

Literary sources do not describe runaway slaves in the same noble light.[62] By and large, the runaway slave is described as weak and disgraced and is used as a metaphor for cowardly behavior. Sallust reports that Catiline rejected enrolling slaves into his cause because he did not want to be associated with runaways. Cicero uses the terminology of runaway slaves (*fugitivi*) to call the corrupt magistrate Verres worse than slaves, runaway slaves, barbarians, and enemies. Epictetus, the formerly enslaved philosopher, argues that free people should not be as cowardly as slaves who run away.[63] Perhaps in part due to a cultural, intellectual, and moral sympathy with suicide at the time, the jurists do not view the suicidal slave in the same light as the runaway slave, despite the similar economic loss the owner would face. More pragmatically, the slave who dies by suicide does not do so to challenge their status as a slave.

Paul's idea that a slave kills themself because of shame following some moral misdeed can be further elaborated if we consider the examples the jurists give of slaves who run away from their owners in order to protect themselves from those very owners. In the scenarios of both the suicidal slave and the self-preserving slave, there is a suggestion that the slave is taking action because they are experiencing shame due to a position the owner has put them in. Self-preservation, in general, is considered a justifiable reason for an enslaved person to be away from their owner's house as it is in the owner's interest. Ulpian, citing Vivian, notes that a slave who flees an enemy, a thief, or from a fire or

---

60. Sen. *Ep.* 77. On the difference between flight and death: Sen. *Ep.* 70.25. On the idea of the reasons why a slave should run away, see Aulus Gellius *NA* 5.14 (on cruelty to slaves and subsequent flight). See Reduzzi Merola 2011, 401–2.

61. On slaves killing themselves in their owners' place, see App. *B Civ.* 4.29, and on slaves killing themselves when their owner is dying, App. *B Civ.* 4.26. On slaves enduring torture for their owner, see Tac. *Ann.* 4.29, Val. Max. 6.8.1, 6.8.5; Sen. *Ep.* 47.4–5.

62. In Petronius' *Satyricon* not only is the character of Giton, who appears as a runaway slave, represented unfavorably, but the terminology of runaway slave (*fugitivus*) is adopted for bad behavior, see at *Sat.* 95–96.

63. Sall. *Cat.* 56.5; Cic. *Verr* 4.112; Epict. *Diss.* 1.9.7–8, 3.26.1–2.

collapsing building is not a runaway.[64] The question of the slave's action might appear obvious, that when facing danger or death, a slave should flee the situation; the owner, in the interest of protecting his investment, would not see the fault in this. Here we have an example of how the physical location of the slave or even being caught in the act of flight does not make the slave a runaway. The reasons Vivian gives for running away are not a consideration of a slave's mental state (like the feeling of shame), but from their desire to keep themself out of physical danger.

In these scenarios of Vivian, the slave escapes with good reason; they do not allow themself to be damaged. If we recall the purpose of defining a *fugitivus*, the reason behind these cases becomes clear. Three correlated ideas come out of this discussion. First, a slave's location relative to their owner did not necessarily matter; second, a slave does not become a fugitive every time they flee; and third, the way to determine if they are a fugitive is whether their reason was good in the eyes of the owner (e.g., for self-preservation) or whether it was bad (e.g., for escape). Rather than the previous scenarios, which gave a general reason for flight, the slave in these cases is fleeing from particular circumstances detrimental to their own person; the slave is protecting themself and protecting the owner's investment from damage. The slave has a good reason for flight when they protect the owner's property even without the owner's consultation.

The majority of the examples of the self-preserving slave, however, are not about external factors like a fire or collapsing building but are about the excessive violence of their owner or other person in charge of them. The examples of Vivian immediately above move on from the slave running out of the collapsing building to the slave who flees an instructor or person to whom he had been lent for immoderate or too savage treatment.[65] Shortly thereafter, Ulpian cites Vivian again in a case of a slave who flees to their mother to get her to intervene on their behalf and lessen whatever punishment their owner has in

64. D. 21.1.17.3 Ulpian, *Curule Aediles' Edict*, book 1.

65. D. 21.1.17.3 Ulpian, *Curule Aediles' Edict*, book 1, "In the same way, a slave who runs away from the instructor to whom he was entrusted for training is not a fugitive, if the reason for his running away is the intolerable treatment which he receives. Vivian says the same, if that is the reason for his running away from someone who borrowed him. He says the same if the slave were savagely used. All this applies to those who, having fled, return to their owners; but, says Vivian, if they do not return, then they are unquestionably fugitives" (*Item ne eum quidem, qui a praeceptore cui in disciplinam traditus erat aufugit, esse fugitivum, si forte ideo fugit, quia immoderate eo utebatur. Idemque probat et si ab eo fugerit cui erat commodatus, si propter eandem causam fugerit. Idem probat Vivianus et si saevius cum eo agebat. Haec ita, si eos fugisset et ad dominum venisset: ceterum si ad dominum non venisset, sine ulla dubitatione fugitivum videri ait*).

store for them for some wrongdoing (*aliud delictum*).[66] While the slave here has done wrong, they are not a runaway: The owner's domination of this slave has not been challenged as the slave fears their owner and their anger or punishment. In contrast, Vivian says if the slave was hiding out without the intent of returning to their owner they are a fugitive. This judgment again rests on the intent: Intending to hide (*causa celandi*) is not a good reason, and the slave is a fugitive. The focus on the will of the slave is seen in the deliberation between the slave who runs with the intent of never returning and the slave who goes to their mother to obtain an easier pardon of some transgression. Paul gives a similar example of a slave who runs off to seek intervention from a friend of the owner.[67]

Ulpian also cites Labeo and Caelius on a slave seeking asylum, sale, or the statue of the emperor. He agrees with the earlier jurists that these slaves are similarly not fugitives as they are not intending to run away (*causa fugiendi*).[68] In the instance of the slave running to their mother for assistance, it is made clear that the slave has done some wrong that their owner plans to punish them for. However, in the other situations of the slave seeking assistance from the owner's friend or the wider community it is not spelled out from what precisely

66. D. 21.1.17.5 Ulpian, *Curule Aediles' Edict*, book 1, "If a slave leaves his owner and comes back to his mother, the question of whether he is a fugitive is one for consideration; if he fled to conceal himself and not to return to his owner, he is a fugitive; but he is not a fugitive if he seeks that some wrongdoing of his may be better extenuated by his mother's entreaties" (*Si a magistro puer recessit et rursus ad matrem pervenit, cum quaereretur, num fugitivus esset: si celandi causa quo, ne ad dominum reverteretur, fugisset, fugitivum esse: sin vero ut per matrem faciliorem deprecationem haberet delicti alicuius, non esse fugitivum*).

67. D. 21.1.43.1 Paul, *Curule Aediles' Edict*, book 1, "A slave who takes himself off to a friend of his owner to seek his intercession is not a fugitive; indeed, even if his thinking is that in the event of his not receiving assistance, he will not return home, he is not yet a fugitive, for flight requires not only the intention but also the act of flight" (*Qui ad amicum domini deprecaturus confugit, non est fugitivus: immo etiamsi ea mente sit, ut non impetrato auxilio domum non revertatur, nondum fugitivus est, quia non solum consilii, sed et facti fugae nomen est*).

68. D. 21.1.17.12 Ulpian, *Curule Aediles' Edict*, book 1, "In Labeo and Caelius, the question is raised whether a slave who seeks asylum or betakes himself to a place frequented by those who declare themselves for sale is a fugitive; I think that a slave who does what is adjudged permissible to do publicly is not a fugitive. No more do I regard as a fugitive a slave who flees to the emperor's statue; for he does not so act with the intention of running away. I think the same of a slave who seeks asylum or other sanctuary, because he does not do so with the intention of running away; but if he first runs away and then takes shelter, he does not cease to be a fugitive" (*Apud Labeonem et Caelium quaeritur, si quis in asylum confugerit aut eo se conferat, quo solent venire qui se venales postulant, an fugitivus sit: ego puto non esse eum fugitivum, qui id facit quod publice facere licere arbitratur. Ne eum quidem, qui ad statuam Caesaris confugit, fugitivum arbitror: non enim fugiendi animo hoc facit. idem puto et in eum, qui in asylum vel quod aliud confugit, quia non fugiendi animo hoc facit: si tamen ante fugit et postea se contulit, non ideo magis fugitivus esse desinit*). See D. 21.1.19.1 on a vendor being held to his word if he promised a slave for sale had never taken refuge at the statue of the emperor (even though these slaves were not considered runaways).

the slave is running. The examples of the slave getting help beyond the owner's house are potentially revealing. They provide a glimpse into the family and social life of a slave: The slave can seek out their mother who does not appear to be in the same household and has a good enough relationship with their owner's friend that the friend may ask for intervention. This appeal to a wider network is also suggestive of a potential problem with the owner as the patriarchal head of household. Is this owner excessively harsh in punishment or asking the slave to do some immoral act? The real-world happenings that led to these cases are lost to us, if they ever occurred, but a slave that can get a legally sanctioned intermediary between them and their owner suggests trouble at the owner's home.

This seeking assistance lies parallel then to the slave who seeks death because of some morally bad act; these are explicitly linked by Ulpian:

> Proculus said . . . if he concealed himself [on the owner's property] until his owner's wrath abated, he would not be a fugitive any more than one who, having in mind that his owner wished to punish him physically, took himself to a friend whom he induced to plead on his behalf. It cannot even be said that a slave is a fugitive who has come to the stage that he hurls himself from a height (otherwise one could declare a fugitive one who goes up to a high point of the house to cast himself down): rather does he desire to end his life.

> Proculus . . . ait . . . sin autem in hoc tantum latuisset, quoad iracundia domini effervesceret, fugitivum non esse, sicuti ne eum quidem, qui cum dominum animadverteret verberibus se adficere velle, praeripuisset se ad amicum, quem ad precandum perduceret. ne eum quidem fugitivum esse, qui in hoc progressus est, ut se praecipitaret (ceterum etiam eum quis fugitivum diceret, qui domi in altum locum ad praecipitandum se ascendisset), magisque hunc mortem sibi consciscere voluisse.[69]

In this case, the slave who hides at home until his owner's anger (*iracundia*) has passed is much the same as the slave who runs to seek intervention from a friend or wishes to end their life. Additionally, while it is not explicit, we can understand that this owner is a bad owner; he is too angry and lets his emotions

69. D. 21.1.17.4 Ulpian, *Curule Aediles' Edict*, book 1.

control him.[70] The self-preserving slave saves themself from their owner *for* their owner and saves the owner from themself. This seeking assistance might be viewed as an alternative to suicide that is permissible as these slaves behave as Roman owners expected and wanted. They do not use their independent thought or agency to seek a better life by escaping their status, but rather preserve their status as slaves. This idea is reaffirmed by Vivian; he deems "ignorant" (*imprudentes*) those too quick to judge as a fugitive a slave outside their owner's house without their owner's consent. He stresses instead that the judgment of the fugitive must be assessed (*aestimare*) by the disposition of the slave's mind (*ab affectu animi*).[71]

The Unwilling, the Unaware, and the Liberated Slave

Moving to a different scenario of motivations for running away allows us to consider the question in a different manner, one that revolves around the concept of good faith (*bona fides*). These last cases of slaves being away from their owners highlight how the jurists envision a slave who is not with their owner. In the first case, a slave who ran away took his *vicarius* (a slave that is in his *peculium*) with him. Caelius says that if the *vicarius* is unwilling (*invitus*) or ignorant (*imprudens*) and returns when they can, they are not a fugitive.[72] Because it was not their intent to escape, the *vicarius* is not a fugitive. The determination of who is a fugitive is tied to the mind, and as we have seen, here the *vicarius* lacks both the knowledge and the intention to be a fugitive.

The following case regards the freeing of a slave and the death of his owner. Ulpian cites Caelius:

---

70. On the owner being angry, see D. 21.1.17.4–5 Ulpian, *Curule Aediles' Edict*, book 1 (discussed above). The owner who lets his anger get the better of him is much discussed in Roman literature, see, for example, Gellius *NA* 1.26 and Seneca, *De Ira* 3.40, Gal. *Aff. Pecc. Dig.* 4, Kühn 5.17–18.

71. D. 21.1.17.3 Ulpian, *Curule Aediles' Edict*, book 1.

72. D.21.1.17.7 Ulpian, *Curule Aediles' Edict*, book 1, Ulpian cites Caelius, "If your slave in running away from you takes with him his *vicarius* and the latter goes unwillingly or not knowing what it is all about and seeks the opportunity to return, he will not be deemed a fugitive; but if he knew at the time of flight what was going on or later became aware of it and chose not to return to you when he could do so, the *vicarius* would himself be a fugitive. He thinks the same to apply to a slave abducted by a kidnapper" (*si servus tuus fugiens vicarium suum secum abduxit: si vicarius invitus aut imprudens secutus est neque occasionem ad te redeundi nactus praetermisit, non videri fugitivum fuisse: sed si aut olim cum fugeret intellexit quid ageretur aut postea cognovit quid acti esset et redire ad te cum posset noluit, contra esse. idem putat dicendum de eo, quem plagiarius abduxit*).

> A slave, sent off to a province by his owner, who learns that the owner is dead and has freed him in his will and who continues in the same office but acting for himself as a freeman is not a fugitive; he did not begin to be a fugitive by lying that he was free, he says, because he did this without the intention to flee.
>
> Servum in provinciam missum a domino, cum eum mortuum esse et testamento se liberum relictum audisset et in eodem officio permansisset tantumque pro libero se gerere coepisset, hunc non esse fugitivum: nec enim mentiendo se liberum, inquit, fugitivus esse coepit, quia sine fugae consilio id fecit.[73]

This passage shows how a slave could shift status easily (*pro libero se gerere coepisset, mentiendo se liberum*) and highlights perhaps why the jurists spend such an effort distinguishing fugitive slaves from other slaves out of the house: The line between a slave and a free person could become confused.

The preoccupation of the jurists in these cases as they construct the legal concept of the fugitive has been with the inner workings of the slave's mind. This concentration on the mind is illuminated in one more fragment of the fugitive discussion. Caelius, the main jurist of Ulpian's treatment, is quoted, "Likewise, rightly [Caelius] says flight is an appearance of a kind of liberty, since he is freed from the power of his owner in that present moment" (*Idem recte ait libertatis cuiusdam speciem esse fugisse, hoc est potestate dominica in praesenti liberatum esse*).[74] Caelius places this idea of flight as the appearance of a kind of liberty right after he has explained that it is the mind (*animus*) of the slave that makes them a fugitive. Caelius' passages, where he discusses a slave who simply begins to act like a freeman upon being granted freedom in their owner's will and the fact that a fugitive has an appearance of a kind of liberty, bring together the tension between a slaveholder's ownership and the fact that the owner does not have total knowledge and control over their property. We see that at times it was difficult to know not only who was a slave and who was a free person, but even for an owner to know if their own slave was still under their power. This is slave law in its purist form; the mental state of being a fugitive is the basic human desire of not wishing to be under the arbitrary rule of another.

The rendering of acting like a free person into a mental defect for the enslaved population serves as the apex of the "slave medicine" the jurists cre-

73. D.21.1.17.16 Ulpian, *Curule Aediles' Edict*, book 1.
74. D.21.1.17.10 Ulpian, *Curule Aediles' Edict*, book 1.

ated; this is unsurprising, given the idea that a slave could come upon the appearance of a kind of liberty easily. Both the desire of the jurists to define the fugitive by their intent and the fact that flight was an appearance of liberty reveals a number of reasons for the jurists' approach. The first and most evident is the commercial reason: the need to be aware of whether the slave one was to buy had a so-called defect. Second, there is a tension between the lack of legal status markers and the great importance placed on that status (free, freedperson, or slave) in Rome.[75] The discovery or attempts to know whether the slave at market had a history of running away mattered to a potential owner, but also to the larger state, which had a vested interest in knowing and controlling the status of its population.

The fugitive slave posed a threat to this division and to Roman status hierarchy. For a slave to be a successful fugitive, they must convince others that indeed they are not a fugitive, or a slave without their owner, but a free person. The phrase "appearance of liberty" (*species libertatis*) is perhaps best known from the opening of Tacitus' *Histories*.[76] Discussing the Roman historiographical practice, he writes that since the start of the Empire, Romans have been subjected to histories either too sycophantic or too harsh. He describes the first (*adulatio*) as a result of being under the thumb of the emperor (literally, "a shameful crime of slavery," *foedum crimen servitutis*) and the second (*malignitas*) as presenting a false appearance of liberty (*falsa species libertatis*). Like the fugitive slave who has too much license, in the *Annals* Tacitus uses the phrase in a morally negative sense about a group of people showing too much license in their speech or actions.[77]

There is a great tension between the facility or difficulty in the recognition of slaves and the Roman preoccupation with status. Seneca reminds his audience that there is no essential difference between the free person and the slave, "Recall that the person you call your slave was born from the same seed, enjoys

---

75. D.1.5.3 Gaius, *Institutes*, book 1, "And so, the greatest division in the law of persons is this: that all men are either free or slaves" (*Summa itaque de iure personarum divisio haec est, quod omnes homines aut liberi sunt aut servi*).

In literature, see, for example, Seneca on the similarity between free people and slaves: Sen. *Ep.* 47.10; Epict. *Diss.* 1.29.58–63 where he incorporates a metaphor involving the fear of a runaway slave being caught by his owner; 4.1.145–46 on liberty in the Empire where Epictetus uses the language of slave detection; and Sen. Rhet. *Contro.* 7.6.22–24 on looking at a slave's sale documents to ensure he is not a wanderer or a fugitive.

76. Tac. *Hist.* 1.1.

77. Tac. *Ann.* 13.24. See also Quint. *Inst.* 12.9.13, 12.10.73. Livy uses the term to describe a peace treaty that left Greek cities with only a false appearance of freedom, 33.31.

the same sky, breathes equally, lives equally, and dies equally to you! You can see a freeborn man in him as much as he can see a slave in you" (*Vis tu cogitare istum, quem servum tuum vocas, ex isdem seminibus ortum eodem frui caelo, aeque spirare, aeque vivere, aeque mori! Tam tu illum videre ingenuum potes quam ille te servum*).[78] While both literary and legal sources have shown, tacitly or openly, the existence of the ambiguities of status, the reasons for their conclusions are very different. For Seneca, a philosopher and politician, the recommendation of harmony with all people instead of those only in the same status agrees very well with Stoic ideas. Seneca also recalls that the Senate was going to have slaves wear distinguishing clothes, but this was not taken up because of the fear that slaves would realize how few the free were in comparison with them.[79] In the case of the runaway slave, the jurists study the mind of the slave because it was informative; it revealed threats to the tenuous boundaries established between free and slave. The desire to understand the mind of the slave must be seen as an aspect of social control in Roman society and one that was so important that certain attributes, like being a runaway, were crafted into a special category of *vitia animi* that only pertained to slaves. Understanding that the runaway slave could appear to be a free person allows us to see that these slaves, through their intention to run away, have rejected the ownership of the slaveholder.

A great amount of attention to humanity and authoritarianism runs through the juristic discussions of the deranged slave and the runaway slave. The discussion first humanizes the slave: Its examination of the mind brings to the fore the slave as person (*persona*). Subsequently, as this desire to know the mind of the slave was an effort to control and secure ownership and the boundaries of status, it recalls the other nature of the slave, as thing (*res*). The jurists' recognition of the slave's mentality and intention created a space of autonomy from the owner. In the case of the Edict of the Aediles, this space of autonomy needed to be controlled and regulated because it revealed undesired characteristics and choices on the part of the slave. The juristic commentary on the Aedilician Edict exposes the relationship between the power an owner has over their slave and the difficulty of knowing their slave's mind and character.

Looking at this evaluative process at the slave market underscores that the value of the slave was in their utility, and part of this utility entails the owner's

78. Sen. *Ep.* 47.10. See also D. 18.1.5, Paul, *Sabinus*, book 5, "because it can be difficult to distinguish a freeman from a slave" (*quia difficile dinosci potest liber homo a servo*).

79. Sen. *Clem.* 1.24.1.

ability to have a level of control on the mind of the slave. In the examined cases, if the slave's behavior was wayward enough, they were deemed mentally defective. Behavior determined whether the slave was good (and therefore mentally healthy) as behavior revealed or led to an understanding of a slave's character and intention. The slave that is deemed to have a mental defect exhibits a mentality that is not beneficial to the owner. The mentally defective slave then is a slave whose will and character are not in the service of the owner. In order to facilitate this evaluation, the jurists create a medicine particular to the slave market. While at times they draw on existing medical and philosophical understandings of madness and adapt them to suit their ends, in the case of the runaway slave they must develop their own pathology. This creation of a "slave medicine" also erases the experience of the enslaved as it frames their actions as not part of the human condition, where, for example, the desire to be free is considered good and rational, but as part of a servile one.

Examining which mental ailments allow for rescission enables us to see which defects rendered a slave unable to be owned in any effective manner. We see this explicitly in the cases of the deranged slave and the runaway slave. As the deranged slave is deemed not to have a will by the jurists and to have a blinded reasoning faculty by Cicero, the owner cannot hope to exhibit their ownership over the slave's mind to ensure that they act according to their desires. The runaway, in contrast, has all of their faculties but the slave has removed their mind (and usually, though not always, their person) from the domination of the owner, and could appear to be a free person—behavior that challenges the understandings of status. The deranged slave and the runaway slave show us a limit of ownership: These slaves can be handed back in an action for rescission because the domination over their minds has failed. These mental defects are so severe that they render the mind, an essential part of ownership, impermeable to the owner (and in the case of the deranged slave, the slave as well).

PART TWO
The Life of the Slave

THREE

Slaves at Work

The variety of economic positions held by slaves made necessary the careful analysis of a slave's abilities and character, which was discussed in the first part of this book.[1] At first glance, the uncertainty of whether a slave will perform their duties in the manner prescribed lies seemingly at odds with the ownership a slaveholder has over their slave's mind and body. This chapter explores the necessary economic relationship between the mental autonomy of slaves and the ownership of slaveholders, thus allowing us to see the scope and capacity of this ownership. Most studies focus on ownership when it is in the process of change, but here we turn to the in-between period that comprises the entirety of the owner-slave relationship. As will be revealed, while potentially precarious, the mental autonomy of the slave was not an inherent threat to ownership as long as the slave made use of this autonomy in order to benefit the owner. For both Roman jurists and literary writers, however, this relationship between the ownership of the slaveholder and the mental autonomy of the slave provoked much consideration and debate in which the abstract and the pragmatic notions of ownership are seemingly in conflict.

This chapter considers how free Romans negotiated between a slave's status as property and unfree and their capacity as a human being for independent thought and action in their life and duties. Here we turn to texts concerned with commercial affairs: the agronomist Columella weighs a slave's ability to be placed in a position of authority with their innate slave character. From there,

1. Among others, see Gamauf 2009; Carlsen 1995; Aubert 1994; and Watson 1987a, 90–114, on the responsibilities of slaves.

the chapter turns to juristic texts to consider the relationship between owners and high-level slaves by examining cases of slaves as account managers and considering the different levels of autonomy individual slaves had. Lastly, we turn to the legal remedies available to third parties who had made contracts with enslaved business agents. This chapter shows that rather than being inherently problematic, the autonomy of slaves was an essential part of the owner-slave relationship in Roman commercial relations.

Columella and the Ingenium Servile

Slaves were allotted countless jobs and tasks, from basic menial labor to managing the accounts of a wealthy household. How did the Romans balance the financial and social need for competent and trusted slaves with the underlying anxieties of a slave society? Slaves in positions of financial trust and responsibility, such as business agents (*actores*), managers (*institores*), and foremen (*vilici*), were a source of concern for owners.[2] The question of balance is particularly warranted considering how preoccupied the Roman jurists were with the idea of slaves breaking their owners' trust.[3] This question places the owner's lack of knowledge about the character and actions of their slave at the forefront, allowing us to consider how one might manifest ownership without having full knowledge of the object of domination, their slave. The risk involved was in part an individual financial one; when an owner appointed a slave as a business agent, the owner could also be held legally accountable. In certain situations, the jurists consider whether the owner was aware of the slave's actions.[4]

Literary texts provide good evidence that a slave's responsibilities should be

2. For the sake of clarity here: an *actor* is a business agent, generally a slave; a *vilicus* is a foreman of an estate, a slave, who is in charge of other slaves; an *institor* is a more general title for a manager appointed to a business by his owner. See Carlsen 1995 and Aubert 1994, 117–200, for a discussion on the role of *actores* and other *institores* of agricultural estates. For a discussion about the legal status of *vilici*, *actores*, and *dispensatores* (stewards), see Schumacher 2010, 31–40. For a comparative discussion of foremen (nineteenth-century American South and Rome), see Carlsen 2010, 75–90.
3. For example: D.11.3.1.5 Ulpian, *Edict*, book 23 (discussed in chapter 4) refers specifically to business managers. *Digest* 40 on manumission includes several provisions for slaves that ought to be freed so long as they took care of accounts well (discussed below). Aubert 1994, 159, makes note of a number of inscriptions thanking their slaves for being faithful, including *CIL* VI 9989 and *CIL* VI 9119. Chapter 4 will take up the issue of when that trust is broken.
4. See, for example, D.14.1.1.22 Ulpian, *Edict*, book 22, and D.14.4.5.1 Ulpian, *Edict*, book 29 (discussed below).

determined by their owner's comprehension of their abilities. Discussing the role of a foreman (*vilicus*) in his work *On Agriculture*, Columella raises the issue of the limits of a slave's *ingenium* (their natural character or talent) and therefore potential responsibilities. Columella adds that along with husbandry, a foreman must have the ability to humor the good workers and show consideration to the less skilled ones. This second more intangible requirement is qualified: the mind of the foreman could only hold these managerial virtues "as far as servile nature allows":

> Not only should he be skilled in agricultural works, but also, as much as a servile nature allows, he should be equipped with qualities of mind so that he gives commands neither too gently nor cruelly, and always encourages some of the better workers while still showing mercy to those less good. In this way, they fear his sternness rather than hate his cruelty.
>
> Nec tantum operis agrestis sit artifex sed et animi, quantum servile patitur ingenium, virtutibus instructus, ut neque remisse neque crudeliter imperet semperque aliquos ex melioribus foveat, parcat tamen etiam minus bonis ita, ut potius timeant eius severitatem quam crudelitatem detestentur.[5]

The foreman must be an *artifex*, a master of agricultural skill, and have certain qualities of mind (*virtutes animi*). This ideal slave foreman has a bit of a paternalistic character: he commands (*imperare*), he fosters (*fovere*), he has mercy (*parcere*), and he has the capacity to be strict rather than cruel. The foreman's strictness rather than cruelty is important because like a slave owner, a foreman should not punish because he is angry or enjoys it, but because, in his eyes, the slave needs discipline or correction.[6] The foreman behaves as a go-between for the owner and the slave-hands[7] and he exhibits qualities of mastery even to the extent of military language; Columella's conception of the foreman goes so far as to grant the foreman the ability to order around other slaves in the same terminology as a general would in giving orders (*imperare*).[8] Columella frames

5. Columella *Rust.* 1.8.10. Bradley 1987b, 21–28, discusses Columella's views on slave management as a method of control. On Columella and slave management, see Howley 2025.
6. See, for example, Sen. *Ira* 3.5.4, 3.40.2.
7. Carlsen 2010, 75–76.
8. Tacitus refers to the static servile character (*ingenium servile*) of one of Claudius' freedmen, Antonius Felix, who, Tacitus says, exercised a king's right while equipped with a servile character (*ius regium servili ingenio exercuit*), Tac. *Hist.* 5.9.3. Tacitus also refers to the freedman with the servile

the nature of a foreman's—a slave's—authority in such a way that the slave remains a slave in name and in fact, but has the power and ability to control other slaves.

Seemingly at odds with this power is Columella's consideration of the slave's *ingenium* as servile.[9] The term *ingenium* signifies something intrinsic and innate. It is etymologically related to the same root as the verb *gigno* (also with present *geno*) and Greek *gignomai*.[10] The *ingenium* here has governance over the *animus*; its being cast as servile affects the formation, ability, and virtues of a person's *animus*.[11] The *ingenium* as formative to the *animus* is seen in other authors as well.[12] But to discuss an *ingenium* as being *servile* recalls Aristotle's theory of natural slavery rather than the Roman model of slavery as a status imposed on others, especially because the practice of manumission made former slaves into freedperson Roman citizens. Columella balances his need for a competent and managerial foreman with his understanding of slave nature. The *animus* of a slave can have certain desired qualities, but these are restrained by the *ingenium servile*.

Columella navigates between his inherent prejudice that slaves cannot have a full set of virtues and his need for a slave with some level of temperance, judgment, and authority. This navigation is not an uncommon one but for Columella the question remains: Does the *ingenium* become this way because he is a slave or is he a slave because of his *ingenium*? While Columella could be discussing the servile nature of that particular slave, it is more likely in this case he

---

character performing the king's right through the use of a particularly military term: *exercere*, to practice or train. The word can mean to work or put to use, but it is often used for the military.

9. See Ernout-Meillet s.v. *ingenium*. See also Hellegouarc'h 1963, 298, discussing the hereditary nature of *auctoritas* and its connection to *ingenium*.

10. Both are from the same PIE root, see de Vaan s.v. *gigno*.

11. Columella refers to the *ingenium animi* again when he is discussing buying oxen and notes that oxen get their *ingenium animi* as well as their size and hair color from their original region and climate, *Rust.* 6.1.

12. On the relationship between *ingenium* and *animus*, see, for example: Seneca the Elder *Controv.* 7.1.13 has a brother discussing the different "temperaments" (*animi*) of two brothers, the one explains that nature has handed him down a different character (*ingenium*) from his brother; the *animus* is what comes from the nature-given *ingenium*.

In the opening of the *Consolatio ad Marciam* (1.3), Seneca the Younger tells Marcia that she has provided a model of a freeman by promoting the writings of her father, Cremutius Cordus (a historian who was accused of treason under Tiberius), who is free in *ingenium*, then *animus*, and then *manus*.

Aulus Gellius (*NA* 7.2) tells of Chrysippus' claim that we were subject to fate but still had control over our own decisions. Gellius discusses how Chrysippus' opponents argued that if fate was in control, then bad people could not be subject to the law as they were not in control of their actions (here the phrase *ingenium mentium* is used as well as the *ingenium* having governance of the *animus*).

was discussing the nature or innate qualities that are part and parcel of slavery. The typical read on Roman slavery, however, would have us believe that the Romans did not adhere to a concept of natural slavery. Yet Columella acknowledges the limitations of a slave because of something intrinsic that, being born out of nature, could not be shaken off by manumission. There certainly was a social prejudice against freedpersons among the freeborn and Tacitus refers to the *ingenia servilia* of freedpersons on several occasions. Tacitus' use of *ingenia servilia* could be rhetorical, but his language choice nevertheless shows that the *ingenia* of slaves and therefore ex-slaves was under consideration and could affect the prospects of a *libertinus*. And it is Seneca who uses the perplexing descriptor *ingenium libertini*, the nature of a freedman, to drive home the idea that there is something innate and static (and undesirable) about formerly enslaved people.[13] Columella and the other authors have conceptions to varying degrees that the status of a slave would permeate his mind; these authors must reflect on to what degree these slaves were "servile" when deciding whether they could perform high-level tasks and be trusted.

The Price of Freedom[14] *(Account Management)*

Despite these hesitancies, Columella and his like would have made use of high-level and trusted slaves or business agents (*actores*) placed in charge of financial accounts. These accounts could be from agricultural estates or city businesses, and the job of the slave was to transact and record the amount taken in and owed on the owner's business. While specific levels of access to accounts varied individually, these slaves played an important role in their owners' financial welfare and in the Roman economy. The slave in charge of accounts was likely to be one of the most trusted and closest to the owner, but there was always a risk of the slave not working to the owner's advantage.[15] An account manager

13. Tacitus too considers the *ingenium* unchangeable in the sense that he describes the *ingenia* of freedmen (*liberti*) as *servilia*, Tac. *Ann.* 2.12.3. Tacitus again describes the *servilia ingenia* of freedmen in the *Histories*, 2.92.3. As noted above, he discusses Claudius' freedman Antonius Felix (*Hist.* 5.9.3) as having an *ingenium servile*. The language of the *ingenium servile* is used by Livy 35.49.8 when discussing the Syrians, who were considered a better fit as slaves than soldiers because of their *servilia ingenia*. Seneca uses *ingenium libertini* in *Ep.* 27.5, discussed in the introduction.

14. After Koops 2020, 52–53, "such extensive discussion [of manumission terms among the jurists] only makes sense if the purchase of manumission was common, and freedom had its price."

15. A slave persuaded to work against his owner by a third party (*actio servi corrupti*) will be discussed in the following chapter.

who betrayed their owner caused not only a financial loss but also one on a personal and potentially social level, as will be explored in the following chapter.[16] Here instead we will look at when this arrangement more or less worked through three juristic cases that discuss account management and illustrate the level of autonomy and trust placed in certain slave business agents. While these three cases feature jurists from the second century CE, we have evidence of this kind of practice as early as the first-century BCE jurist Alfenus Varus, and in certain situations later jurists cite Varus and the Augustan jurist Labeo, meaning that we can understand this to be the standard practice during the lifetime of people like Seneca, Columella, and Pliny.[17]

Promises of manumission contained in these cases served to ensure honest and accurate account management. These promises of manumission are contained in slave owner's wills; as Egbert Koops has noted, the will is a means of recording a "negotiated agreement and mak[ing] it actionable."[18] Given that in Roman law an owner cannot sue their slave for mismanaging their accounts, the promise of manumission written down in a will, in this case for good account management, was as close to a contract for freedom as a slave could hope to get. In this way, we see how a brokered trust is created to offset some of the uncertainties of slave ownership.[19] The *Digest of Justinian* preserves examples of these manumission orders, often scrubbed of historical details and sometimes fictionalized.[20] The language of these manumissions is largely formulaic, but the individual cases are recorded because of the different circumstance in which manumission was to take place.

The first case is as follows: a *statuliber*—a slave who will be freed in a will on the condition that he completes an allotted task—has made some computational errors in his accounting. His manumission was conditional on rendering these very accounts. The jurist Sextus Caecilius Africanus discusses whether this slave met the condition and should be freed:

---

16. Watson 1987a, 102–14, on the social effects of a slave on his owner through acquisitions.
17. See especially Pomponius quoting Labeo: D. 40.7.21pr Pomponius, *From Plautius*, book 7 and D. 40.4.8 Pomponius, *Sabinus*, book 5. But also, for example, Alfenus Varus: D. 40.1.6 Alfenus Varus, *Digest*, book 4; Ulpian referring to Labeo: D. 33.8.8.5 Ulpian, *Sabinus*, book 25. See Koops 2020, 49, and Morabito 1981, 105–10.
18. Koops 2020, 52.
19. Incentives for manumission were not limited to these skilled slaves, and, for example, birthing a requisite number of children could also gain a person their freedom: for Columella, more than three children would do the trick (*Rust.* 1.8.19); the jurist Julian discusses a case involving freeing a woman once she had borne three children (D. 40.7.3.16 Ulpian, *Ad Sabinum*, book 27), see Koops 2020, 41n20.
20. Koops 2020, 37, following Morabito 1981, 170–72, notes that there are about seventy of these testamentary orders in the *Digest*.

> Rendering accounts is nothing more than discharging balances; still if through the fault of both *statuliber* and heir, but without bad faith on the slave's part, less is paid than is due, and the accounts are deemed to have been rendered in good faith, the slave will be free. If we held differently, no one conditionally manumitted would ever achieve liberty, if an underpayment were made through oversight. [Julian] says that this should be accepted if, when a slave is directed to render accounts, he renders accounts in error but without deceit in such a way that the master is also in error over the computation.

> Quamvis rationes reddere nihil aliud sit quam reliqua solvere, tamen si et statuliberi et heredis culpa, sine fraude tamen servi minus solutum sit et bona fide redditas esse rationes existimatum fuerit, liberum fore: et nisi ita observetur, neminem, qui sub condicione ita manumissus esset, umquam ad libertatem perventurum, si per imprudentiam minus solutum esset. Haec ita accipienda ait, si quando is, qui rationes reddere iussus sit, per aliquem errorem sine dolo malo ita rationes ediderit, ut dominus quoque circa computationem erraret.[21]

Africanus offers us a definition of rendering accounts (*rationes reddere*): It is the simple matter of returning the money due to the owner or heir.[22] From there, Africanus' reasoning becomes less direct. The intention of the conditionally manumitted slave (as is evident in the language of *sine fraude* and *bona fides*) becomes part of the determination of whether a slave who rendered the accounts incorrectly should be freed. While it is the slave's fault (*culpa*), this fault is one akin to negligence. This is made clear too by the role the heir plays: The heir is also at fault because they did not check the math, so to speak, or simply because the *culpa* of the slave transfers to the heir.

Africanus then explains why, when having accounts rendered correctly would seemingly be the main priority of this endeavor, the honest effort of the slave ought to be considered. First, it appears this version of favoring liberty applies only when the heir has also (either by his own or transferred negligence) failed to correct the mistake. But Africanus also gives us a truth about this system of incentivized work for freedom: There probably were minor errors in rendering accounts from time to time, but if the manumissions promised in these sorts of agreements were not made good on, they would fail to incentivize

21. D.35.1.32 Africanus, *Questions*, book 9.
22. Koops 2020, 38, to understand how potential complications could arise, as he notes, "The Roman jurists consider it near-normal that the accounts of master and slave become entangled."

bona fides rendering of accounts.[23] Africanus bolsters his judgment with an equally ahistorical fragment of his teacher Julian, but with one notable difference: Julian's example is not a testamentary manumission, but one *inter vivos* (while both parties were alive). In the example of Julian, we have a negotiated agreement between an owner and slave where both parties are active participants with something to lose. This is not to suggest they were on equal footing. The slave owner always had the upper hand at the end of the day—they could take whatever they wanted from the slave, financially or physically, and even fail to make good on the promise of manumission. And surely some owners did. But the focus on the intent of the slave—this is a "good slave" in the eyes of the jurists—suggests that the failure to settle up in cases such as this was not the norm.

The price of freedom, then, is the enslaved accountant's apparent honest effort and the owner's acceptance of it over the accurate rendering of accounts. We should view these kinds of testamentary manumissions in the same manner. Africanus' focus on the intention of the slave rather than their accidental error underscores that this slave chose to act in their owner's best interest. The liberation of an honest slave (although one that made a mistake) does two things. First, it honors the agreement between owner and slave, which was the morally right thing to do for a respectable Roman, and second, with these high-level slaves, this can be viewed as more than a generalized idea of controlling the slave population.[24] A very specific skill is wanted from this slave, and they have the ability to choose to render the accounts truthfully and to the best of their ability, thus serving the mutual best interests of their owner and, given their limited options, of themself.

A second scenario of account management considers when the trust of a slave was taken too far. As can be seen in this very detailed case, the more important and trusted the slave and the more lackadaisical the owner, the more harmful the betrayal would be both in terms of finance and *familia*. The jurist Quintus Cervidius Scaevola deliberates on whether a slave, who was meant to be freed via *fideicommissum* ("trust") once they had rendered accounts, still ought to be freed when the slave willfully mismanaged accounts among other

23. Some account keepers of course could choose not to render accounts *bona fides*, see Koops 2020, 39.

24. Dari-Mattiacci 2013 rightly emphasizes this negotiatory aspect of the owner-slave relationship, in particular for these bookkeeping slaves, over a more generalized idea of social control. See also Roth 2010, 91–120, on the carrot-stick relationship between business and manumission and Bradley 1987b, 81–112, on social control.

misdeeds. Fideicommissary manumission is a form of testamentary manumission that directs the heir to formally manumit the slave, often after the slave has fulfilled some condition—here, to render accounts.

> Freedom was given to Stichus thus: "I ask my heirs, and commit it to their good faith, to manumit Stichus after he has rendered accounts." A large sum was due from the chest entrusted to the man after the testator's death; he has not entered in the accounts certain moneys collected from the tenants; he had despoiled the inheritance by secretly opening the storage rooms, removing furniture and clothing, and emptying the stores. Would fideicommissary freedom be due to him only when he had restored the sums he had embezzled and all the things he had stolen? He replied that he should not be given fideicommissary freedom before he had made good the arrears and the losses for which he was responsible.
>
> Sticho libertas data est: "ab heredibus meis peto fideique eorum committo, ut rationibus redditis Stichum manumittant." quaesitum est, cum ampla pecunia ex arca post mortem testatoris sibi commissa reliquetur et quasdam summas a colonis exactis rationibus non intulerit hereditatemque spoliaverit apertis clam horreis sublatisque supellectili et veste et apothecis exhaustis: an non prius ei fideicommissa libertas debeatur, quam ea, quae mala ratione reliquatus est quae furatus est, reposuerit. respondit non prius ei fideicommissam libertatem praestandam, quam et reliqua et omnia, quae per eum abessent, restituisset.[25]

While Scaevola does not indicate explicitly that the slave was a business agent (*actor*), his narrative of events underscores the amount of access certain slaves had into the depths of their owners' finances.[26] The slave's offenses here are not limited to rendering the accounts improperly; he also owed money, was embezzling, and he plundered the inheritance by stealing goods (*spoliare*). *Spoliare* can have reference to the pillaging that takes place after a military campaign and also to piracy.[27] The language puts the owner in the position of the victim, being robbed right out from under him. Notably, as the will is upheld upon

25. D.40.7.40pr Scaevola, *Digest*, book 24. I follow the emendation taken from the Greek as represented in Brunt's translation: *ex arca* "from the chest" rather than *exacta*. The translation may require Brencmannus' emendation of *quae furatus est* to *quaeque furatus est*.
26. On the fact that a former *actor* would not be required to render accounts following manumission D. 40.5.19pr Scaevola, *Digest*, book 24. See Aubert 1994, 193–94.
27. Columella too imbued his slave with militaristic terminology: *imperare*, Columella *Rust.* 1.8.10. Ernout- Meillet s.v. *spolium*. See Sall. *Cat.* 11.6, Quint. *Inst.* 6.1.3.

restitution, the disloyalty of the slave does not outweigh the slave's right to fideicommissary manumission; he still becomes free. The owner's desire to free the slave holds despite the actions of the slave.

The slave has put not only his owner at financial risk but also, by disrupting the inheritance, the heir as well. The fragment of Scaevola highlights the amount of latitude and responsibility a particular slave could have. Following the death of his owner, a single slave was entrusted with a large sum of money in addition to his duties with respect to the accounts. The slave also had access to storage rooms containing valuables, and the autonomy and capability to find methods to remove the stolen goods from his owner's property. The slave's knowledge and ability to store and sell the wares were no doubt those skills that the owner prized when they were in his interest. We saw that Columella attempted to balance his need for a slave foreman (*vilicus*) who could have judgment and a level of authority over other slaves with his belief that the *ingenium servile* is limited and should not be given too much license. Roman jurists attempted to maintain the intent of wills to the best of their ability, but here the force of the will is truly seen. The slave would be freed after he returned the stolen goods and money. The slave had betrayed his owner and the owner had failed to ensure that the slave in whom he had placed so much trust and power was working in his interest. By leaving Stichus in a position to plot and carry out theft and plunder, we see the level of autonomy a slave could have and the difficulties that arise in attempting to control that autonomy. Why manumit this slave at all? Perhaps this is the best negotiating tool the heir has to get the goods or their value restored. There might be a desire to manumit this slave, after restoration, because the heir would have no interest in having such a highly talented and knowledgeable slave whom he could not trust in his household. Or perhaps we might read this more cynically, that the slave could in theory be freed, but he would never be able to make up the money to restore the balance.

Given situations such as this, Columella counsels vigilance and attentiveness. He advises that an owner ought to be an active presence on his farm and that if he must be away from his land, he ought to put free farmers (*liberi coloni*) in charge rather than slave foremen (*vilici servi*) as they are more reliable. The agronomist goes as far as to say that if a landowner does not yield as much from his land as his tenants do, it is on account of the greatest negligence or greed on the part of the slave-hands. In his discussion, Columella highlights the difference between leaving one's land in the charge of free farmers in contrast to slaves: While it is tolerable to leave free farmers in charge of grain-producing land (though not vineyards or orchards), slave foremen will wreck even grain land. He attributes this to slaves' general greed (e.g., renting out oxen needed for labor and skimming off the top), laziness (e.g., ploughing *nec industrie*), and their desire to scheme against their owner. The scheming comes in a number of forms: mismanaging the daily records either by deceit or negligence (*vel fraude vel neglegentia*), theft or not being vigilant guardians against others, computing the accounts of the stored grains incorrectly, and perhaps worst of all, a business agent (*actor*) and slave-hands (*familia*) plotting against the owner.[28]

A final case of fideicommissary manumission shows how independent a slave can be while still working in the service of his owner. Due to the serious illness of his owner, an enslaved business agent (*actor*) had been managing his owner's accounts without the owner signing off on them for many years. The will of the owner stated that the slave was to be free under the provision that he render a full account of his transactions and settle any outstanding debts. Scaevola reasons that the slave should be freed provided he rendered the accounts and gave back faithfully (*ex fide*) all that was owed, even though his owner was unable to sign off on the slave's work.[29] The management of the accounts in this case presents the opportunity for the slave to behave independently and in a competent, trustworthy manner. This is a representation of the ideal good slave, autonomous yet obedient, as the slave has been managing his owner's accounts honestly and proficiently without oversight for a number of years while the owner himself was too sick to work. This case might be seen to represent the ideal of ownership as well; the slave obeys without any supervision from the owner. Here we see a confrontation between the Roman economy's dependence on competent slaves and the reality that those slaves existed and functioned beyond the watchful eye of their owner.

---

28. Columella *Rust.* 1.7.6–7.
29. D. 40.7.40.3 Scaevola, *Digest*, book 24, "A slave was manumitted by will in these terms: 'Let my slave and steward Stichus be free if he has rendered a complete account to my heir of his administration and given satisfaction for it, and I wish him, when he is free, to be given twenty coins and his peculium.' If he is ready to render to the heir accounts of which he was in charge for many years without a signature by the testator [certifying that they were correct,] would he be free under the will, considering that because of ill health the testator was unable to sign the accounts, though he did sign the will? He replied that if the accounts were rendered honestly and any sums due paid in, he would be free" (*Servus testamento ita manumissus est: 'Stichus servus meus actor si rationem omnem actus sui heredi meo reddiderit quoque nomine satisfecerit, liber esto eique, cum liber erit, dari volo viginti et peculium suum'. quaesitum est, an, si rationes, quas egit per multos annos sine subscriptione testatoris, heredi reddere paratus sit, liber ex testamento fiat, cum propter gravem valetudinem testator non potuerit rationibus subscribere, testamento tamen subscripserit. respondit, si ex fide ratio redderetur reliquaque inferantur, liberum fore*).

After the owner has empowered the slave with the instruments to do them great financial and social harm or benefit, it might seem that the owner retains a very tenuous mastery over the slave. The difficulty here is that along with the necessary financial acumen, the attribute of character that is sought—trustworthiness—is both impossible to guarantee and entirely contradictory to the institution of slavery. These cases of conditional manumission offer a solution to this problem of trust between owner and slave, both incentivizing the enslaved account manager and allowing owners to have their slaves take the reins of any number of enterprises.

Fictions of Freedom[30] (Indirect Agency)

Roman private law did not recognize indirect agency, meaning that an agent (X) could not make a formal contract with a third party (Y) that would bind the principal (Z—even if Z wanted X to do this).[31] The acquisition of property or profit was a different matter, however, if the acting agent was a dependent of the *paterfamilias*. In this category were both children in power and slaves over whom the *paterfamilias* had absolute authority. By legal right, whatever profit or property these dependents acquired went to the *paterfamilias*. There were times when it was advantageous or desirable for the *paterfamilias* to allow a son or a slave to manage an amount of property or money as if it were their own. This allowance was called a *peculium* and was composed of money or property (including pretty much any moveable good such as clothes, livestock, or other slaves, but also immovables such as land). Legally, a slave could not own property and the *peculium* remained the owner's property but was under the slave's control.[32] The *peculium*, which existed already at the time of Plautus, allowed for some autonomy for the slave as it was a discrete account or set of property

30. After Nicholas 2008, 202n1, discussing slave contracts, "Since a slave could not in any event incur civil rights and duties a fiction of freedom was also necessary."

31. See G. 2.95, D. 45.1.126.2 Paul, *Questions*, book 3, on the Roman inability to take possession or ownership through another free person. For exceptions, see Aubert 1994, 42. On the lack of indirect agency, see Abatino and Dari-Mattiacci 2020; Abatino, Dari-Mattiacci, and Perotti 2011; Johnston 1999, 99–101; Aubert 1994, 40–41; Gordon 1983, 341–49.

32. That a slave owner allowed or did not prohibit a slave from making some profit for himself does not mean the *peculium* was the property of the slave as Cohen has recently argued, see Cohen 2023, esp. 49–82. On the autonomy the slave had in the management of the *peculium*, see G. 2.86–7; D.41.1.10pr–1 Gaius, *Institutes*, book 2; and D.41.2.49.1 Papinian, *Definitions*, book 2; see also Aubert 1994, 66–67.

apart from the rest of the owner's.[33] While the *peculium* served many purposes, one important possibility it facilitated was the slave as manager for a particular business of the owner. The slave could run a business without much consultation or involvement of the owner in day-to-day affairs. But slaves, under the power of their owners and acting as channels to them for profit and problems, could not go, or be brought to court; it would thus be risky for another party to enter into a contract with someone who had no legal personality in private suits.

The advent of certain legal remedies provided protections against this risk. In order to implement these remedies certain sleights of hand like name-swapping and fictions of freedom were needed in order not to violate the Roman law of obligations (i.e., contract law, among other things), which found its force in binding the two contracting people together (usually two *patres*).[34] To create remedies in which the owner of a slave would be bound for a contract made by the slave, the praetor changed out the name of the slave for the owner in the *formula* for the legal remedy. Barry Nicholas renders the *formula* as such: "if B, who is the slave of C, were a free man, then if he would owe A, condemn C to pay A."[35] Instead of having the slave (B) pay the third party (A), the owner (C) must now pay. And because B is a slave, and thus without the ability to incur civil liability in this kind of contract, a legal fiction must also be deployed: if B were a free person.[36] While all know they are not a free person, they will be treated as one for the purpose of this case. A slave in this position would surely see the dizzying nature of their situation: free in a *formula*, for this transaction to be valid—free on paper, so to speak. Slaves did have what is called natural liability, a kind of latent liability that only rose to the surface if they were freed. These Praetorian remedies did not take the liability of the slave and place it on

33. On the Plautine reference, see Stewart 2012, 60, 78. There is some discussion on the *peculium* being referenced in the Twelve Tables, see Kirschenbaum 1987, 33n11. On the origins of the *peculium* more generally, see Kirschenbaum 1987, 33–35; Diósdi 1970, 19–30.

Ulpian gives us (quoting Celsus citing Tubero), the oldest juristic reference to the *peculium*, D. 15.1.5.4 Ulpian, *Edict*, book 29, "Tubero, however, defines *peculium* to be (as Celsus states in the sixth book of his *Digest*) what the slave has separate and apart from his master's accounts with the permission of the latter, after deducting therefrom anything which may be due to his master" (*Peculium autem Tubero quidem sic definit, ut Celsus libro sexto digestorum refert, quod servus domini permissu separatum a rationibus dominicis habet, deducto inde si quid domino debetur*).

34. On the fictions of freedom and name-swapping, see Nicholas 2008, 199–202. On the law of obligations, see D. 15.1.41 Ulpian, *Sabinus*, book 43 and D. 15.1.44 Ulpian, *Edict*, book 63 as well as Johnston 1999, 99–105 and Aubert 1994, 70–84.

35. Nicholas 2008, 202n1.

36. On legal fictions, see Ando 2015.

the owner (the slave's liability remained, but was dormant while they were enslaved), but rather created an additional liability for the owner.[37]

Different scenarios led to different actions. For example, if an enslaved agent was following the orders of their owner in making a contract, a third party could be fully compensated; the liability of the owner was unlimited (*actio quod iussu*—action on the order).[38] But, if the enslaved agent acted with their *peculium* and without express instruction from their owner, the owner would only be liable up to the amount of that slave's *peculium* (*actio de peculio*—action on the *peculium*).[39] The difference between these two actions then was whether the principal (the owner) had knowledge of and consented to what the slave was doing with their *peculium*; this made the owner more liable.[40] If a competent and trustworthy slave could be found, the owner was protected from more financial risk if they were ignorant of their slave's actions; the remedies were set up in such a way that encouraged the owner's hands-off approach.[41] Roman ownership is conceived of in such a manner that anything the slave acquires belongs to the owner, but here the owner's liability for an enterprise is limited depending on their own knowledge of the slave's actions. The owner is incentivized and able to be ignorant of their slave's plans and transactions. In commercial relations, economic liability concerns outweigh the desire for an owner to have complete access to and control over their slaves' minds.

As noted, the *peculium* of a slave could have other slaves in it (*servi vicarii*). When discussing another of these Praetorian remedies, Ulpian gives a presen-

---

37. For this reason, these remedies come to be called the *actiones adiecticiae qualitatis*, emphasizing the "added-on nature" of the liability. These were the *actio exercitoria, actio institoria, actio de peculio, actio de in rem verso* and *actio quod iussu* (the *actio tributoria* was not strictly speaking part of the *actiones adiecticiae qualitiatis*). Aubert 1994, 70–84, on the history of the development of *actiones adiecticiae qualitatis* and the *actio tributoria*, on the scholarly debates about these *actiones*, and on the remedies on the *peculium* more generally, see 40–117. Watson 1965, 185, suggests that the *actiones* must have developed in the mid-Republican period, but there is not a firm date before the mid-first century BCE. Lenel (1927) suggests the order in the perpetual edict as *actio exercitoria, actio institoria, actio tributioria, actio de peculio, actio de in rem verso*, and *actio quod iussu*; see also Kirschenbaum 1987, 47–72 and Valiño 1967, 339–36.
38. On the *actio quod iussu*, see Aubert 1994, 50–52. A slave does not need to have a *peculium* for the *actio quod iussu*.
39. On the *actio de peculio*, see Aubert 1994, 65–70.
40. Johnston 1999, 103–5. Aubert 1994, 50, "The principal's interests required that this type of remedy be available only when it was well established that he had commissioned (implying *voluntas* expressed through *iussum* or *praepositio*), or given his consent (implying *patientia* and *scientia*) to, the agent's activity."
41. Kirschenbaum 1987, 31, 31n2. It has also been suggested that for elite, well-off Romans, the idea of engaging in the day-to-day of business appeared unseemly and this "laissez-faire" approach appealed to them.

tation of the different levels of management and responsibility. These different levels allow for a nesting of knowledge that can limit the owner's liability. The *actio exercitoria*, the action against the shipowner, compelled the principal (the shipowner or *exercitor*) to pay a third party because of the actions of the ship's captain (a slave in this case):

> If a ship is managed by a slave with the consent of a son-in-power (or by an underslave with the consent of the slave) to whose *peculium* he belongs, the son will be liable in full, but the father or owner, unless he consented, will be liable only up to the amount of the *peculium*. Of course, if the father or owner did consent to the ship's being so managed, he will be liable in full, as will the son if he also consented.
>
> Si tamen servus peculiaris volente filio familias in cuius peculio erat, vel servo vicarius eius navem exercuit, pater dominusve, qui voluntatem non accommodavit, dumtaxat de peculio tenebitur, sed filius ipse in solidum. Plane si voluntate domini vel patris exerceant, in solidum tenebuntur et praeterea et filius, si et ipse voluntatem accommodavit, in solidum erit obligatus.[42]

In this text of Ulpian, sons and slaves are interchangeable as they are indistinguishable generally in Roman commercial law: The masterly liability for slave transactions is the same as the fatherly liability for the transactions of sons because both are members of the *familia*. The pairing of sons and slaves here, and in much of Roman private law, conflates their positions and can be sugges-

42. D. 14.1.1.22 Ulpian, *Edict*, book 23. On this passage, see Di Porto 1984, 304, where he notes that this was "the fundamental organizational structure for limited responsibility in a collective enterprise." Abatino and Dari-Mattiacci 2020 argue on the other hand that these set-ups were more extensions of a family business model rather than large-scale businesses. On agents more generally, see also Abatino and Dari-Mattiacci 2020; Abatino, Dari-Mattiacci, and Perotti 2011; Aubert 1994; Wacke 1994; Kirschenbaum 1987; Di Porto 1984.

D.14.4.3pr Ulpian, *Edict*, book 29, "If a slave has two owners and both of them know that he is trading, the action lies against each of them. If one of them knows and the other does not, the action lies against the one who knows, subject to a deduction of all that is owed to the master without knowledge. If suit is brought against the ignorant master, it must be by way of action on the *peculium*; so a full deducation must be made of anything owed to the master with knowledge, just as it would be if he himself had been sued on the *peculium*. This is in line with what Julian says in the twelfth book of his *Digest*" (*Sed si servus communis sit et ambo sciant domini, in utrumlibet ex illis dabitur actio: at si alter scit, alter ignoravit, in eum qui scit dabitur actio, deducetur tamen solidum quod ei qui ignoravit debetur. Quod si ipsum quis ignorantem convenerit, quoniam de peculio convenitur, deducetur etiam id quod scienti debetur et quidem in solidum: nam et si ipse de peculio conventus esset, solidum quod ei deberetur deduceretur, et ita Iulianus libro duodecimo digestorum scripsit*). See also D. 14.1.4.2 Ulpian, *Edict*, book 29 and D. 14.1.6.1 Paul, *Short Notes*, book 6.

tive of the kinds of social and familial expectations a slave owner would place on a slave even though they do not have legally recognized kinship ties with their owner. A *servus peculiaris* (a slave that is part of a *peculium* of either a slave or a son-in-power) or *servus vicarius* (again a slave in a *peculium*, but this refers specifically to a slave of a slave) runs this ship. The slave in charge of the *peculium* is called a *servus ordinarius*. If the slave in the *peculium* is following orders, he is following the will (*voluntas*) of the slave in charge. If this is so, then the owner will be liable to the extent of the slave in charge's *peculium*. However, if the slave in the *peculium* was following an order from the owner, then the owner will be liable to the full extent of damages (even if that exceeds the *peculium* of the *servus ordinarius*).

Two developments in this passage have bearing upon our question of ownership and the mind of the slave. The first is the knowledge the owner has of this slave's actions (as *voluntas* here implies knowledge). The relative ignorance or knowledge of the owner is built into these remedies. Second, not only is the *voluntas* of the *servus ordinarius* legally taken into account, but the *voluntas* is one that the owner would generally find in accordance with their own, even if they did not know precisely what it was. While these Praetorian remedies were in place for when problems arose, this business model must have been largely successful, otherwise it would not have been tenable. An owner must have confidence in their reading of a slave's character and ability, specifically whether a slave will use their independence in a way that will benefit their owner. This enslaved ship captain in the *peculium* of another slave had both the means and transport to escape if he chose to do so.

A slave owner could use various tactics to attempt to ensure loyalty and efficiency on the part of an enslaved agent. Legally speaking, an owner always retained rights to any profit the slave made and could take back the *peculium* (*ademptio peculii*); however, the loss of the *peculium* would certainly not foster any kindly feelings or determination on the slave's part to perform their duties for their owner well.[43] As we have seen from the cases of conditional manumission above, one avenue to ensure an enslaved person's compliance came from the potential for manumission (even if never realized).[44] Other incentives were

43. Kirschenbaum 1987, 36–37. Kirschenbaum 1987, 34–35, notes that some farm slaves were allowed some land and animals to make their own profit.

44. If the slave was an *institor* his manumission would not increase the liability of the owner, see especially D. 14.3.19.1 Papinian, *Replies*, book 3; similar scenarios: D. 26.7.37.1 Papinian, *Questions*, book 11; D. 26.7.58pr Scaevola, *Digest*, book 11.

Aubert 1994, 77, speculates that the *actio institoria* comes from the second-century BCE prae-

the possibility to make some money for themselves, or possible family ties with other members of the enslaved household or the owner.[45]

These slaves in financial and managerial positions clearly did not make up the vast majority of the slaves in the Roman Empire; however, considering this structuralized gradation of knowledge and responsibility, an owner of a business (or many businesses) would find themself in need of several slaves with a particular mental acuity, good business sense, and trustworthiness. The grades of knowledge and administration between an owner and their slave can be seen in the following passage of Ulpian, which discusses the action for distribution (*actio tributoria*) and action on the *peculium* (*de peculio*). The *actio tributoria* existed for situations in which the *peculium* of a slave became insolvent with the owner's knowledge. Whatever was left in the *peculium* was meant to be distributed among the slave owner and the creditors.[46]

> I am liable to an action for distribution if I know that an underslave of my slave is engaged in trade. If I do not know, but my slave in charge of the *peculium* (*ordinarius*) does, I am liable to an action on the *peculium* of the underslave, as Pomponius says in his sixtieth book; I may deduct from the *peculium* of the underslave what is owed to me, but not what is owed to my *ordinarius*. If we both knew, he says, I shall be liable not only to an action for distribution but also to an action on the *peculium*, the former in respect to the underslave, the latter in respect to the *peculium* of the *ordinarius*, and the plaintiff will have to choose which of these actions to bring. Either way there will be a distribution of what is owed to me and what is owed to my *ordinarius*, when, if my *ordinarius* had been unaware of the actions of his underslave, whatever was owed to him by the underslave would be entirely deducted.

> Si vicarius servi mei negotietur, si quidem me sciente, tributoria tenebor, si me ignorante, ordinario sciente, de peculio eius actionem dandam Pomponius libro sexagensimo scripsit, nec deducendum ex vicarii peculio, quod ordinario debetur, cum id quod mihi debetur deducatur. Sed si uterque scierimus, et trib-

---

tor and jurist M. Junius Brutus, who owned several agricultural estates and a bathhouse; one of the few mentions of his legal opinions (Cic. *Fin.* 1.12) regards estate management. See Aubert 1994, 52–58, on the *actio institoria* more generally.

45. Kirschenbaum 1987, 34, on how slaves made extra money including tips, gifts, and hiring himself out when he was not working for his owner. On slaves purchasing their freedom, see D. 33.8.8.5 Ulpian, *Sabinus*, book 25.

46. See Aubert 1994, 68–69.

> utoriam et de peculio actionem competere ait, tributoriam vicarii nomine, de peculio vero ordinarii: eligere tamen debere agentem, qua potius actione experiatur, sic tamen, ut utrumque tribuatur et quod mihi et quod servo debetur, cum, si servus ordinarius ignorasset, deduceretur integrum, quod ei a vicario debetur.[47]

There are three levels here: the owner, the *servus ordinarius*, and the *servus vicarius*, who also has a *peculium* (which might contain even more slaves). It is not simply that the owner should not know the day-to-day affairs of the business, but generally if the owner knew that an underslave was "conducting business" (*negotia*), they would have more responsibility for the debts. If a middleman (the *servus ordinarius*) is introduced into the equation, then the owner is more protected because they are one grade removed from the business of the underslave. The second part of the passage indicates that the *servus ordinarius* could also not be aware of the specifics of the business that his underslave had conducted, which would further lower the liability ceiling for the owner. Sound business sense would indicate that anyone who could afford to run their businesses in this fashion would be inclined to and, in this vein, an owner would need several high-level competent slaves that they felt could make financial decisions without consulting them.

This section began with two small adjustments to a legal formula. A legal fiction dictated that for the purpose of the contract the slave was to be treated as a free person and the name of the slave was switched with the owner's in order for the owner to have liability. These adjustments went a long way: They opened up a world of economic potential by allowing Roman commerce to become more layered and sophisticated. This was a major benefit for slave owners and allowed the owners to capitalize on the reality of their situation. There is a necessary relationship between ownership (as the point of the *peculium* is for the owner themself to make a profit) and the internal freedom that these high-level slaves needed to manage their owners' affairs successfully. We see that commercial law is set up in such a manner that the mental autonomy and agency of the slave is exploited for the benefit of the owner. And while Columella fixates on the limitations of the *ingenium servile*, here the juristic litera-

---

47. D.14.4.5.1 Ulpian, *Edict*, book 29. There is a dittographic error in the translation of the final sentence of this passage in the 1985 Watson edition. See Di Porto 1984, 306, where he notes that this passage stresses the importance of the *ignorantia*, *scientia*, and *voluntas* of not only the *dominus* but also the *servus ordinarius*. See also Abatino and Dari-Mattiacci 2020 on this passage.

ture that stems from this fiction of freedom might be seen as representational of the ideas of mental autonomy in the philosophy of Epictetus, who holds that all are free in mind, or Seneca's idea that the ownership of the mind is not equal to knowledge of it.[48]

The question about the ownership of the mind of a slave comes up indirectly; we find it in discussions of commercial law such as when slaves serve as account managers and business agents for their owners. In this economic sphere of high-level slaves, the jurists consider the respective levels of knowledge the owner and their slave had in a specific business enterprise in order to determine the liability of the owner if anything went awry. While the philosophers and jurists consider the mental autonomy of free people and slaves for very different reasons and audiences, they are reflecting on a similar idea. The claim here is not that contemporary and later jurists were actively in conversation with those of the philosophical class (though there is no reason to suspect they were not), but that there was a similar awareness and concern over the mental autonomy of slaves in these different circumstances and among these different groups of people.

48. See discussion of Epict. *Diss.* 1.1 and Sen. *Ep.* 27 in the introduction.

FOUR
Corrupting Slaves

He will say he was pleased with the slave at first and for that reason put him in charge of accounts. But afterwards the slave turned to vice both on account of his own license and the negligence of his owner who trusted him excessively; he had been corrupted [into taking bribes] by many before this.

Initio autem dicet hunc sibi placuisse servum, et ideo supra rationes esse positum; sed postea et licentia sua et securitate domini, qui illi plurimum crediderit, isse in vitia, a multis corruptum antequam ab hoc.

—[Quint.] *Decl.* 353.3

The previous chapter discussed how a slave's mental autonomy operated as an instrument to benefit the owner financially. In that situation, the mental autonomy of slaves functioned as Roman owners wanted it to—in their service. This chapter explores when the mental autonomy of the slave is not in the service of the owner either through outside influence (*actio servi corrupti*) or the slave's own initiative (noxal liability) and consequently reflects on who is at fault: the slave, the outsider, or the owner who failed to control their slave. The questions that arise from this betrayal are ones of trust: Was the owner's trust unwarranted? How does an owner decide to trust a slave? Should an owner ever trust a slave? These questions allow us to consider a particular weakness of ownership. While ownership was relatively well protected, legally speaking, this chapter examines certain factual insecurities of ownership;[1] namely, that an owner is unsure whether their slave will behave as they were asked. While agricultural

1. On factual vs. legal insecurities, see the introduction.

slaves who spent most of their time doing physical labor away from their owners could cause trouble, the owner had the ability to physically punish or restrain the slave. High-level slaves, on the other hand, expose the fragile nature of this kind of ownership because these slaves were placed in a position of trust and had access to the world outside their owner's house.

Generally, if a slave misbehaves, it falls on their owner to punish, sell, or, if need be, surrender them. The action for making a slave worse (*actio servi corrupti*) goes further; it provides a remedy if it was believed that this bad behavior was the result of a third-party actor. The jurists discussing this remedy consider what constitutes a decrease in the value of the slave and give the owner of a degraded slave the right to sue the person responsible. These considerations illustrate the qualities of a slave about which Roman owners were most concerned. This chapter examines the variety of ways how the mind of the slave may be corrupted by another person and the ramifications of this corruption.

Persuasion and the **Actio Servi Corrupti**

The juristic literature about the *actio servi corrupti* stems from the Praetor's Edict, which the jurist Ulpian quotes: "The praetor says: 'If a man is alleged to have harbored another man's male or female slave or to have fraudulently persuaded him or her to do anything in order to make him or her worse, I shall give an action against him for double the sum therein involved'" (*Ait praetor: 'Qui servum servam alienum alienam recepisse persuasisseve quid ei dicetur dolo malo, quo eum eam deteriorem faceret, in eum quanti ea res erit in duplum iudicium dabo'*).[2] The action is not concerned with the deed the deceitfully swayed slave performed, but with the fact that the deed makes the slave himself (or herself) worse (*deteriorem facere*). The worsening of the first part of the edict is

2. D.11.3.1.pr Ulpian, *Edict*, book 23. Longo 1966 argues that the only true part of the Edict is the *persuadere* part, and argues that the harboring slaves part was added later.

Scholars have studied the *actio servi corrupti* together with other actions (Bonfiglio 1998; Longo 1966; Albanese 1959) including the *actio iniuriarum* (the Praetorian action against outrage, D. 47.10), the *actio doli* (the Praetorian action against fraud, D. 4.3), and the *actio furti* (on theft, D. 47.2; 13.1) or in order to form a better understanding of delicts (Reduzzi Merola 2011). Barbara Bonfiglio (1998) also focused her attention on the language used in the *actio servi corrupti*. There are seventeen passages from five jurists on this clause of the Edict. Our earliest commentary of the clause, probably created at the end of the Roman Republic, is by Alfenus Varus. The other sixteen passages are from four jurists; passages from the works of Ulpian and Paul predominate.

tied to the physical: the removal of another's slave from their possession; the second part lies in the mental realm—did this person willfully persuade a slave to bad behavior? The attention of the jurists discussing the *actio servi corrupti* focuses more on the question of fraudulent persuasion, as it requires an examination of the motivation behind the third party's actions and generally has a broader scope and implication than the question of harboring.

From the earliest times in Roman legal history, legislation protected the property rights of owners. The *lex Aquilia*, a plebiscite likely from the early third century BCE that replaced legislation from the Twelve Tables, continued to remedy wrongful loss of property (*damnum iniuria datum*) during the Empire.[3] In its two relevant chapters, the *lex Aquilia* states that a person would be liable for the highest value of the property in the past year if they (1) slayed (*occidere*) another's slave or four-footed livestock, or (2) burnt, rent, or spoiled (*urere, frangere, rumpere*) the property of another.[4] As the *lex Aquilia* specifically discusses slaves and much of the juristic commentary on it pertains to slaves, it is worth considering why there was additional need for the *actio servi corrupti*, which was likely introduced by the praetor in the Late Republic. The distinction lies in that the cases of the *lex Aquilia* largely pertain to physical harm, whereas the *actio servi corrupti* is generally concerned with character. The enslaved victim's character only comes into consideration in Aquilian liability with regard to issues such as contributory negligence: for example, in the infamous case of the barber shaving a slave near some people playing ball, Ulpian argues against another jurist that when the ball inevitably hits the hand of the barber, who then slices the throat of the slave, it would also be sensible to blame the slave who chose a barber so careless as to set up shop around a ball game.[5] But it is not until the *actio servi corrupti* that character is the location of damage to the slave.[6]

As we will see in their discussions of the corruption of slaves, the jurists come to an exploration of the will and morality of the slave, typically encapsu-

---

3. A plebiscite is a law passed by the assembly of the plebeians. For the *lex Aquilia*, which has a vast literature, see for an introduction Sirks 2015, Cursi 2016 with recent bibliography, and in more detail Zimmermann 1996, 953–1049. On the date, see Zimmermann 1996, 953–61.
4. D. 9.2.2 Gaius, *Provincial Edict*, book 7; D. 9.2.27.5 Ulpian, *Edict*, book 18.
5. D. 9.2.11 Ulpian, *Edict*, book 18. See also D. 9.2.23.4 Ulpian, *Edict*, book 18, on the increased value of a killed trickster slave because he had yet to name his accomplices before he was slain. It is the owner's interest in catching out his co-conspirators that raises his value and not the value of the damage he has done. This is considered reasonable as any damage he has done to his owner's accounts would be an internal financial issue between owner and slave.
6. The *actio servi corrupti* at times was brought concurrently with other actions, in particular we see this for questions of *stuprum* (defilement), where for example an action for theft (D. 47.1.2.5) Ulpian, *Sabinus*, book 43), *iniuria* (outrage D. 7.1.66 Paul, *Edict*, book 47; D. 48.5.6 Papinian, *Adulterers*, book 1), and the *lex Aquilia* (D. 48.5.6 Papinian, *Adulterers*, book 1) could also be brought.

lated by the word *animus*. The juristic literature questions what makes a slave worse and in doing so considers what physical, intellectual, or moral characteristics give a slave their value. The jurist Paul writes that the action revolves around the "estimation of utility" (*aestimatio utilitatis*) from before the slave was damaged or worsened.[7] And while the *aestimatio* of a slave is irrevocably tied to price, it is also necessarily tied to a more basic or intrinsic value, the utility and goodness of an individual slave.[8] The legal language of the sources revolves around the verb *corrumpere*, to break, damage, or corrupt;[9] the corruption could pertain to either the mind (*animus*) or body (*corpus*).[10] In the language of the edict, the liable person has persuaded the slave, or changed their mind, and so the slave makes themself worse. And while this could be physical—a free person could persuade a slave to jump off a roof or to run away[11]—the majority of the casuistic examples that the jurists explore fall in the mental realm; their preoccupation is with the mind and character of the slave.

The jurists who interpret this law frame their discussion around the meaning of persuasion, which Ulpian defines as "more than to be compelled and to be forced to obey" (*plus quam compelli atque cogi sibi parere*). Ulpian adds that "persuasion is a neutral concept" (*sed persuadere τῶν μέσων ἐστίν*) as one can persuade (here the simplex *suadere*) someone by giving good advice as well as bad.[12] The issue is not persuasion itself, but being persuaded into doing some-

7. D. 11.3.6 Paul, *Edict*, book 19, "for this action is concerned with the assessment of the value of the slave in the past" (*praeteritae enim utilitatis aestimatio in hoc iudicum versatur*). On *aestimatio* in this passage, see Bonfiglio 1998, 121–46.
8. See du Plessis 2013 generally and du Plessis 2010, 57–59, for a discussion on the value (*pretium*) of slaves.
9. See Ernout-Meillet on *corrumpo*, s.v. *rumpo* on the moral meaning to worsen, spoil, or corrupt.
10. D. 11.3.9.3 Ulpian, *Edict*, book 23, "But there is a question, whether the evaluation of the slave ought to be made to this extent: what damage the slave is subjected to either in body or in mind, that is, only by how much the slave is made lesser, or rather including other things as well" (*Sed quaestionis est, aestimatio utrum eius dumtaxat fieri debeat, quod servus in corpore vel in animo damni senserit, hoc est quanto vilior servus factus sit, an vero et ceterorum*). *Vilior*: the term has a moral component ("dirt cheap"); the *servus* is made cheaper, less worthy. It is not his price that has gone down, but his own worth. See Ernout-Meillet s.v. *vilis*.
11. On legal remedies for this sort of thing, see D. 11.3.1.4 Ulpian, *Edict*, book 23; D. 47.2.36 Ulpian, *Sabinus*, book 41, but Bonfiglio 1998, 176, following the *Index Interpolationum*, considers the passage as a whole potentially interpolated; however, she notes it is not clear whether the jurists Ulpian is citing are interpolated.
12. D. 11.3.1.3 Ulpian, *Edict*, book 23, "*Persuadere autem est plus quam compelli atque cogi sibi parere. Sed persuadere τῶν μέσων ἐστίν, nam et bonum consilium quis dando potest suadere et malum.*" The idea of persuasion as a form of corruption is seen also in D. 11.3.1.5 Ulpian, *Edict*, book 23 (discussed below); D. 47.2.36 Ulpian, *Sabinus*, book 41 (see previous note); D. 47.10.26 Paul, *Edict*, book 19, where the person who persuades a slave is doing so with malicious intent toward the owner (discussed below). See also C. 6.2.4 and 9.20.2.

thing negative and self-destructive. 'To persuade' here takes on a very forceful meaning; both *compelli* (to be compelled) and *cogi* (to be forced) are words suggestive of violence.[13] However, the *actio servi corrupti* is not concerned solely with a physical act, but anyone "who incited a slave to do or to contemplate something wrong" (*qui igitur servum sollicitat ad aliquid vel faciendum vel cogitandum improbe*).[14] Here again the verb used to describe the act of persuasion is a very active one, *sollicitare* (to incite). Barbara Bonfiglio suggests that *sollicitare* is used not to avoid repetition, but with a particular purpose, that is "to indicate an activity stemming from psychological pressure."[15] As these were generally skilled or high-level slaves, they would have been expected to make use of some sense of intelligence or decision-making capacity. Nevertheless, there is a concern about the susceptibility of the slave's character to persuasion. The passage explicitly removes the action from the slave—both the legal action and the act of making up one's mind are in another person's hands—even if that is not the specific intention of the edict.

The main focus of this juristic literature is thus not on the action of the slave—the *actio servi corrupti* speaks only indirectly about the actions of the slave—but on the actions of the third party: what they did to make the slave worse. Persuasion and compulsion should be things only an owner can impose on their slave. The acknowledgment of a slave's ability to be compelled and to act in a way different than ordered suggests a threat to ownership as it infringes on a basic aspect of it: the right to make use of the slave. In the edict, the parameters of *persuadere* are defined as whatever makes a slave worse; this underscores the idea that a slave can be considered worse if they have been moved to not only do but to contemplate something untoward (*cogito improbe*). Ulpian reasons that a slave is damaged if their thought or state of mind has been altered. The *actio servi corrupti* implicitly denies the slave the decision to remain loyal or to betray their owner.

The language of persuasion and influence also illustrates one way in which

---

13. *Compelli*: Ernout-Meillet s.v. *pello*. *Pello* has a very physical meaning, to push, urge, beat, with the military meaning of to rout. *Compello* has the sense, in particular in classical prose, of to address with a sense of blame, accost, and is used to accuse people of crimes in a judicial sphere. *Cogi*: see Ernout-Meillet s.v. *ago*.
14. D. 11.3.1.3 Ulpian, *Edict*, book 23, "Therefore, the praetor adds: 'fraudulently, in order to make him worse.' For no offense is committed unless the slave is persuaded to do the sort of thing which will make him worse. So it appears that this edict condemns anyone who incited a slave to do or to contemplate something wrong" (*et ideo praetor adiecit 'dolo malo, quo eum deteriorem faceret': neque enim delinquit, nisi qui tale aliquid servo persuadet, ex quo eum faciat deteriorem. qui igitur servum sollicitat ad aliquid vel faciendum vel cogitandum improbe, hic videtur hoc edicto notari*).
15. Bonfiglio 1998, 26–27. See Ernout-Meillet s.v. *cieo*.

slaves were measured as good or bad—their resistance or susceptibility to others:

> But is the person liable only if he has driven an honest slave to wrongdoing, or is he also liable if he has given a bad slave encouragement or shown him how he could commit an offense? The better view is that he is also liable if he has shown a bad slave how he could commit an offense. Indeed, even if the slave would have run away or committed the theft anyway, if the person gave his approval to the slave's intention, he is liable; for wickedness ought not to be increased by the approval of others. So whether one makes a good slave bad or a bad slave more so, one is held to have made him worse.
>
> Sed utrum ita demum tenetur, si bonae frugi servum perpulit ad delinquendum, an vero et si malum hortatus est vel malo monstravit, quemadmodum faceret? et est verius etiam si malo monstravit, in quem modum delinqueret, teneri eum. immo et si erat servus omnimodo fugiturus vel furtum facturus, hic vero laudator huius propositi extitit, tenetur: non enim oportet laudando augeri malitiam. sive ergo bonum servum fecerit malum sive malum fecerit deteriorem, corrupisse videbitur.[16]

There are three kinds of action in this passage of the jurist Ulpian: to urge a good slave to delinquency, to encourage a bad slave, or to show an already bad slave how to do a bad act. The corrupter pushes (*perpellere*), exhorts (*hortari*), and demonstrates or teaches (*monstrare*) bad behavior. The jurist creates a distinction between an honest slave (*bonae frugi servus*) and a bad slave (*malus servus*) and uses the most violent language on the good slave (*perpellere*: to push violently, to enforce).[17] Presumably a slave deemed honest would need more incentive or compulsion to turn to delinquency. The good slave is not the only concern of the jurists; Ulpian reasons that a corrupter who teaches a bad slave new ways to do wrong is liable. The exposure to new ideas (*monstrare*) is dangerous because it again highlights a change in mindset and an act (showing, teaching) that should be in the purview of the owner alone, or at the very least under their orders. It also brings us to the Roman idea that knowledge can be dangerous to minds that are not meant to be developed.[18]

The phrasing of the jurist puts the would-be corrupter in the role of judg-

16. D. 11.3.1.4 Ulpian, *Edict*, book 23.
17. Bonfiglio 1998, 59–60, on the meaning of *perpellere* here. See, for example, Tac. *Ann.* 6.33.
18. See below, Columella *Rust.* 1.8.6–7 refers to the *rudes animi* of slaves.

ment. They are meant to see the bad actions of the slave and, as a good Roman, put a stop to them, but instead they first encourage (*hortari*) and then become a praiser (*laudator*) of the slave's intended act. If this passage is genuine, *laudator* is a strong word for the morality of the act that is working against the corrupting free person, described as praising a person of lower status.[19] The edict and the juristic literature concerning it are meant to protect one free person's property from the malicious meddling of another. However, the language of persuasion used is one of psychological tampering and at times verges on the militaristic. It is not a sly suggestion that Ulpian considers, but words of mental pressure and stress that drive a change in a slave's character. The emphasis of the language of persuasion as forced takes the decision to betray the owner out of the slave's hands. It takes the reasoning faculties away from the slave; the *actio servi corrupti* sets up a seeming theft of the intellect and ethics of the slave from the owner, and from the slave themself.

Rudes Animi *and the Control of Knowledge*

This section discusses different situations in which we see the potential deterioration or corruption of slaves. The concern with third parties influencing slaves is not limited to the jurists. Columella provides a list of provisions for owners to use in order to protect their slaves from any harmful outside agents. His ideas about the susceptibility of slaves to persuasion at the hands of a third party prefigure the concerns about the persuasion of slaves found in the juristic discussion of the *actio servi corrupti*. Columella himself advocates the manipulation of one's own slaves into working more diligently.[20] Here, it is the *animus* of the slave that Columella is particularly focused on.

> The foreman should not grant audience to diviners and witches, since both sorts of people compel undeveloped minds with their empty superstition to waste money and then to shameful acts. Nor should the foreman know the city or any market, except for the purpose of making purchases or sales specifically

19. There is a relative consensus, however, that this sentence (*immo . . . malitiam*) is interpolated both because of the sudden mention of *fugere* and *furtum facere* and because the moralizing seems better fitted to the sentiment of the Justinianic period; see Bonfiglio 1998, 58–60; Longo 1966, 151; Longo 1961, 202; Albanese 1959, 19n25.

20. For Columella, the question of responsibility and trust is answered by observation and attempts to manipulate the slave's *ingenium*, see *Rust.* 1.8.15–16, discussed in chapter 1.

pertaining to his own affairs. For, as Cato says, the foreman ought not to be a dawdler. Nor should he leave the limits of the farm, unless it is to learn something new about cultivation, and then only if it is in the neighborhood so that he can return. He should not allow footpaths and new passages to be made in the land. Nor should he receive a guest except a close friend or family member of the owner.

> Haruspices sagasque, quae utraque genera vana superstitione rudis animos ad inpensas ac deinceps ad flagitia compellunt, ne admiserit, neque urbem neque ullas nundinas noverit, nisi emendae vendundaeve pertinentis ad se rei causa. Vilicus enim, quod ait Cato, ambulator esse non debet nec egredi terminos, nisi ut addiscat aliquam culturam, et hoc si ita in vicino est ut remeare possit. Semitas novosque limites in agro fieri ne patiatur, neve hospitem, nisi amicum familiaremque domini necessarium receperit.[21]

The minds of Columella's slaves are *rudes animi*, undeveloped minds, and the remainder of the passage pertains to controlling information and access to those minds. Columella shares the language of Ulpian; diviners and witches compel (*compellere*) the minds of slaves.[22] A diviner or other trickster might swindle money from his slave, but Columella is more preoccupied with any shameful behavior (*flagitia*) the slave might perform as a result of their encounter. The shade of the bacchant or epileptic slave perhaps colors Columella's concern about soothsayers and witches.[23] Columella's rural belief that urban life was corrupting is seen in his desire to keep his foreman at home. His dilemma, to protect the slave by keeping him indoors or to make use of him but risk his becoming corrupt, highlights why discussion regarding the mind of the slave was so prevalent in Rome. Elsewhere he counsels having an illiterate slave as an account manager so any harm he could do would be minimal.[24] His concern for potential betrayal overshadows his desire for an effective accountant.

The agronomist must balance, on the one hand, the need for his slave to conduct his business—bringing him into contact with the marketplace and many other people—with, on the other, the conception that slaves did not have

---

21. Columella *Rust.* 1.8.6–7.
22. See above *compelli* D. 11.3.1.3 Ulpian, *Edict*, book 23.
23. On the bacchant slave and epileptic slave, see chapters 1 and 2, respectively. See Padilla Peralta 2017 on this passage and slave religiosity.
24. Columella *Rust.* 1.8.4.

the strength of mind to see through or withstand trickery or corrupting influences. As a result, Columella uses the language of resisting influence: The slave must not know (*noscere*) the city or the marketplace, except regarding the owner's business, and he must not acquire any new knowledge (*addiscere*) regarding anything but cultivation. For Columella, fear about his slave's corruption is directed at the new and unsanctioned knowledge that an outside character could expose a slave to—the *monstrare* of Ulpian's description of persuasion. We see in these two different sources a shared concern about the illicit influence on slaves; in Ulpian, the corruption of a slave because of another's demonstration of bad behavior, and in Columella, its prevention.

Columella proposes a number of ways to prevent exposing the slave to outside knowledge. Some of the provisions are about physically keeping the slave away from external influences: No wandering, no new pathways to make leaving the estate easier. Other provisions regard people: The slave can fraternize only with someone who has the owner's best interest at heart. Columella's prescriptions also allow us to see the life of the foreman of a farm. Certain slaves had the license to leave their owners' farms and interact with various people outside the sphere of their owners' influence, leaving them open to corruption. The *animi servorum* are of concern here; it is their deterioration that is at stake for Columella, as it is when Ulpian is reflecting on the value of the slave in relation to the damage done.[25] Regarding the concern about influences over the mind, we see a similarity to Epictetus (discussed in the introduction) in the very fact that the mind of the slave is presented as free. The mind is free to be influenced, persuaded, or corrupted regardless of the status of the person. In Columella's fears about external influences, the mental autonomy of the slave emerges; it is up to the slave to allow their mind to be swayed or to withstand corruption.

In the commentaries on the *actio servi corrupti*, the jurists include a list of harms that are actionable. They bear similarities to Columella's concerns (see table 1). Some of these actions are crimes—committing outrage, theft, or inciting another person's slave—and if the slave were caught, the owner would have to pay a penalty. Some of these actions would fiscally damage the owner and others involved, such as a slave running away or wandering off, but more directly, convincing a slave to mismanage their own account, to falsify or adulterate their owner's accounts, or to confuse accounts entrusted to them. The

---

25. D. 11.3.9.3 Ulpian, *Edict*, book 23, quoted in note 10 above. Cf. D. 47.10.26 Paul, *Edict*, book 19.

Table 1. A free person is liable under the *actio servi corrupti* if they persuaded a slave . . .

Form of Corruption	Text	Citation
To commit an outrage	*Iniuriam faceret*	D. 11.3.1.5 Ulpian, *Edict*, book 23
To commit theft	*Furtum faceret*	D. 11.3.1.5 Ulpian, *Edict*, book 23
To incite another man's slave	*Alienum servum sollicitaret*	D. 11.3.1.5 Ulpian, *Edict*, book 23
To run away	*Fugeret*	D. 11.3.1.5 Ulpian, *Edict*, book 23
To be a wanderer	*Erro esset*	D. 11.3.1.5 Ulpian, *Edict*, book 23
To mismanage his personal account	*Peculium intricaret*	D. 11.3.1.5 Ulpian, *Edict*, book 23
To falsify or adulterate his master's accounts	*Rationes dominicas intercideret, adulteraret*	D. 11.3.1.5 Ulpian, *Edict*, book 23
To confuse accounts entrusted to him	*Rationem sibi commissam turbaret*	D. 11.3.1.5 Ulpian, *Edict*, book 23
To practice evil arts	*Malis artibus deditus esset*	D. 11.3.1.5 Ulpian, *Edict*, book 23
To be seditious	*Seditiosus esset*	D. 11.3.1.5 Ulpian, *Edict*, book 23
To spend too much time at public entertainments	*In spectaculis nimius esset*	D. 11.3.1.5 Ulpian, *Edict*, book 23
To join them in a tavern	*In popinam illum duxerit*	D. 47.10.26 Paul, *Edict*, book 19
To play dice	*Alea luserit*	D. 47.10.26 Paul, *Edict*, book 19
To become a lover	*Amator existeret*	D. 11.3.1.5 Ulpian, *Edict*, book 23
To suffer defilement	*Stuprum pateretur*	D. 11.3.2 Paul, *Edict*, book 19
To suffer adultery or defilement	*Adulterium stuprumve* <*pateretur*>	D. 48.5.6pr Papinian, *Adulterers*, book 1
To become extravagant	*Luxuriosum fecit*	D. 11.3.2 Paul, *Edict*, book 19
To become obstinate	*Contumacem fecit*	D. 11.3.2 Paul, *Edict*, book 19

language of tampering with accounts is one of moral wrongdoing. *Intercidere* means to cut through or falsify.[26] And while *adulterare* does mean to falsify, it also means to commit adultery, or in Roman terms, to corrupt another's wife.[27]

---

26. Pliny the Younger also uses the verb to describe the corrupted actions of a slave (*intercidere commentarios, Ep.* 6.22.4, discussed below). Persuading slaves to tamper with accounts and sale documents is also seen in D. 47.2.52.23–4 Ulpian, *Edict*, book 37, "If someone persuaded my slave to remove his name from, say, a document of purchase, Mela wrote, and I think, that I can proceed against him for theft. But if the slave were persuaded to transcribe my document, then, if the slave be suborned into doing so, the action for making a slave worse would be available; if the inciter himself made the copy, the action would be that for fraud" (*Si quis servo meo persuaserit, ut nomen suum ex instrumento puta emptionis tolleret, et Mela scripsit et ego puto furti agendum. Sed si servo persuasum sit, ut tabulas meas describeret, puto, si quidem servo persuasum sit, servi corrupti agendum, si ipse fecit, de dolo actionem dandam*). Schiller 1930, 841, invokes this passage in his article on the use of the *actio servi corrupti* to protect trade secrets. For a counterargument, see Watson 1996.

27. Ernout-Meillet s.v. *alter.* D. 48.5 focuses on adultery (in the traditional sense). For our purposes, D. 48.5.6pr Papinian, *Adulterers*, book 1, discusses the adultery (*adulterium*) among free people and the use of the *lex Julia*, and for a female slave the *lex Aquilia*, the charge of *iniuria*, or the *actio servi corrupti*.

The association is an act that strikes at the very center of a Roman's house; the owner has been cuckolded via his accounts. The use of a term that has overtones of infidelity brings the morality of the act to the fore.

Similarly, *turbare*, to confuse, relates to the noun *turba*, the term used for the urban crowd of Rome. The use of *turbare* can be seen as a reflection by an elite Roman on the effect a slave has on their owner's accounts; it is not an orderly mind that has contaminated the accounts, but quite literally a mob mentality. *Turbare* also emphasizes that the slave's actions are not technical and precise, but stirred up and disordered.[28] Some charges, such as taking up evil arts, inciting another's slave, or being seditious, could be dangerous for the owner.[29] Still others, such as spending too much time at the games, being someone's lover, and allowing oneself to become defiled or luxurious, speak more to the slave's character and a potential alteration that would leave the slave less suitable for a life of servitude. It would also be a challenge or embarrassment to the owner.[30] Many of these charges echo Columella's concerns such as running away or wandering off (what Columella describes as an *ambulator*)—or fall under the rubric of what Columella refers to as shameful acts (*flagitia*)—practicing evil arts, becoming a lover, a drunk, or defiled, or watching too many games. Elsewhere, Columella even prescribes giving a slave-woman to a foreman to help prevent him from becoming wayward.[31]

The question of influence is important; while a slave may have been motivated by money or some other tangible benefit, the slave in any of these scenarios could have chosen or even felt obliged to act because of some personal connection with their so-called corrupter. The third-party influence could easily have been a family member or friend. This might explain why Columella does not want the slave to interact with people outside of the owner's own network as it breaks the legally constructed *familia* of owner and slave, including

---

On adultery or the sexual corruption of slaves, see D. 1.18.21 Paul, *Duties of Assessors*, sole book, where the sexual corruption of slaves is bad for the household; D. 47.1.2.5 Ulpian, *Sabinus*, 43, which mentions the *actio servi corrupti*; D. 47.10.9.4 Ulpian, *Edict*, book 57 and D. 47.10.25 Ulpian, *Edict*, book 18.

28. For a definition of *turba*, see D. 47.8.4.2 Ulpian, *Edict*, book 56, "Labeo says that uproar is named from the general category, tumult, and the word comes from the Greek to create an uproar" (*Turbam autem appellatam Labeo ait ex genere tumultus idque verbum ex Graeco tractum* ἀπὸ τοῦ θορυβεῖν). Maltby s.v. *turba*. See Hellegouarc'h 1963, 515, discussing *turba* and the terminology for plebs.

29. D. 47.11.5 Ulpian, *On the Duties of Proconsul*, book 5, on bringing *infamia* to your owner.

30. Du Plessis 2013, 165, discusses the *actio servi corrupti* in terms of the removal of the slave in body and mind from the *potestas* of the owner, "This curious remedy seems to have been linked to the Roman understanding of 'character'."

31. Columella *Rust.* 1.8.5.

whatever obligations accompanied it. Along a similar line, it is worth keeping in mind that these are charges of making a slave, not a person, worse; a number of these characteristics are illicit in slaves alone and echo the unwanted servile behavior made into "mental defect" (*vitium animi*) seen in chapter 1.

The morality of slaves then can be seen as a priority for an owner, to own slaves who would certainly hold loyalty to them and their house as a part of being a good slave. Referencing his Republican predecessor Cato the Elder, Columella suggests that slaves not be allowed guests who were not intimates of the owner (and perhaps would not gain from a slave tampering with accounts). Ulpian and the jurist Gaius hold the corruption of the slave to be a loss of loyalty to the owner. Gaius goes as far as to say that the mind of the slave "is made worse if he is persuaded to disrespect his owner" (*corrumpitur animus servi et si persuadeatur ei, ut dominum contemneret*).[32] The mind of the slave (*animus servi*) is considered deteriorated because their opinion and feelings toward their owner have changed. *Contemnere* is a significant word: It can mean to defy or despise, but it indicates a loss in value, to hold a person as lesser and not to fear them.[33] If a third party can persuade a slave to disrespect (*contemnere*) their owner, they succeed in throwing the owner-slave relationship off balance. This suggests that the morality and internal considerations of a slave have a role in their value, changes that the *actio servi corrupti* served to remedy. As seen, the *actio servi corrupti* also functioned to situate moral judgment outside the slave; the guilt placed on the third-party actor removes the reasoning faculties and will from the slave. In this sense, the double nature of slaves as human beings and property is first recognized and then denied. This is the way in which the slave is recognized as a human being with all the capacities that entails. On the other hand, these characteristics are enumerated in order to put them at the mercy of someone else, removing these capacities and the slave's humanity with them. Both Columella and the jurists go to lengths to disarm the slave: Columella describes the character of the slave as limited, and the jurists echo that in the case of the *actio servi corrupti*. But in so doing, they implicitly recognize the subjectivity of the slave. When the mental autonomy of the slave is no longer in the service of the owner, the intellect and the capacity to reason is removed from the slave's control. But while this is a nice legal solution, and

32. D. 11.3.15 Gaius, *Provincial Edict*, book 6. The passage is generally thought to be classical (Bonfiglio 1998, 32; Albanese 1959, 111; Schiller 1930, 839–40).

33. Bonfiglio 1998, 33, on *contemnere*. Cf. D. 1.12.1.10 Ulpian, *Duties on the Prefect of the City*, sole book.

legally the ownership of the now-less-valuable slave is still intact, the factual issue remains: The slave has picked up a bad habit, and their previous relationship with their owner remains altered. The slave did decide to betray the owner. Nothing can fix this: There is either trust to rebuild or there will be no trust—that relationship is forever altered.

The Role of Free People

Slaves were everywhere in the Roman world, with countless different jobs and levels of autonomy, serving as channels to their owners and Roman households. Slave corruption serves as a barometer for the character of the three people involved: the owner, the third-party corrupter, and the slave. It also functions as a yardstick for the general state of affairs because the owner-slave relationship is deeply protected and its corruption ruins the paternalistic ideal of the Roman household.

Too many wayward slaves brought on financial and social detriment, while having control of one's slaves was a part of being a good Roman and respected *paterfamilias*. Columella takes a strict approach to prevent losses on account of excessive trust in slaves. Discussing farming, he reasons that so long as the land is good, the owner's care should allow for good harvests. As noted earlier, Columella reasons that a farm is better left out of the hands of a foreman because of the chance that great negligence or greed will seize the slave. Columella explains:

> There is no question that both of these errors are mostly committed or fostered by the faults of the owner, since he can either prevent such a person from being in charge of the business or, if he is already installed there, take care that he is removed.

> Quae utraque peccata plerumque vitio domini vel committi vel foveri nihil dubium est, cum liceat aut cavere ne talis praeficiatur negotio aut iam praepositus ut summoveatur curare.[34]

This is where the owner has failed; as Columella reasons, the owner should have been able to prevent the negligence or greed of the foreman because he has the

34. Columella *Rust.* 1.7.5–7.

power and duty to remove such a person. His failure to do so not only ensures the mismanagement of his farm, it fosters it. Columella uses the language of cultivation and care (*foveri, curare*) to describe an owner's failure. The owner should have been tending the health (*salubritas*) of his farm, but instead by his own fault or defect (*vitium*) he has brought about its ruin. Columella in fact begins this reflection by expressly stating, "since it is certain that the slaves are corrupted by being so far away from their owners" (*quoniam quidem et illi tam longa dominorum distantia corrumpuntur*).[35] Columella's harshest criticisms fall on the owner, not on the negligent or greedy slave. Corruption is a failure of the owner's domination because he did not ensure that the *vilicus* was working well. Here, too, as in the *actio servi corrupti*, the free Roman, in this case the owner, takes on the blame rather than the slave. Columella assigns responsibility to the owner, as through his ownership he is meant to have control over his slaves. With the removal of blame from the slave, Columella cements the idea that the slave's internal choice to act is a part of the owner's property.

In part 1 of this book, we saw the evaluative process Roman owners engaged in to attempt to know the character and qualities of slaves. Nevertheless, the jurist Ulpian, in discussing the *actio servi corrupti*, notes that "bad slaves" were at times freed. He writes, "For even bad slaves may gain their liberty, and sometimes subsequent events provide good reason for manumission" (*nam et mali servi forsitan consequuntur libertatem et posterior causa interdum tribuit manumissionis iustam rationem*).[36] Ulpian's statement recognizes the potential for change in a slave. However, the language can be seen as more skeptical; they are still bad slaves (*mali servi*) and only sometimes (*interdum*) does a later reason present itself as a just reason for manumission. The juristic literature on the *actio servi corrupti*, along with the actions on the *peculium* and account mismanagement seen in the previous chapter, highlight some owners' hands-off approach and others' inability to control their slaves. Here, the statement forms a critique of an owner who rewards a bad slave. The owner has failed to show their dominance over their slave's insubordinate character.

Some owners, on the other hand, are not bad because of their lack of attention, but because they listen to their slaves too much. In Tacitus' account of the Year of the Four Emperors, one reason Tacitus gives for Otho's plotting to take Galba's throne is goading from the would-be emperor's slaves and freedmen:

---

35. Columella *Rust.* 1.1.20.
36. D. 11.3.7 Ulpian, *Edict*, book 23. Bonfiglio 1998, 121, holds this as genuine contra Albanese 1959, 43–44.

> Otho's mind was not flabby like his body. The closest of his freedmen and slaves—who were more corrupt than is normal in a private house—held out to their greedy master the court and extravagance of Nero, affairs, marriages, and all the other pleasures of tyranny. If he dared to act all these would be his, but they reproached him that if he did not act they would fall to someone else.
>
> Non erat Othonis mollis et corpori similis animus. et intimi libertorum servorumque, corruptius quam in privata domo habiti, aulam Neronis et luxus, adulteria matrimonia ceterasque regnorum libidines avido talium, si auderet, ut sua ostentantes, quiescenti ut aliena exprobrabant.[37]

There is a balance to be struck between owners knowing what slaves know and knowing their character, but not allowing themselves to be corrupted by slaves (though perhaps in Otho's case, this was just a small push). Otho, in order to win over the troops following the murder of Galba, is described as acting "like a slave in every way for the sake of getting mastery" (*et omnia serviliter pro dominatione*).[38] Listening to slaves too carefully can be dangerous.

The third party found corrupting a slave must pay a legal penalty, and it also carried a social stigma. This free person becomes a *servi corruptor*,[39] and their actions toward the slave define them. The language attached to the corrupter is negative and holds a tone of morality. Pliny the Younger describes the corrupter of a slave, Atticinus, as being charged with the corruption of the slave of a secretary (*corrupto . . . scribae servo*) in order to intercept and tamper with documents (*commentarios interciderat*), among other things.[40] Pliny writes that Atticinus attempted to defend himself from charges, but proved himself disgraceful while he defended himself (*dum defenditur turpis*) and depraved while he accused others (*dum accusat sceleratus*). Pliny uses the same language as the jurists to describe the corruption (*servus corruptus, intercidere*).[41] The emphasis on the corrupter and his moral character serves to take those features away from the slave, diminishing the consideration of a slave's capacity for moral judgment. The actions of Atticinus were illegal, but the language describing the corruptors of slaves has a morality that speaks to the fact that these corruptions were intrusions into the very house of another Roman citizen.

37. Tac. *Hist.* 1.22.
38. Tac. *Hist.* 1.36.
39. *Corruptor* used as descriptor in D. 11.3.9.3 Ulpian, *Edict*, book 23.
40. Plin. *Ep.* 6.22.4.
41. See D. 11.3.1.5 Ulpian, *Edict*, book 23, "to falsify his owner's accounts" (*ut rationes dominicas intercideret*), discussed above.

From the perspective of the third party, literary authors use servile corruption to indicate the bad character of a person and disruptions to the Roman household. Tacitus, for example, uses the death of Petronius to critique Tigellinus and Nero. Tigellinus, described as jealous of not rivaling Petronius in his knowledge of pleasures, corrupted a slave of Petronius to inform to the emperor that he was part of the Pisonian conspiracy (*corrupto ad indicium servo*). Because cruelty was Nero's worst vice, Tacitus explains that Petronius was not allowed to offer a defense.[42] Similarly, in the first details of the reign of the final king of Rome, Tarquinius Superbus, Livy illustrates his arrogance and deceit through a tale of how "he ruined an innocent man by casting a false accusation" (*oblato falso crimine insontem oppressit*). Tarquin had called a morning meeting of the Latins but delayed his arrival until the evening. While they were waiting and even after Tarquin arrived, the Latin Turnus Herdonius gave a speech against the new Roman king, calling him arrogant and a usurper. In revenge, Tarquin bribed one of Turnus' slaves with gold (*servum Turni auro corrupit*) to allow his enemies entrance into Turnus' quarters in order to place a collection of swords in various hiding places. Tarquin then claimed that divine providence made him aware that Turnus had been planning on murdering him at the council meeting the day before and that therefore he must have a great number of weapons stashed away. Turnus' quarters were searched, the planted swords found. Livy reports that Turnus' slaves tried to protect their owner (presumably not the bribed slave). The swords, however, were taken as dispositive; Turnus was not allowed to defend himself and was then drowned.[43] Livy, Pliny, and Tacitus—no strangers to civil unrest—use the corruption of slaves not only as a symbol of rot at the heart of the Roman *familia* but also as a political metaphor in which the household is representative of the state.[44]

We see an example of this language of servile corruption in moments of political upheaval such as in the opening of Tacitus' description of the fall of the Julio-Claudian dynasty: "The labor I am undertaking is full of disasters: dark with battles, divided by unrest, savage even in peace" (*Opus adgredior opimum casibus, atrox proeliis, discors seditionibus, ipsa etiam pace saevum*). He continues, enumerating wars, fires, exiles, and terror among other troubles, and concludes with a remark on social relations, "slaves were corrupted against their

42. Tac. *Ann.* 16.18.
43. Livy 1.51.2.
44. On the representation of the Roman *familia* as the state, see Pliny himself in *Ep.* 8.16.3, "For the household is a kind of republic and quasi citizenship for slaves" (*nam servis res publica quaedam et quasi civitas domus est*). Pliny echoes Seneca *Ep.* 47.14, "They judged the household to be a little republic" (*domum pusillam rem publicam esse iudicaverunt*).

owners, freedmen against their patrons, and those who had no enemies were ruined by their friends" (*corrupti in dominos servi, in patronos liberti; et quibus deerat inimicus, per amicos oppressi*).[45] Detailing the power struggle between Nero and his mother, Agrippina, following the death of Britannicus in 55 CE, Tacitus again uses the presence of corrupted slaves as an indicator of real danger. Dismissing charges that she was plotting against Nero as mere rumor, Agrippina asks her accusers, Burrus and Seneca, under orders from the young emperor, to point to real evidence: "Or let someone come forward who can prove the urban cohorts have been bribed, the loyalty of the provinces shaken, and finally, the slaves and freedmen corrupted into wickedness" (*aut exsistat qui cohortes in urbe temptatas, qui provinciarum fidem labefactatam, denique servos vel libertos ad scelus corruptos arguat*).[46] Servile corruption is a means to understanding that things are not as they should be.

The Role of Slaves

The owner who cannot control his enslaved *familia* and the person who inserts themself between owner and slave are both treated with high-handed moralism and dramatics. In the first place, this represents interference in a Roman house, which was in the aristocratic mind the center of the family and finance. The case of Otho discussed above suggests another reason for the moralizing tone of the jurists and literary writers: the corrupting influence a slave can have on a free person. We have already seen that a slave can corrupt a fellow slave (*alienum servum ut sollicitaret*).[47] Both Quintilian and Seneca warn of the danger of those closest to us. In discussing the education of boys, Quintilian notes that there is just as much danger of corruption of character at home as at school. He reasons that the teacher at home (a slave) might be disgraceful (*turpis*) and that bad slaves are just as capable of being a bad influence as are well-born people of few scruples.[48] Again the corrupter is *turpis*. The corrupting slave teacher and the corrupting Atticinus[49] are on equal moral footing, both capable of making another person worse. Seneca takes on a more global tone, describing corruption as a disease:

---

45. Tac. *Hist.* 1.2.
46. Tac. *Ann.* 13.21.
47. D. 11.3.1.5 Ulpian, *Edict*, book 23 discussed above.
48. Quint. *Inst.* 1.2.4.
49. Plin. *Ep.* 6.22.4, discussed above.

> It is not permitted, I say, to travel a straight path. Our parents drag us down a wrong path, or our slaves do. No one errs by himself, but each person spreads madness to those nearest him and receives it from them in turn. For there are defects of nations in individuals, because the nation gave its vices to them. While someone makes another person worse, he is made worse. He learned a worse way of life and then he taught it. The effect is a great vileness because the worst in every person is piled up into one heap.
>
> Non licet, inquam, ire recta via; trahunt in pravum parentes, trahunt servi. Nemo errat uni sibi, sed dementiam spargit in proximos accipitque invicem. Et ideo in singulis vitia populorum sunt, quia illa populus dedit. Dum facit quisque peiorem, factus est; didicit deteriora, dein docuit, effectaque est ingens illa nequitia congesto in unum quod cuique pessimum scitur.[50]

The slave is a channel that goes directly to the owner and his household, but here they bring vice rather than profits into the collective. Seneca envisions a worldview where slaves are just as likely as parents to make you worse. Slaves and parents, both seemingly odd choices as would-be corrupters, are placed in the same role. The first, slaves, are not necessarily in a position to influence, and the second, parents, are supposed to be a nurturing influence. Seneca stresses that anyone can corrupt. The corrupter, free or slave, first learns (*discere*) and then teaches (*docere*) degradation; as Ulpian held in the passage of the *actio servi corrupti*, a slave is corrupted if he is taught (*monstrare*) to do a bad act, but here, instead, it is the slave doing the teaching. In the above passages, Pliny, Quintilian, and Seneca emphasize the ability of slaves to be bad influences. For Pliny it is more indirect; by corrupting the slave of the secretary, Atticinus debases himself. Quintilian and Seneca specifically compare the corruption a slave is able to do with that of a free person (well-born and slave teachers, parents and slaves, respectively). They concede here that slaves are able to morally alter free people, as a free corrupter is able to morally alter the slave. These literary authors speak to the ability of slaves to hold influence over their free counterparts more than the juristic literature allows. However, we can see that the literary and juristic sources, though differing in approaches and intents, both consider the dual image of the slave as mentally autonomous but also as owned and unfree.

In the cases of the *actio servi corrupti*, the attention has been on the actions

50. Sen. *Ep.* 94.54.

of the third party influencing another's slave or the owner who has failed to show proper domination over their slaves. Cases of noxal surrender instead examine the actions of a slave and consider the liability of the owner for the misdeeds of the slave. Owners, just like fathers with children in power, were responsible for any delicts (civil wrongs akin to common law torts) committed by their dependents. The owner of a slave who had done a civil wrong had the option to surrender their slave or pay damages to the plaintiff. It appears that surrendering the slave was the original method of resolving delicts in which the slave was found to be the perpetrator.[51] Later, the owner could choose to pay the extent of the damages or surrender the slave, meaning that the owner's liability was effectively limited to the higher value.

The principle underlying noxal surrender was that the wrong followed the wrongdoer (*noxa caput sequitur*). This results in a number of interesting scenarios for a slave who was found to have committed a delict. For example, Labeo (cited by Ulpian) considers who should be held responsible for the damages if the slave had subsequently been manumitted:

> If, at the instigation of his owner, a slave should perpetrate an outrage, the owner can certainly be sued in his own respect. But if the case be put that the slave has been manumitted, Labeo was of the opinion that the action should be given against the freedman himself, because the wrong attaches to the wrongdoer, and a slave is not obliged to obey his owner in everything; equally if the slave should kill someone at his owner's behest, we proceed against him himself under the *lex Cornelia*.
>
> Si iussu domini servus iniuriam fecerit, utique dominus conveniri poterit etiam suo nomine. Sed si proponatur servus manumissus, placet Labeoni dandam in eum actionem, quia et noxa caput sequitur nec in omnia servus domino parere debet: ceterum et si occiderit iussu domini, Cornelia eum eximemus.[52]

In this case, which was discussing the delict of *iniuria* (outrage or "affronting another person"), Ulpian notes that if the slave is following orders, the owner should be held liable for the full amount of the damages. He then cites Labeo, who complicates the scenario: If the slave was freed (why the delict-committing

51. Nicholas 2008, 223. On noxal liability and slaves, see Buckland 1908, 98–130, and especially Watson 1987a, 67–76.
52. D. 47.10.17.7 Ulpian, *Edict*, book 57.

slave is freed is not commented upon, but it is perhaps expressly to put the responsibility onto the slave), the slave themself will be held responsible for the damages for two reasons. First, *noxa caput sequitur*, and, second, a slave does not need to obey their owner in all things. *Noxa caput sequitur* was rather unwavering—if the slave was sold, the new owner would be noxally liable for them.[53] The body was the location of the wrongdoer's responsibility; even at times it appears that a corpse or a part of the body would do.[54] The body here sums up the wrongdoer; the slave is handed over like the property they are.

There is still a second reason that Labeo gives for placing the liability on the newly freed slave: "a slave is not obligated to obey his owner in everything." The slave (as the freedperson was a slave when they committed the offense) is meant to reason and to understand morality and the law. The slave has the choice, though surely there would be consequences, of not doing as they were told. The latent liability of the slave shows how the slave is held in a different position than a very young child (*infans*) or deranged person (*furiosus*) who, once older or if healed, would not be held liable for past actions.[55] Labeo's predecessor Alfenus Varus explicitly draws on the moral reasoning of the slave as he notes "typically a slave does not obey the orders of his owner in all cases with impunity" (*servus non in omnibus rebus sine poena domino dicto audiens esse solet*). The older jurist then adds that the slave who got in a fight in order to help their owner would not be held liable once freed, but would be in cases of murder, theft, or piracy.[56] The case of murder is echoed in the quote of Labeo; even while enslaved, the slave had enough of a legal personality that they could face charges under the law on murder (*lex Cornelia de sicariis et veneficiis*) regardless of whether they were following their owner's orders.[57] The *exemplum* of a

---

53. D. 9.4.7pr Ulpian, *Edict*, book 3, which is why in the Edict of the Aediles (the regulations on the slave market, discussed in chapters 1 and 2), it was stipulated that the seller must make the purchaser aware if there was any noxal liability tied to the slave; cf. D. 21.1.1.1 Ulpian, *Curule Aediles' Edict*, book 1.

54. D. 9.4.1 Gaius, *Provincial Edict*, book 2, "The force and effect of such actions is that if judgment is given against us we can avoid having to pay the amount of the condemnation by handing over the body of the wrongdoer" (*quarum actionum vis et potestas haec est, ut, si damnati fuerimus, liceat nobis deditione ipsius corporis quod deliquerit evitare litis aestimationem*). On the corpse, hair, and fingernails, see G. 4.81 with de Zulueta 1953 *ad loc.* and Buckland 1908, 111.

55. See, for example, D. 50.17.40 Pomponius, *Sabinus*, book 34; D. 9.2.5.2 Ulpian, *Edict*, book 18; D. 6.1.60 Pomponius, *Sabinus*, book 29; D. 21.1.23.2 Ulpian, *Curule Aediles' Edict*, book 1; D. 47.10.3.1 Ulpian, *Edict*, book 56; D. 48.8.12 Modestinus, *Rules*, book 8; G. 3.106–109.

56. D. 44.7.20 Alfenus Varus, *Digest*, book 2. Watson 1968b, 298–99, discusses the difficult position in which the slave is placed in this case. The slave might be pardoned if he was following orders and the offense or crime was not too extreme (D. 43.24.11.7 Ulpian, *Edict*, book 71, with Watson 1987a, 132–33).

57. On slaves and criminal liability, see Robinson 1995; Robleda 1976; Del Prete 1972; Kaser 1940;

slave choosing to virtuously disobey their owner goes back to the beginning of the Republic when Livy tells the story of Vindicius, a slave who reveals that his owner was plotting to restore the monarchy.[58]

On the other hand, the jurists limit the owner's liability by creating a narrow definition of knowledge (*scientia*). Unlike Columella, who counsels a watchful eye and criticizes inattentive owners, Ulpian construes knowledge to mean the following with respect to noxal actions: "wherever knowledge on the part of the owner is required, 'knowledge' must be understood to include instances where he could have prevented the slave but did not do so" (*ubicumque scientia exigitur domini, sic accipienda est, si, cum prohibere posset, non prohibuit*).[59] Paul too considers similar blocks to an owner's "knowledge" in the context of delicts committed by slaves:

> Or suppose the slave is on the other side of a river and commits some harmful act within the sight but against the will of the owner. In such cases it seems better to say that 'knowledge' should be taken to mean knowledge on the part of someone who has the power to prevent.
>
> vel cum trans flumen sit servus, vidente quidem, sed invito domino noxiam noceat? rectius itaque dicitur scientiam eius accipiendam, qui prohibere potest.[60]

Along similar lines as this owner who can only helplessly watch their slave commit a wrong without any hope of stopping them, Ulpian notes that when the owner is a defendant in a noxal case they must have the slave in their power (*in potestate*). *In potestate* here has a very physical meaning and betrays a reality of slave ownership: If the slave had run away or gone abroad, the slave owner naturally did not have the physical ability to surrender them.[61] This works in

---

Buckland 1908, 98–130. If the slave had been freed in the meantime, he would nevertheless be punished as a slave, that is, more harshly, see D. 48.19.1.1 Ulpian, *Disputations*, book 8.

58. Livy 2.5.9–10. On the tale of Vindicius, see Mouritsen 2011, 68; Kleijwegt 2009, 319–30; Daube 1946.

59. D. 9.4.3 Ulpian, *Edict*, book 3, "In all noxal actions, wherever knowledge on the part of the owner is required, 'knowledge' must be understood to include instances where he could have prevented the slave but did not do so. For it is one thing to instigate the commission of a delict by a slave and quite another to allow him to commit one" (*In omnibus noxalibus actionibus, ubicumque scientia exigitur domini, sic accipienda est, si, cum prohibere posset, non prohibuit: aliud est enim auctorem esse servo delinquenti, aliud pati delinquere*).

60. D. 9.4.4 Paul, *Edict*, book 3.

61. D. 9.4.21.3 Ulpian, *Edict*, book 23, "We must accept the words 'in power' to mean that the defendant has the means and ability to produce the slave. Otherwise, if he is on the run or gone abroad,

the owner's favor—they will not be liable if the slave has left town (unless the owner told them to do this)[62]—but it also shows how few ownership protections exist in this circumstance. The slave has chosen to leave the power of the owner and it seems they have done so successfully.

Noxal surrender presents a potential problem for ownership as it explicitly took property away from the owner and handed it over to the victim. This is particularly true if the slave was acting without the owner's order or knowledge. We might even imagine that this is one reason why the discussion of manumission was prevalent in the juristic literature on noxal surrender. The owner could choose this path and not lose the slave on the same semantic level (or have to pay the financial penalty). The concern with choice can also be seen in a case Ulpian gives us in which he cites two other jurists (Urseius who cites Proculus). A slave owned by two people killed another slave belonging to one of his owners. Proculus reports that if it was not with the consent of the other owner, a noxal action was not a good idea as it would incentivize slaves in such positions to commit wrongs in order to be surrendered to their preferred owner: "so that it not be in the power of the slave who he might serve alone" (*ne sit in potestate servi, ut tibi soli serviat*).[63] These are the kinds of factual insecurities that an owner could not know or necessarily plan for, but that could affect their ownership of a slave.

By reading these sources with questions of mental freedom in mind, we can access the relationship between owner and slave in a more nuanced manner and understand that it is not a simple binary of the absolute ownership of the slaveholder and the mental autonomy of the slave. The slaveholder's ownership

---

he cannot be deemed to be in power" (*'In potestate' sic accipere debemus, ut facultatem et potestatem exhibendi eius habeat: ceterum si in fuga sit vel peregre, non videbitur esse in potestate*).

62. D. 9.4.21 Ulpian, *Edict*, book 23, considers this situation.

63. D. 9.2.27.1–2 Ulpian, *Edict*, book 18, "If a slave in common ownership, mine and yours, kills another slave of mine, the *lex Aquilia* lies against you if he did it with your consent. Urseius reports that this was the opinion held by Proculus; but he says that if the slave did it without your consent, a noxal action will not lie in case it might be in the power of the slave to decide which he might serve exclusively; and I think this is correct. Again, if a slave owned by you and me in common is killed by the slave of Titius, Celsus writes that if either of us sues, he should recover the assessed value of his share or noxal surrender will have to be made of the assailant as a whole, because this solution is not susceptible of division" (*Si servus communis, id est meus et tuus, servum meum occiderit, legi Aquiliae locus est adversus te, si tua voluntate fecit: et ita Proculum existimasse Urseius refert. quod si non voluntate tua fecit, cessare noxalem actionem, ne sit in potestate servi, ut tibi soli serviat: quod puto verum esse. Item si servus communis meus et tuus sit occisus a servo Titii, Celsus scribit alterum ex dominis agentem aut litis aestimationem consecuturum pro parte aut noxae dedi ei in solidum oportere, quia haec res divisionem non recipit*). Watson 1987a, 74, holds that there would then be no Aquilian action in this case.

may be understood as absolute in the sense that an owner may largely do what he wishes with his slave: he can educate him, chain him, or free him. This represents the owner's physical domination and the slave's physical subjection. However, the owner's inability to know what the slave thinks and feels, that is, to know with certainty that the slave will do what the owner wishes and have the owner's best interest in mind, reveals a more tenuous form of domination. The owner must continuously assess and reassess the slave's mind without the surety that exists in the corporeal relationship between owner and slave. And in that assessment, we encounter Roman owners and jurists considering and reflecting on the subjectivity of the slave in question even if we are not able to recover it directly.

The law goes to great lengths to shield the owner from what Romans would consider servile misbehavior, which allows us to see how open to influence, corruption, and danger the owners and their households were from slaves. In times of crisis, such as a slave running off with their owner's account books, the mental autonomy and agency of the slave is legally denied so that the owner may claim damages, and also perhaps to save a little face after being swindled by their slave. But we must view this denial as a fiction not because we know that the value of these slaves was in that very same autonomy and agency, but because the Romans did.

PART THREE

The End of the Owner-Slave Relationship

FIVE
Exits from Slavery

> Why should I make good on my slave's too loud retort, insolent look, or muttering under his breath with whips and chains? Who am I that it is a sin for my ears to be offended? Many have pardoned their enemies: should I not pardon the indolent, the indifferent, and the babblers? Age makes excuse for a boy, sex for a woman, liberty for a stranger, family ties for a member of the household.
>
> Quid est quare ego servi mei clarius responsum et contumaciorem vultum et non pervenientem usque ad me murmurationem flagellis et compedibus expiem? Quis sum, cuius aures laedi nefas sit? Ignoverunt multi hostibus: ego non ignoscam pigris neglegentibus garrulis? Puerum aetas excuset, feminam sexus, extraneum libertas, domesticum familiaritas.
>
> —Sen. *Ira* 3.24.2–3

The story of Roman slavery that we are typically told is one that ends in manumission, and it would seem eccentric to not include a chapter on the practice even though most enslaved people died enslaved. There are good reasons for the scholarly focus on manumission: it is perhaps the most idiosyncratic aspect of the Roman version of the institution of slavery, at least considering the rate at which the Romans practiced it.[1] Specific reasons why Romans manumitted with a frequency otherwise unheard of in the ancient world depend on the individuals involved, but there are prevailing theories generally to do with the Roman economy and domestic stability, especially concerning social control,

1. The actual rate of manumission is unknown to us; see Mouritsen 2011, 120–41, on this question. Summarizing the data, he notes at 140 that "manumission was both very common and very selective." On some tentative conclusions based on epigraphic data, see Mouritsen 2007 and 2004.

incentivization, and appeasement.[2] Slaves, at least those who had some contact with their owners, were aware of this possibility for manumission. Thus, a slave unhappy with their situation was still encouraged to behave rather than run away or otherwise resist because they might someday be manumitted. Slave owners would go so far as to tell their slaves that they were planning on manumitting them, which surely would encourage good behavior in hopes that the owner would not change their mind.[3] The owner could revoke a promise of manumission; Tacitus tells the story of Pedanius Secundus, prefect of the city, who was killed by his slave when he allegedly revoked an agreement for manumission for which the price had already been set.[4] Cicero, discussing the fall of the Republic and the loss of freedom under Marc Antony, notes that honest and hardworking slaves could expect to be freed after six years. The number of years is a reference to the years when the Republic was "enslaved," but the metaphor would not hold if the potential for manumission were not a possible reality.[5]

This chapter is about close ties and close saves between owner and slave; manumission emphasized the relationship between owner and slave and encouraged careful consideration before any ruptures in ownership occurred. Manumission was almost entirely at the prerogative of the slave owner, and it was only under exceptional circumstances that external approval was required. This chapter focuses on manumission under such circumstances as they showcase the virtues and qualities of character that were desired in a freed citizen populace. Here I will focus on two causes of exits from slavery: (1) manumission due to kin relations ("close ties"); and (2) extraordinary situations that bring about manumission ("close saves: virtuous slaves"). An exit from slavery occurs either when the slave acts like a good potential citizen or, as we will see, at times when the slave owner falls short of their duties as slave owner ("close saves: vicious masters"). The end of the chapter steps back to consider the dynamics between legal status and enslaved identity more generally through a reading of Dio Chrysostom's Fifteenth Discourse and the jurists' discussion of suits for freedom (D. 40.12).

2. See Mouritsen 2011, 141–202, for these different readings of manumission.
3. Petr. *Satr.* 71.1–3; Tac. *Ann.* 15.54.2; and Plin. *Ep.* 5.5.2, 8.18.5 for related scenarios.
4. Tac. *Ann.* 14.42–45. Tacitus gives an alternative explanation: the owner and the slave who murdered him were sexual rivals (*sive amore exoleti incensus et dominum aemulum non tolerans*). Following the *SC Silanianum* (10 CE) all of the slaves of the house (four hundred in number) were executed. Tacitus records that the plebs did not want the execution of so many, but Nero ordered it be done in an edict. The jurist C. Cassius Longinus gave a speech (according to Tacitus) arguing that the slaves must be executed because they failed to protect their owner and were likely complicit. See the epilogue to this book, Harries 2013, and MacMullen 1986 for discussion.
5. Cic. *Phil.* 8.32. Bradley 1984, 85, expresses his skepticism about the length of time.

While manumission was an archaic institution, Augustus introduced laws at the beginning of the Empire to limit the number and kind of slaves that owners could free. Following this, a just reason (*iusta causa*) had to be provided for certain kinds of manumissions to be granted.[6] The *iustae causae* of manumission presented here show slaves behaving and acting with the virtues of a citizen (such as *fides* or *virtus*) and engaging in particularly Roman practices (such as the giving of *beneficia* or defending honor) before they are manumitted; these slaves can be seen to be performing aspects of citizenship. As we will see, these manumissions can then be read as a possible negotiation between owner and slave, as well as a means of settling the potential ethical dilemma that the performance of citizenship poses to Roman slave ownership.[7] In the decision to manumit their slave, the owner is performing their final act of ownership and a final act of assessment and scrutiny: in the cases I examine, the reasons for manumission are based on particular qualities that, while generally shown through action, originate in the realm of feeling and character, or the mind. Following these manumissions, the slave's relationship with their owner and with the community at large is altered; the owner and slave become patron and freedperson, and Rome gets a new citizen.

Close Ties

In the passage from *De Ira* above, Seneca discusses various reasons for the kindly and forgiving treatment of others. A slave may show insolence and disobedience with their responses and looks, but the behavior should be pardoned: Just as boys are pardoned because of their age (*aetas*), women their sex (*sexus*), and strangers their liberty (*libertas*), slaves ought to be forgiven because they are members of the household (*familiaritas*). Others are pardoned because of something inherent in their status; the slave instead is pardoned because of their relationship with their owner.[8] This principle guides Seneca's lenient punishment of slaves—one makes excuses for one's family—and Seneca here includes domestic slaves.

6. I will discuss this in more detail below. On the forms of manumission and its regulation, see Mouritsen 2011, 66–92. From a legal perspective, see Watson 1987a, 23–34; Buckland 1908, 437–597; and Atkinson 1966 (on the Augustan laws).
7. On negotiation, see Vlassopoulos 2021; Koops 2020; Dari-Mattiacci 2013.
8. *Familiaritas*, etymologically tied to *familia*, is the idea of being intimate or having a familial sort of relationship with others. Hellegouarc'h 1963, 68–71, connects *familiaritas* with *amicitia*. *Familiaritas* is often tied to *intimus* as well (Nep. *Att.* 19.4; Cic. *Fin.* 1.69).

Generally, following the statute law of Rome, slaves had no family ties; they were not legally recognized as parent and child, husband and wife, or brother and sister. But as is widely evidenced in their commentaries, the Roman jurists did have a concept of kin relationships both among slaves and between owner and slave. This is seen clearly in the *lex Aelia Sentia* (4 CE), a part of Augustus' wider restrictions on manumission.[9] This law is concerned with the qualities and character of a slave being released from slavery; it stipulated that if the owner was under twenty or the slave under thirty, the owner must seek permission to manumit by stating a just reason (*iusta causa*), which would be approved by a counsel (*consilium*). A slave under thirty manumitted without a *iusta causa* and the subsequent approval of the *consilium* did not become a citizen.[10] William Buckland has argued that the reason for this age restriction on slaves was because before thirty, one could not be sure that a (former) slave could bear the duties of citizenship.[11]

The jurists give several acceptable *iustae causae* including blood relations, past services (such as protecting an owner), and future services (such as becoming a business manager or wife).[12] In the remaining fragments of Ulpian's four-book commentary on the *lex Aelia Sentia*, he is rather general: a "connection by blood, for account is taken of kinship" (*vel si sanguine eum contingit, habetur enim ratio cognationis*).[13] Ulpian is more detailed in his work on the duties of provincial governors, giving a long list of kinship relationships that specifically underline the close connections between owner and slave: a son, daughter, or

9. The *lex Aelia Sentia* focused on the individual owner and slave with provisions including age restrictions for both parties, the nullification of manumissions to defraud creditors or patrons, and also that slaves who had been chained, tortured for wrongdoing, or forced to fight beasts would become *dediticii* upon manumission. On the *lex Aelia Sentia* and the other Augustan laws on manumission (*lex Fufia Caninia* and *lex Junia*), see Mouritsen 2016, 406–10 and 2011, 80–92; Atkinson 1966; Buckland 1908, 533–51.
10. They became instead Junian Latins, which has been described as being free for life, but a slave in death. On this defective form of freedom and citizenship, see Koops 2014.
11. Buckland 1908, 542–43.
12. On the particular *causae*, see G. 1.13–32, 36–41, 65–70; *Tit. Ulp.* 1.13; and more generally, D. 40.2. G. 1.19; D. 40.2.25 Gaius, *Manumissions*, book 1 (on being manumitted to become a *procurator*, but not a *tutor*, because someone who needs a *tutor* is not of age to manumit; see Buckland 1908, 539–40). D. 40.2.19 Celsus, *Digest*, book 29, and D. 40.2.20.2 Ulpian, *Duties of Consul*, book 2 (on manumission for the purposes of marrying a slave). G. 1.18; D. 40.2.14.1 Marcian, *Rules*, book 4 (on the fact that women could not use the *causa matrimonii* unless the woman was a freedwoman herself). D. 40.2.15pr Paul, *lex Aelia Sentia*, book 1 (on slaves being freed if a young owner had to free a slave as a condition for him to become an heir). D. 40.1.20pr Papinian, *Replies*, book 10, and D. 40.2.20.1 Ulpian, *Duties of Consul*, book 2 (on manumission if a slave was given to a young owner for the express purpose of manumission). D. 40.2.9.1 Marcian, *Institutes*, book 13 (on once the *causa* is approved it is held even if it is wrong).
13. D. 40.2.11 Ulpian, *Duties of Proconsul*, book 6 and D. 40.2.12 Ulpian, *lex Aelia Sentia*, book 2.

sibling by birth; someone nursed by the same woman (*collactaneus*), a guardian (*educator*), teacher (*paedagogus*), or wet nurse, including the children of these four; a ward (*alumnus*), a slave who carried their owner's books to school (*capsarius*), a manager (*procurator*) if the slave is over eighteen, or a virgin or other woman for the purpose of marriage (to take place within six months).[14] While Ulpian begins with blood relations, the category is widened to include adopted relations, those that will be related by marriage (or business), or who served as caretakers of their owners in their childhood. Here we see the idea of the Roman family encompassing the household, both free and slave.[15] These slaves are not granted exceptional manumission solely because of kindly feelings on the part of their owner (though that may have instigated it); these slaves are manumitted because they have a predetermined role in a Roman family and were likely already performing that role. For example, Plutarch tells the story that Cato had his wife nurse their son alongside infants of slaves so that "they might come to have a familial affection for her son" (κατεσκεύαζεν εὔνοιαν ἐκ τῆς συντροφίας προς τὸν υἱόν).[16] Plutarch's example of a *collactaneus* is of one born within the household (*verna*). An owner sought manumission because of the affection he had for a slave; the *consilium* granted the manumission because the slave was already in practice part of a Roman household, and this legitimated the tie in the eyes of the law. Manumission serves as a form of social birth; the former slave would gain not only a free legal status, but social status within a Roman family.

Ulpian counsels judges that these relationships provide cause for manumission so long as they are based in "affection" (*affectus*) and "legally just feelings" (*iustae affectiones*) and not "excess" (*luxuria*) or "sexual indulgence" (*delicia*).[17] A recent heir may choose to manumit their teacher, wet nurse, or *collactaneus*. An owner may have children who were enslaved if he had a child with one of his slaves or, alternatively, the owner may be a freedperson themself, now able to purchase family members in order to free them. Ulpian's moralizing, however, seems to apply most prominently not to freeing one's children or former nanny, but to manumissions that take place for the purpose of marriage. As noted, the former owner and the enslaved woman had six months to marry

14. D. 40.2.11, 13 Ulpian, *Duties of Proconsul*, book 6.
15. On this, see, for example, Fitzgerald 2000, 4, "The Roman concepts of the *domus* and *familia*, both of which may include relations and slaves, indicate that on some level slaves and free living under the same roof formed a unit."
16. Plut. *Cat. Mai.* 20.3.
17. D. 40.2.16pr Ulpian, *lex Aelia Sentia*, book 2.

before the manumission would be nullified (female owners could manumit slaves for the purpose of marriage only if they themselves were freedwomen).[18] In one of the most coercive aspects of the Roman institution of slavery, these women were freed into a particularly defective form of freedom. While in a better situation than remaining enslaved—the owners would have sexual access to them either way—these women, unlike other freeborn or freed Roman women, could not divorce their husbands without their consent (specifically, they could not sue for the return of their dowry), nor could they retain their property separately from their husbands.[19] Nevertheless, they were married, and thus rather than the owner just freeing his pregnant slave so his child might be born free (but out of wedlock), here the child is born free and legitimate—these are the kind of legally just feelings Ulpian has in mind.

Family ties are taken into account at the other end of the spectrum as well. In his discussion of regulations on the slave market (found in D. 21.1), Ulpian considers the return of a group of slaves sold together (as a unit) on account of one being ill:

> Healthy slaves are generally returned on account of those who are diseased when they cannot be separated without great inconvenience or affront to family ties. Suppose that they wish to return the parents but keep their son or vice versa. The same is true in respect of brothers and those linked in a servile quasi-matrimonial relationship.
>
> Plerumque propter morbosa mancipia etiam non morbosa redhibentur, si separari non possint sine magno incommodo vel ad pietatis rationem offensam. Quid enim, si filio retento parentes redhibere maluerint vel contra? Quod et in fratribus et in personas contubernio sibi coniunctas observari oportet.[20]

Paul seconds this opinion for brothers.[21] So while slaves were legally not allowed

18. D. 40.2.13 Ulpian, *Duties of Proconsul*, book 6. On women, see D. 40.2.14 Marcian, *Rules*, book 4.
19. See especially Huemoeller 2020, in which she argues at 137 that these women, "freed-wives" in Huemoeller's terminology, "inhabited a middle ground between the poles of free and enslaved." See also Wacke 2001, but with critiques from Huemoeller 2020, 127, on idealizing the nature of these marriages.
20. D. 21.1.35 Ulpian, *Curule Aediles' Edict*, book 1.
21. D. 21.1.39 Paul, *Curule Aediles' Edict*, book 1.
Ulpian takes in parallel that when one of a set of animals is returnable, both must be returned: D. 21.1.38.14 Ulpian, *Curule Aediles' Edict*, book 2, "We say the same of a batch of slaves sold at a single price, unless they cannot be split up, for example, actors or mimes" (*Haec et in hominibus dicemus pluribus uno pretio distractis, nisi si separari non possint, ut puta si tragoedi vel mimi*). At other times owners would free slaves in their wills and give them dowries, see Watson 1987a, 34.

to marry, here Ulpian respects "persons joined together in a slave dwelling" (*personae contubernio sibi coniunctae*). *Contubernium* refers to slave marriages in contrast to legal Roman marriage (*conubium*).[22] In Ulpian's concession to the slave family, we can see the divergence from a strict reading of the *ius civile* in the jurist's reasoning. *Persona*, too, is suggestive. *Persona* can simply mean person, but the original meaning of *persona* refers to the theater mask; that is, something one puts on and can remove. It comes to mean character, both in the sense of a role someone plays and the moral and mental qualities that constitute a particular person.[23] Ulpian's language, using *persona* and *contubernium* to describe a slave marriage, preserves the letter of the law where slaves could not marry while also making room for the actuality that slaves had families. Ulpian states this all as *plerumque*, "generally, commonly," his words in no way obliging an owner to act in such a fashion, but stating an ideal that reflects reality. This is carried through in *oportet*, "it is fitting," that is, it is not compulsory, but it is right. Ulpian does not grant that slaves could marry (*conubium*) or in any way diverge from the strictures of the *ius civile*; he interprets and works around these constraints such that the *ius civile* is upheld, but nonetheless carves out a space for contemporary sentiments.

Ulpian gives his reasoning for not separating slave families, stating that it is a great disadvantage (*magnum incommodum*) and offends the reason of *pietas* (*ad pietatis rationem offensam*). The Roman virtue *pietas* was highly desirable and was part and parcel of the functioning of elite Roman society. What is unexpected here is that it is used in the description of a slave family; these are slaves behaving as a social unit within which *pietas* is an implicit virtue. *Pietas* fits into the generalized idea of *humanitas*, which reigns throughout Ulpian's discussion; it is from this idea that the notion of keeping slave families together comes about. Emperors and jurists often discussed questions of manumission under this wider framework of *humanitas* from the second century on. *Humanitas* serves as a bridge between the strict legal structure of the *ius civile* and a more comprehensive interpretation of law that intertwined social etiquette and morality with the older legal system.[24] While selling brothers and other unof-

22. On the use of *contubernium* as an indication of the "slave marriage" and as distinct from legal marriage (*conubium*), see D.40.4.59pr Scaevola, *Digest*, book 23; Tac. *Hist.* 1.43; Cic. *Verr.* 2.5.104.

23. Mantovani 2010, 37. While slaves were considered both *res* and *persona*, Ulpian referring to slaves as *personae* highlights the transiency of whatever role, or in this case, status, someone is currently in, which reflects the Roman construction of slavery as a changeable and malleable status.

24. *Humanitas* encompassed several extolled Roman virtues including *pietas*, *aequitas*, *clementia*, and *benignitas*. It is often related to the Greek words *philanthropia* and *paideia* (see Gell. *NA* 13.17, see also *NA* 19.14.1). On other terminology related to *humanitas*, see Woolf 1998, 54–55, where he offers *benevolentia*, *observantia*, *mansuetudo*, *facilitas*, *severitas*, *dignitas*, and *gravitas*, among

ficial slave family units together was in one way kindly, it was also a form of appeasement and an implicit threat—no one need heed this. Columella too concerns himself with the slave family unit with an eye toward controlling his slaves. He counsels that a foreman (*vilicus*) should be given a slave woman to live with (*contubernalis*) so that she may help keep him under the owner's control and aid in his duties.[25]

We can understand *humanitas* as a unifying Roman cultural paradigm that served as a marker for distinguishing someone's ability to participate in Roman imperial society. It should not however be viewed as benign when applied to people outside of elite Roman male culture, since it served as a form of social control as well as a pathway into Roman society.[26] *Humanitas* does double duty in the passage from the Edict of the Aediles: It allows the jurist both to recognize the slave family unit—like a Roman family this is a relationship governed by *pietas*—and at the same time to hold the slaves outside of Roman society. Nevertheless, the attempt at preservation of slave kin relations in both cases, during a return on sale and as a justification for early manumission, shows that the Roman jurists certainly had a conception of the slave family unit.

The *familiaritas* that arose between owner and household slaves and the concessions made to the slave family by the jurists are important because the family was the primary social unit in Roman society. Seneca excuses his slaves' faults on account of this *familiaritas*. However, he is not unaware of the pragmatic benefit that will befall the owner on account of this: the loyal behavior of the slave. Cato too protects his own son by situating him such that he would gain the affection and loyalty of his slaves from birth. In each of these scenarios—

---

others. The term gained currency in the Late Republic and was used by Cicero to discuss relationships among Romans themselves and between Romans and foreigners (Cic. *QF* 1.1.27–8, *Cael.* 25; see discussion in Woolf). The Hadrianic or Antonine jurists were the first to begin to incorporate the concept of *humanitas* into their arguments, see Palma 1992, 23. Palma 1992 (at 42–47) discusses the shift in this period to a "less rigid" interpretation of the cases under the justification of being more compassionate (*humanior*) or more kindly (*benignior*) and by the time of the Severans, the idea of *humanitas* was entirely embedded into the work of the jurists. Paul Veyne (1993, 342) offers a definition, "*Humanitas* means literary culture, the virtue of humanity, and the state of civilization," and, at 343, "*Humanitas* was thus a merit rather than a universal trait." Riccobono (1965, 590) describes *humanitas* as "il sentimento di pietà umana." See Crifò 1993; Casavola 1976, 131–75 (in particular 157–60); Riccobono 1965, 583–614; Maschi 1948, 263–362. On *humanitas* in Roman culture, see Woolf 1998; Veyne 1993, 342–69; Schadewaldt 1973, 43–62.

25. Columella *Rust.* 1.8.5. See also, for example, Columella *Rust.* 1.6.3, 1.6.19–20, 12.3.7.

26. Woolf (1998, 54–55) discusses the system of *humanitas* as a control on foreigners entering into Roman society, and viewing *humanitas* as the gatekeeper into Roman civic life applies well to the situation of slaves. The ability of slaves to understand and assimilate into Roman culture is important for understanding Roman manumission practice in the Empire.

when Seneca invites his slaves to speak freely,[27] Cato rears slaves alongside his son, and Columella allows his foreman to have a slave-wife—the owners are promoting good behavior and simultaneously exposing their slaves to the Roman family and its customs.[28] Family ties are perhaps the most clear-cut reason to seek special permission to free a slave as manumission hereby constructs a legal connection to a Roman *familia* and serves to legitimize familial feelings through the law.

Close Saves: Virtuous Slaves

In contrast to accidents of birth or position, here we will consider the character of an enslaved person as a reason for manumission. This section looks at four fragments from the jurists Scaevola, Paul, Marcian, and Ulpian to examine scenarios in which enslaved people exhibit qualities of mind that are desirable in the free, and at times even elite, populace. The first case, a passage of Scaevola, considers manumission for the honest completion of assigned work, similar to the cases discussed in chapter 3. The subsequent cases (Paul and Marcian) look at unplanned and extraordinary behavior that leads to a scenario in which a slave owner who was acquainted with Roman social *mores* might feel it was right, or was pressured, to manumit the slave, and thus seeks the approval of a *consilium*. A consideration of Roman honor and honorable behavior underlies the passages of Paul and Marcian; the final fragment, from the jurist Ulpian, examines explicitly the question of slaves in Roman honor culture.

In the first case, Scaevola complicates a typical formulation for fideicommissary freedom:

> "Let my slaves Stichus and Damas be free, if they render accounts"; the question was asked whether not only accounts but making good of anything removed by their design or fraud was due from them for them to attain their liberty; the reply was that there is inherent in the condition of rendering accounts everything in any way pertaining to the conduct and good faith of the slave.

27. The pragmatic benefits are made explicit in Sen. *Ep.* 47.4 where he contrasts slave owners who converse openly with their slaves, which leads to loyalty under judicial torture, and those that must be tight-lipped around their owners. I discuss this passage in chapter 1.

28. We see this practice of Roman acculturation in Columella's advice (at 1.8.5) to allow a foreman to invite other slaves to his table.

> 'Stichus et Damas servi mei, si rationes reddideritis, liberi estote;' quaesitum est, an non solum rationes, verum si qua alia consilio et fraude eorum amota sunt, praestari ab his debeant, ut ad libertatem perveniant. Respondit rationum reddendarum condicioni contineri omne, quod quoquo genere servi actum fidemque respiceret.[29]

Fideicommissary manumission was a direction in a will for the heir to manumit a slave, usually after the slave has completed a particular task (e.g., rendering accounts).[30] While this is not a kind of manumission that would require the approval of a *consilium*, there is an examination of the slaves' past behavior: Did they complete whatever was required before manumission? Scaevola's answer to this legal inquiry shows that "rendering accounts" (*rationes reddere*) is not enough as the act serves as a shorthand for the slave's entire behavior and character. *Fides*, or faithfulness, is an important financial concept in Roman society, and a slave who exhibited *fides* to his owner over financial matters was a slave ready to engage in the free Roman economy. It has even been stated that *fides* was "the key virtue of a freedman."[31] Whether the slave exhibited this faithfulness because of the hope of manumission or because they actually felt loyalty to their owner is beside the point. The slaves are not freed solely because of the money they have made or successfully managed for their owner, but for their accuracy and honesty, which is shown through their behavior. The conditional nature of the manumission highlights the importance of this—if Stichus and Damas have rendered the accounts in such a way that reveals positive action and faith on their part, they will be free. The demonstration of *fides* on the part of slaves shows that they understand not only economic relations in Rome, but social ones, as *fides* highlights the idea of loyalty and trust in both business relations and those between friends. The virtues displayed by these slaves are not simply virtues of a good slave, but of a good citizen.[32]

---

29. D. 40.5.41.11 Scaevola, *Responses*, book 4.
30. For a longer discussion of fideicommissary manumission, see chapter 3.
31. Mouritsen 2011, 61. See also Morgan 2015, 51–55, on *fides* between owner and slave. On *fides* as the connection between two parties, the foundation of *amicitia* and the patron-client relationship, and on *fides* and legal warranty, see Hellegouarc'h 1963, 23–35.
32. The opposite could also work: the will of a centurion (D. 40.4.51.1 Papinian, *Responses*, book 14) asks that his slaves not be sold, but freed, if they deserved it. Papinian interprets who then deserves liberty from a negative: those who had not been removed from the office of their duty nor from the administration of the centurion's commercial business (*ab honore ministrandi vel administrandae rei negotio removit*) among other things. In his failure to show *fides*, the slave is removed from these esteemed positions. In the most literal sense, the slave has lost his *honor*, which will have social and potentially legal (status) ramifications.

Turning to manumissions *inter vivos*, which would require the approval of a *consilium*, the jurist Paul gives a list of past circumstances that are reasons enough to make manumission an honorable act.

> Past events can provide several grounds for manumission; thus, the slave may have aided the owner in battle, protected him against brigands, healed him in sickness, uncovered a plot. And it is a long business, should we wish to make a list, since many services can occur for which it is honorable to grant freedom by a formal decision; the person before whom the procedure takes place will have to evaluate them.
>
> Ex praeterito tempore plures causae esse possunt, veluti quod dominum in proelio adiuvaverit, contra latrones tuitus sit, quod aegrum sanaverit, quod insidias detexerit. et longum est, si exequi voluerimus, quia multa merita incidere possunt, quibus honestum sit libertatem cum decreto praestare: quas aestimare debebit is, apud quem de ea re agatur.[33]

The examples that Paul lists are noteworthy. While there is evidence that slaves did fight in the army, the law and rhetoric of the Romans were such that they expressly forbade slaves in the military.[34] Being a soldier was the prerogative of a free person. However, Paul is not referring to the standard service that a slave could offer an owner at camp, but specifies that the slave assisted in battle, performing some extraordinary feat—conduct considered out of the ordinary for an enslaved person. The slave who assists the owner in battle behaves as a soldier; in that moment he exhibits a basic level of bravery or *virtus*. A slave noticing their owner being robbed in the street could feign ignorance, be afraid, or even use the moment to their advantage for theft or flight. Keeping their owner safe from thieves reveals aspects of character; perhaps risking their life, the slave shows their honesty and loyalty, again a form of *fides*. Caring for their owner when they are ill could show their love and concern for their owner's life, which could be suggestive of the *affectio* and *familiaritas* that existed in some owner-slave relationships. As we saw earlier, Ulpian considered the affection between owner and slave a just reason for exceptional manumission, and Seneca urges owners to forgive any shortcomings on the part of the slave because

33. D. 40.2.15.1 Paul, *lex Aelia Sentia*, book 1. See also D. 40.8.5 Marcian, *Rules*, book 5, on manumission as a reward for determining who murdered their owner.
34. On slaves in war, see Lenski 2009; Welwei 1988; and Rouland 1977.

of this *familiaritas*.[35] The care of a sick owner could also suggest that the slave was a doctor.[36] And lastly, detecting plots can indicate intelligence, but perhaps more importantly, again the loyalty of the slave. A slave hearing in the marketplace of a plot against their owner could easily allow the information to go neglected or even offer to help. Detecting a plot to overthrow the new Republic was how, as Livy tells it, the first slave was given his freedom and Roman citizenship.[37] Valerius Maximus relates that he is inclined to comment on a slave's loyalty because of its rarity.[38]

Paul's list of examples is not just a collection of the virtues of a good slave, otherwise they would not be the exceptional reasons that allow an owner to free a slave and grant them citizenship. The language Paul uses is important: These actions make it honorable (*honestum*) to manumit the slave. Even if the slave is being calculating in their efforts to help their owner, the actions are enough. Through their criteria for manumission, Scaevola and Paul provide their conception of a good citizen. Following the reasons he gives for manumission, Paul elaborates on how to judge whether the actions of the slave merit (*aestimare*) manumission. First, the owner will have to evaluate his gratitude for the act versus the financial and personal value of the slave.[39] Then, the *consilium* that grants the formal decision to allow this exceptional manumission evaluates the slave with the concerns of society in mind. At this point, the question of financial worth drops away and the evaluation is one of the character and qualities that make up their person.

These manumissions show a confidence in the (former) slave as a citizen with all the rights and duties citizenship brings, but there were at times tensions when slaves became citizens. For example, in Seneca the Elder's *Controversiae* 7.6, a tyrant is said to have granted slaves the right of killing their male owners and raping their owner's female family members. When one slave refrains from killing his owner and raping his owner's daughter, the owner manumits him and then gives him his daughter to marry. The owner's son thinks his father is insane (*dementia, insanus*) for manumitting the slave and making him his sister's husband-to-be and so he sues his father.[40] The manumission of a slave

35. As cited above, D. 40.2.16pr Ulpian, *lex Aelia Sentia*, book 2 and Sen. *Ira* 3.24.2–3.
36. For slave doctors being manumitted, see D. 40.5.41.6 Scaevola, *Replies*, book 4.
37. Livy 2.5.9–10.
38. Val. Max. 6.8praef.
39. In the Empire, we have uses of *aestimare* for both monetary values and moral ones, for example, Tac. *Ann.* 1.17 and 1.73. See Habinek 1998, 45–59 (discussed in chapter 1).
40. Sen. *Controv.* 7.6pr.

behaving decently or honorably and the acceptance of him as a Roman citizen was not always easy or agreed upon. While it is the owner's prerogative to manumit their slave, they can experience such backlash, in particular if they are so ready to forget their former slave's status.

In the following case of exceptional manumission, a slave engages in a kind of generosity that is explicitly tied to free status, *liberalitas*. The jurist Marcian presents a cause for manumission that pertains to a slave's relationship with his owner's life and honor: "It is a rightful ground of manumission if a slave has freed his owner from the danger of death or dishonor" (*iusta causa manumissionis est, si periculo vitae infamiave dominum servus liberaverit*).[41] In describing a good reason for an exception to the rules of the *lex Aelia Sentia*, Marcian provides two scenarios, both governed by the verb *liberare* ("to free"); a slave that frees his owner from danger of death or from dishonor (*infamia*) creates a just reason for his manumission. The language choice is significant; the slave must liberate their owner. Both the saving of their owner's life and honor are beyond a slave's assigned tasks (*ministerium*); it cannot be part of the slave's job, let alone be expected, for a slave to free their owner from anything. Here we see that slaves were not manumitted for their *ministeria* done well, but for voluntary actions beyond the *ministerium*. The action of saving their owner's life or from *infamia* is an action that a slave does of their own free will.

In free Roman society, this kind of supererogatory act would be considered a *beneficium*. Cicero, for example, tells us giving a *beneficium* is something that is under a person's own power (*in nostra potestate*).[42] The manumission in the Marcian case is granted because the slave has done a service for his owner beyond what was called for in his *ministerium* and is rewarded for these actions with the *beneficium* of manumission.[43] However, in this situation, before the *beneficium* of liberation by the owner, it is the slave who is doing the first act of liberation. These actions of the slave that bring about the *beneficium* of manumission must be understood as *beneficia* in their own right.

Seneca argues that when a slave has finished their *ministerium* they have the

41. D. 40.2.9 Marcian, *Institutes*, book 13.
42. Cic. *Off.* 1.48.
43. Manumission is discussed as a *beneficium* both in legal and literary sources; see, for example, Tac. *Ann.* 13.26.4-5 and D. 1.1.4 Ulpian, *Institutes*, book 1.
See Sen. *Ep.* 81.6 on the relationship between *officia* and *beneficia* as well as Griffin 2013, 37, and Saller 1982, 17-20, on the uses of and interchange between *officium* and *beneficium*.

capacity to choose how they will spend their remaining time and what sort of character and qualities they will exhibit. The slave then has the choice to provide a *beneficium*. To give a *beneficium* is understood as an action of a free person, and to understand the practice of giving *beneficia* exhibits an understanding of Roman cultural practice. He reasons that a slave can be just (*iustus*), strong (*fortis*), magnanimous (*magni animi*), and have virtue (*virtus*); a slave can therefore give *beneficia* because *beneficia* are a part of virtue.[44] Seneca's argument for slaves being able to give *beneficia* is in two parts. The first is that not everything a slave does is a part of their *ministerium*, and when they go over and above that, the slave is performing a *beneficium*. The second related point is that the slave is only a slave in body; their mind is free (*mens quidem sui iuris*), and their will is not controlled by their owner and cannot be sold (*mancipio dari non potest*).[45] Seneca explains that the slave constructs the *beneficium* from the space where they are free from their owner and the restrictions of the law (*leges*).[46] His use of legal language (e.g., *sui iuris*, *mancipium*, *lex*) to create an internal freedom for slaves underscores his challenge to the legal construction of the slave as wholly owned and under the power of their owner. The mind is not affected in Seneca's antiessentialist view of slavery.

The idea of a slave giving a *beneficium* is interesting for a number of reasons. First, Seneca is questioning the general conception of the nature of *beneficia* and its tie to elite society by arguing that slaves can give *beneficia*. *Beneficia* are also important to our study because they come from someone's own volition (a *beneficium* cannot be forced, otherwise it is not a *beneficium*) and they play a central role in the Roman honor system. Giving *beneficia* can help one accrue honor and esteem among friends and society at large, whereas withholding *beneficia* can do the opposite.

In his list of owners receiving *beneficia* from their slaves, Seneca relates a story about two enslaved people who during the siege of Grumentum defected from the losing side in order to sneak back to their old mistress' house and rescue her while the victors, their new "allies," were pillaging. Seneca contrasts the virtuous behavior of these enslaved rescuers with the destruction of the victors.[47] The enslaved men protected their mistress with the greatest care while the Roman soldiers had taken leave of appropriate behavior until satisfied with

44. Sen. *Ben.* 3.18.2–4. On the question of whether slaves can give *beneficia*, see Giannella 2019.
45. Sen. *Ben.* 3.19–20.
46. Sen. *Ben.* 3.21.1.
47. Sen. *Ben.* 3.23.2.

their spoils. The enslaved rescuers then gave themselves back to their mistress as slaves once the danger was over (*dominam sibi ipsos dedisse*). The men were not seeking to challenge their status as slaves with their actions, and they willingly took up their enslavement again. Here Seneca shows how a slave can give their owner a *beneficium* without any challenge to their status; the *beneficium* does not exempt a slave from their *ministerium*. Nevertheless, the men are freed immediately: "She manumitted both of them at that very moment and she did not think it unworthy to get her life back from those over whom she once had the power of life and death" (*Manu misit utrumque e vestigio illa nec indignata est ab his se vitam accepisse, in quos vitae necisque potestatem habuisset*).[48] Seneca counters the question of whether an owner should be ashamed to have their slave save their life. He juxtaposes the saving of the mistress with the fact that she has the power of life and death over her slaves; however, here it is the enslaved who have this power in their choice to save her.

Seneca emphasizes that owners and other free people should not look down on receiving *beneficia* from slaves, suggesting that many people did. Seneca uses this story to propose that it is all the more noble and good to be saved by one's own slaves than just anyone because it indicates good will on the part of the slaves toward their owner, which is something to be esteemed. Following this tale, Seneca discusses the honor in *beneficium*: "Why should the status of a person diminish the gift rather than the gift itself elevating the status of the person?" (*Quare potius persona rem minuat, quam personam res ipsa cohonestet?*)[49] The act of giving a *beneficium* gives one honor;[50] this resonates with the idea in Paul's fragment that many actions make it honorable to manumit a slave. A similar sentiment is seen in the passage of the jurist Marcian: The *beneficium* of delivering an owner from the danger of death or *infamia* elevates a slave out of their enslavement. Seneca's conviction that slaves can perform *beneficia* parallels the jurists' reasoning that slaves are able to perform unexpected and—in the eyes of many Romans—un-slave-like acts that are worthy and even demanding of manumission. While the owner need not heed it, the honorable slave places moral pressure on the owner to manumit.

The verb *liberare* in the passage of Marcian performs two functions: freeing the owner from their danger of death or *infamia* and then freeing the slave

48. Sen. *Ben.* 3.23.3.
49. Sen. *Ben.* 3.28.1.
50. Hellegouarc'h 1963, 386, "l'*honos* est la conséquence et, plus précisément, la récompense de la *virtus*."

themself. In the action of liberation, the slave succeeds in the first step to their own liberty. From a Roman perspective, the slave in this moment ceases to behave like a slave and is instead behaving not only like a free person, but like a Roman. The slave has an active role in the pursuit of their own liberty as a slave who prevents the dishonor of the owner and has, in that moment, control over their owner's honor; conversely, they could choose not to act. We can understand then that these shifts in and around Roman honor culture begin in the mind of the slave. While it is easy to imagine scenarios where a slave saves an owner from the danger of death, *infamia* is very different. Both actions can show courage or bravery, worthy Roman virtues; however, while all humans are subject to mortality, *infamia* is not a part of the human condition, but the Roman one.

A slave who saves their owner from *infamia* shows themself to have an understanding of Roman social and legal relations. *Infamia* means 'dishonor' not only at a social level, but an *infamis* was a person who lost the ability, among other things, to go to court or run for office.[51] The idea of slaves affecting the honor of a free person allows us to examine how the Romans conceived of an unfree person understanding and participating both within and along the periphery of this critical aspect of their society. It also encourages us to entertain a related premise: Can slaves have honor at a societal level? Joseph Hellegouarc'h notes that *honor* is connected to action more so than related honor words such as *existimatio*, *fama*, and *laus*.[52] For example, *honor* is tied to public office in the sense that the honors one has are the duties one bears. This is important for the question of a slave's relationship to honor because it is from their actions that they might influence their owner's or their own honor. While *honor* does have many meanings and contexts, such as the differences between what is honorable for a Roman woman or a Roman man, here we are not considering honor among slaves (i.e., within the *familia*—a microcosmic form of honor),[53] but a slave engaging in free Roman (male) honor. Within this formu-

---

51. A. H. J. Greenidge, in his monograph on the subject, defined *infamia* (1894, 13): "Amongst the kinds of moral unfitness which produced disability in this given case, that known as the *infamia* holds the first place. . . . It is the subject of the special disqualifications based on an injury to reputation (*laesa existimatio*). The questions to which it gives rise are partly moral, partly juristic: since the institution itself depended on the theory that a moral taint involved a civic disability. It was this civic disability, conceived consciously as based on a moral imperfection, that was generally spoken of by the Romans as *infamia*." On *infamia*, see also Edwards 1993.
52. Hellegouarc'h 1963, 383–87.
53. In *Empire of Honour*, Jon Lendon (2005, 96–97) briefly discusses this microcosmic possibility of slaves who can be considered honorable. He focuses on the honor system of the *familia*; the slave foreman, for example, can have honor in relation to other slaves.

lation, a foreigner can be honorable, but only once he has understood what exactly the Roman parameters of honor entail.[54] The relationship between slaves and honor is doubly complicated because they are both within and outside of Roman society. They are not citizens and are often not even Latin-speaking; however, some slaves, in particular domestic slaves, and especially those born in the owner's house (*vernae*), are essentially Roman slaves and a significant part of the household unit. In order for a slave to behave honorably, they must understand and engage with Roman honor and the concepts that impacted honor, such as *iniuria* and *infamia*.[55]

Flipping the Marcian case on its head, Ulpian looks directly at the issue of dishonor and slaves. After a quotation of the Praetor's Edict on outrage (*iniuria*) against slaves, Ulpian's lengthy commentary provides us with a detailed consideration of this question.[56] Ulpian's commentary approaches outrage from two perspectives; the first is a consideration of how a slave might negatively affect the honor of a free person. Stemming from possible punishments for this attack on a free man's honor, a second scenario emerges: A slave can suffer outrage in their own name. These two perspectives demonstrate the different ways that slaves interact with and participate in honor culture beyond the honor of their owner.

The first part of the commentary is a relatively straightforward protection of an owner's right to sue against physical damage of his property. Ulpian provides the text of the edict, "The praetor says: 'Where a man shall be said to have thrashed another's slave contrary to sound morals or to have submitted him to torture without the owner's consent, I will give an action'" (Praetor ait: "*Qui servum alienum adversus bonos mores verberavisse deve eo iniussu domini quaestionem habuisse dicetur, in eum iudicium dabo*").[57] Ulpian then begins to parse the forms of outrage in a programmatic statement that lays the background for the legal ability of a slave to suffer an outrage in their own name. Ulpian's meditation on permissible and illicit forms of slave violence is revealing in that he considers both legal consequences and personal feeling:

54. Woolf 1998, 63, makes this point about *humanitas*.

55. It isn't my specific intention here to argue against Orlando Patterson's "constituent elements" of slavery (1982, 13, quoted in the introduction). While I have some reservations about his model, this would not be a good argument against it because the number of slaves that might occupy this position are infinitesimal. See also Brown 2009, 1233, on not conflating Patterson's social death with "a handy general definition of slavery."

56. On the tie of *iniuria* to honor, see Lendon 2005, 96 and Greenidge 1894, 26.

57. D. 47.10.15.34 Ulpian, *Edict*, book 77. Much of this discussion is adapted from Giannella 2023. See also Fusco 2010, 427–33, on the *persona servi* as developed here. Watson (1987a, 61) suggests that some more detail may be missing from the second half of the edict.

> If someone inflicts an outrage upon a slave in order to inflict it on his owner, in my view the owner can bring the action for outrage in his own right; but even if the beating was not directed to his owner, the outrage done to a slave himself should not be left unavenged by the praetor, especially if it occurred through thrashing or through torture; for it is obvious that a slave himself feels such things.
>
> Si quis sic fecit iniuriam servo, ut domino faceret, video dominum iniuriarum agere posse suo nomine: si vero non ad suggillationem domini id fecit, ipsi servo facta iniuria inulta a praetore relinqui non debuit, maxime si verberibus vel quaestione fieret: hanc enim et servum sentire palam est.[58]

The language he uses to describe the possible scenarios is important. In the first scenario, if a person commits an outrage upon a slave serious enough that it can be considered an outrage upon the owner, the slave's suffering is not legally important other than as a vehicle to their owner. With the outrage of the slave effectively erased, Ulpian suggests that the action should be in the owner's name rather than that of the slave.

Turning to offenses not directed at the owner, the potential outrages—described as a *suggillatio*, most literally a bruise—are physical, which is not surprising as the jurists tend to place the value of the slave on the body. The examples of physical abuse noted are significant as they are particularly servile; Ulpian here argues that the praetor should not leave the outrage unavenged especially, he emphasizes, if the violence is in the form of thrashing or being interrogated under torture. These acts of servitude perhaps are perceived by the Roman jurist as more shameful when they are not sanctioned by the owner or, perhaps because they are shameful, the slave should not have to endure them unless under the owner's sanction. On the most basic level of interpretation, a slave could be irreparably harmed by this violence and the owner should be able to seek damages, but on this somatic level there are other laws, namely the *lex Aquilia*, that deal directly with wrongful loss of property.[59] Ulpian notes that the praetor should investigate these offenses because clearly the slave would be affected (*sentire*) by them. As we will see below, the first part of Ulpian's argument will culminate in an exploration of what sort of juridical weight *sentire* carries with outrages of physical violence. We must be careful not to ascribe too

58. D. 47.10.15.35 Ulpian, *Edict*, book 77.
59. On the *lex Aquilia*, see Zimmermann 1996, 902–1049.

many humanitarian consequences to this argument, because while it does recognize the real affective significance of outrage for a slave, this recognition is always in the service of and for the financial recompense of the owner.

Ulpian then considers the meaning of the phrase "contrary to sound morals" (*adversus bonos mores*) and its deployment in the justification of violence against another person's slave.[60] It is important to note, however, that there were in Ulpian's understanding some kinds of physical violence against another person's slave that were considered morally sound: The paternalistic correcting or chastising of a slave and punishment, even if they lead to physical and psychological harm, were both permitted. In order to illustrate particular circumstances under which a person can lawfully beat another person's slave, Ulpian turns to an example provided by the Augustan jurist Labeo: A slave committed an outrageous act against a magistrate "if he made a brazen attempt on the magistrate's office and insignia" (*nam si honorem ornamentaque petulanter adtemptantem ceciderit*).[61] In this instance, the beating of the slave is not with the intention of outrage but for the correction of such an act. In the eyes of the jurist this surely deserves correction and is thus antithetical to the charge of outrage.

In addition, the original victim in the scenario is a municipal magistrate (*magistratus municipalis*), a government official in a province rather than an ordinary citizen, and the attack is directed specifically at his office and adornments of office. There probably isn't a way for a slave to attack a magistrate without it being *petulanter*, or in an insolent manner, so its inclusion in Ulpian's (or Labeo's) passage may rather emphasize the scandalous nature of this attack. The outrage committed by the slave is seemingly overdetermined at this point; the attack is directly on government administration (the magistrate's office), the slave as actor of outrage is behaving beyond their station, and the wronged magistrate is likely a man of some repute, thus the status differential between the perpetrator and the victim is great and in the wrong direction.[62] The language used to raise the question of when it is acceptable for a municipal magistrate to beat another person's slave is not *verberare*, which primarily means to thrash and can also mean to beat or strike more generally, but rather the more

60. D. 47.10.15.38 Ulpian, *Edict*, book 77.
61. D. 47.10.15.39 Ulpian, *Edict*, book 77.
62. Gaius notes that one reason an outrage is deemed aggravated (*atrox iniuria*) is because of the person it is done to, such as if done to a magistrate (*magistratus*) or a senator by a low person (*senatori ab humili persona*). The other reasons are the severity of the deed itself or the public location of the attack, see G. 3.225.

vivid *loris rumperit*—the magistrate has literally broken the slave with a whip.[63] Perhaps this level of outrage on the part of the slave is necessary to justify the punishment as being according to good morals. We might wonder, for example, if the punishment would still be justified if the slave had physically attacked the magistrate but made no attempt on his office. In any event, the slave has an effect on a freeman's honor but they are not freeing their owner from dishonor, as in the Marcian case. Here, the extreme level of outrage perpetrated by the slave cancels out any potential outrage of the slave being beaten without their owner's permission and there is no consideration of whether a slave feels their punishment.

Ulpian is careful to delineate the parameters of *verberare* ("thrashing") and *quaestio* ("torture") before noting that according to Labeo, if the person torturing the slave is excessive (*modum tamen excesserit*), the owner will have an action even if they initially gave their permission.[64] The reasoning why this turn from sanctioned to unsanctioned violence leads to an action on outrage is worth considering. If the concern here was about the physical damage to the slave, an action under the *lex Aquilia* would apply.[65] An action on outrage may be granted because of the excesses of the interrogator; a person acting beyond their station or right is a hallmark of outrageous action. It's possible that the owner is perhaps disrespected, but this depends on whether this excess was done with the intention of outraging him, and there is no indication of this in the text. We are left instead with Ulpian's earlier explanation that a slave acutely felt (*sentire*) thrashing and torture. For *sentire* to make any sense here we must understand its meaning to go beyond the physical, as a slave would physically feel sanctioned violence just as well as unsanctioned violence, and physical feeling is not particular to torture or thrashing. We should instead consider that the slave would feel this particular form of extra violence on a psychic and affective level, and for this reason the action on outrage is granted. Notably, there is no discussion, as we will see in the second part of Ulpian's interpreta-

63. *Rumpere* is one of the categories of the *lex Aquilia* on wrongful loss of property, see D. 9.2.27.5 Ulpian, *Edict*, book 18.

64. D. 47.10.15.40–42 Ulpian, *Edict*, book 77. Ulpian includes punching in his framework whereas Gaius (G. 3.222) does not.

65. See a comparable case (D. 9.2.5.3 Ulpian, *Edict*, book 18) on a schoolmaster using excessive violence in the correction of a slave student, and where, notably, Ulpian cites a case proposed by Julian in which a shoemaker beats his student apprentice (a free boy) too much and the boy loses an eye. Julian holds that there is no action on outrage because "he struck him not with the intent to outrage, but in order to correct and teach him" (*quia non faciendae iniuriae causa percusserit, sed monendi et docendi causa*).

tion, about what kind of slave the action applies to. All slaves experience the shame of this form of violence. While in this scenario slaves as a category are treated collectively, there are suggestive markers of possible hierarchies when we move beyond violent manifestations of shame alone.

This leads directly to Ulpian requoting the second part of the Praetor's Edict: "If anything else has been done, I will, having looked into the matter, grant an action" (*Si quid aliud factum esse dicetur, causa cognita iudicium dabo*).[66] Ulpian then elaborates:

> Thus, the praetor does not promise an action for every outrage in the name of the slave; if the slave be lightly struck or mildly abused, the praetor will not give an action: but if he be defamed by some act or lampoon, I think that the praetor's investigation into the matter should take into account the standing of the slave; for it is highly relevant what sort of slave he is, whether he be honest, an overseer, or a steward, or only a common slave, a menial laborer, or whatever. And what if he be in fetters, or known to be of bad character, or branded? The praetor, therefore, will take into account both the alleged outrage and the person of the slave said to have suffered it and will grant or refuse the action accordingly.
>
> Itaque praetor non ex omni causa iniuriarum iudicium servi nomine promittit: nam si leviter percussus sit vel maledictum ei leviter, non dabit actionem: at si infamatus sit vel facto aliquo vel carmine scripto puto causae cognitionem praetoris porrigendam et ad servi qualitatem: etenim multum interest, qualis servus sit, bonae frugi, ordinarius, dispensator, an vero vulgaris vel mediastinus an qualisqualis. et quid si compeditus vel male notus vel notae extremae? habebit igitur praetor rationem tam iniuriae, quae admissa dicitur, quam personae servi, in quem admissa dicitur, et sic aut permittet aut denegabit actionem.[67]

As these offenses are not directed at the owner, it is not any minor outrage but only a severe one that can be brought in the name of the slave (*servi nomine*). Notably in Ulpian's commentary on this part of the edict, the descriptive language of violence that is largely particular to slaves falls away, and instead the potential outrages shift to a deed or slander that might defame (*infamatus*) the

66. First quoted by Ulpian at D. 47.10.34 and then again in section 43 of the same fragment.
67. D. 47.10.15.44 Ulpian, *Edict*, book 77.

slave. Ulpian introduces the question of reputability, weighing the outrage against the character and position of work that the slave has rather than the specific type of violence. Outrages *servi nomine* are evaluated not solely by the act but by the character or sphere of activity of the slave.

Ulpian considers the character and status of the slave as "the nature of the slave" (*qualitas servi*), in the interrogative "what sort of slave" (*qualis servus*), and as the "person of the slave" (*persona servi*). These classifications of the slave speak to both their occupation and moral character. The attention that Ulpian draws to the *ordinarius*, a type of overseer slave in charge of a *peculium*, and a *dispensator*, a steward in charge of finances, highlights the economic importance of not allowing certain slaves to suffer outrages. A *mediastinus*, *vulgaris*, or *qualisqualis* slave, meaning a common slave, menial laborer slave, or regular sort of slave, respectively, has less to lose in the jurist's eyes. By distinguishing slaves by their title or lack thereof, Ulpian measures the slave's reputability in direct relationship with their position in the owner's house.

In terms of character, Ulpian distinguishes the *bonae frugi* slave, an honest and productive slave, against the fettered (*compeditus*), ill-reputed (*mala notus*), or branded (*notae extremae*) slave. The jurist has drawn three levels of slave quality: the good slave (*ordinarius*, *dispensator*, *bonae frugi*), the average slave (*mediastinus*, *vulgaris*, *qualisqualis*), and the bad slave (*compeditus*, *mala notus*, *notae extremae*).[68] Ulpian advises that the praetor should allow for these levels of quality and character to be factored in when determining if a slave has lost position and been disgraced by the actions or mockery of another. These titles and descriptors are ones that are imposed on slaves and usually important to the inner workings of a Roman house; here, instead, they are now being taken into account in a court of law.

These slaves, who have a reputation to lose, or in other words have some degree of honor, are not slaves who just have a good name within their owner's house. An *ordinarius* or *dispensator* shamed or maligned by mockery may not be able to carry out their duties effectively. We might think too of the kind of slaves whom free people tried to curry favor with; anecdotes documenting an anxiety about free people who attempt to get on the good side of powerful slaves are found throughout the literature of the imperial period. For example, Seneca, in his letter on owners and slaves, urges his fellow citizens to live on

68. Elsewhere Ulpian notes that slaves ought to be given the proper amount of food according to their rank and position (*ordo et dignitas*), D. 7.1.15.2 Ulpian, *Sabinus*, book 18.

kindly terms with their slaves, and notes that the people who are too embarrassed or disgusted to dine and associate with their own slaves "are the very same ones I catch kissing the hands of other people's slaves" (*Hos ego eosdem deprehendam alienorum servorum osculantes manum*).[69] He is mocking these people, calling them *delicati*, which can mean pleasure seekers, but it is also a term used in inscriptions to mean a favorite slave, in particular a young sex slave.[70] Despite Seneca's scorn, these sorts of anecdotes suggest that we do have some instances of slaves of reputation in Roman society even if that society, according to the author, is morally bankrupt.

The jurist Marcian's assertion then that a slave can affect *infamia*, a concept clearly woven into Roman private and public life, is revealing: An owner had to place his trust in both his slave's character and their understanding of honor and dishonor. How is a slave to know what constitutes an injury to reputation? *Infamia*, in the sense of being deprived of one's civic positions, affects not just the social reputation of a man, but his very status in society. A slave must be familiar with what will cause *infamia* and be able to navigate through the workings of Roman society to attempt to stop it and ensure that their owner remains honorable. Marcian's description of the slave protecting his owner's honor shows a slave who controls an aspect of their owner's honor and dishonor. A slave, like women and sons, can certainly negatively affect their owner's honor by their own choices and behavior. Slaves can bring honor to their owners; even in the most conservative estimation and inactive sense, a slave can bring honor to their owner simply by being alongside them, let alone being a well-behaved or life-saving slave.[71] The slaves discussed in these cases of extraordinary manumission are freed because of virtuous actions that originate in the mind and character of the slave, outside the scope of their assigned duties to the owner. Like the slave who saved their owner from thieves and proved themself brave, or the one who cared for their owner when they were sick and proved their affection and loyalty, the slave who understood the stakes of honor in Rome and acted to protect their owner from dishonor not only exhibits behavior worthy of manumission but also exhibits themself as having the necessary qualities and understandings of a good Roman citizen.

---

69. Sen. *Ep.* 47.14.
70. On *delicati*, see Fitzgerald 2000, 47–54.
71. Fitzgerald 2000, 5, provides the anecdote of Petronius' Eumolpus, who, after an imagined shipwreck, concerns himself not with the loss of his property, but that unattended he is unable to recognize his own dignity (Petron. *Sat.* 117).

Close Saves: Vicious Masters

In a text on restrictions to testamentary manumission, Marcian notes that a slave who uses violence to terrify their owner into freeing them will not be freed.[72] The slave here presents behavior antithetical to the virtues desired in a Roman citizen and belies understanding—or care of understanding—about a slave's relative place in a Roman household. The case though is suggestive of something else too: This owner does not have control of their slaves. To be compelled by force (*vi coegerit*) and thoroughly terrified (*perterritus*) are attributes that are right, in the Roman understanding, for the mind of the slave and not the owner. The representation here is the inverse of the idealized owner-slave relationship: the slave compels, the owner acts. Fear of slaves was a constant topic in Roman literature; the reality was, of course, that many owners, in being terrified or savage, fell short of the ideal. My interest here is not to psychoanalyze or exculpate the long-dead slave owners, but instead to point out how these failures of character at times led to the loss of the slave, usually through state action. The sheer quantity of slaves in Rome was a cause of anxiety,[73] and Columella, writing about agricultural slavery, describes conditions for enslaved people who were chained in the farm prison (*ergastulum*) and notes that they should not be wanting in clothes or other necessities because "when harmed by cruelty and greed, they are to be feared more" (*saevitia atque avaritia laesi magis timendi sunt*).[74]

Authors like Gellius, Galen, and Seneca tell tales of elite, educated slave owners losing their cool, overstepping, or otherwise performing slaving wrongly. The commentary here is largely one of breaking philosophical and social *mores*; owners ought to punish a slave only while they are in a rational and not emotional state of mind.[75] There were particular instances, however,

---

72. D. 40.9.9pr Marcian, *Institutes*, book 1, "A man will not be free who has used violence to compel his owner to manumit him, even if under terror he has given him freedom in his will" (*Ille servus liber non erit, qui vi coegerit, ut eum dominus manumittat, et ille perterritus scripsit liberum eum esse*). This text of Marcian (Lenel fr. 53) seems to pick up from a fragment (Lenel fr. 52, D. 40.4.23) that pertains to testamentary issues that might affect manumission. In a similar case (D. 40.9.17pr Paul, *On Liberty*, sole book), Paul notes that Marcus Aurelius nullified manumissions that were done at the compulsion of the people (*populus*).

73. Sen. *Clem.* 1.24.1, "A motion was once made in the Senate to distinguish slaves from free people by their clothing; but then it was discovered how dangerous it might be if our slaves began to count us" (*Dicta est aliquando a senatu sententia, ut servos a liberis cultus distingueret; deinde adparuit, quantum periculum immineret, si servi nostri numerare nos coepissent*).

74. Columella *Rust.* 1.8.17–18.

75. Gellius (*NA* 1.26) relates the story of Plutarch remaining calm while arguing philosophical points

where the behavior of the owner was so egregious that the state intervened. Despite owners' dramatically titled power of life and death, over time during the Empire, there were some restrictions on what an owner could do with their slave—though enforcement of such infringements on an owner's right would have surely been uneven. The state would intervene, for example, when a slave sought refuge at the statue of the emperor. A magistrate would then investigate, and if the behavior of the owner was found to be unacceptable, the magistrate could force a sale.[76] This was not an exit from slavery for the enslaved person, but from enslavement to this particular individual, and one that came at presumably great cost: There was no guarantee that their future would be an improvement, and sale meant possibly leaving behind family and friends. The situation the enslaved person found themself in which would drive them to instigate this change (and for the magistrate to agree) must have been far beyond the typically dismal and undignified conditions enslaved people faced every day. The owner in this case is compensated for their loss of a slave as it is a sale, but presumably whatever the owner had done to the slave would lower the sale price.

An anecdote from Seneca about Vedius Pollio serves as an apparent early instantiation of seeking refuge at the statute of the emperor. Augustus was dining at the house of Vedius Pollio (whom Dio Cassius pejoratively notes was an equestrian and a son of a freedman) when an enslaved server broke a crystal cup. Pollio ordered the server to be put to death by being thrown into a pool with giant eels. The enslaved server, possibly a youth, broke free from those holding him, ran to Augustus, and begged at his feet that he be given an alternate means of death than being eaten. Here the living emperor embodies the place of refuge. Augustus, so disturbed by Pollio's method of punishment, which Seneca describes as coming more from rage (*saevitia*) than excess (*luxuria*—already a bad quality), does not force a sale but orders that all of Pollio's crystal glasses be destroyed, his fish pond filled up, and the enslaved server released (*mitti*). We might understand *mitti* here to mean the server was freed,

with an enslaved man he is having beaten for some misdeed; Galen (*De an. aff. dign. et cur.* 4; Kühn vol. 5 17–18) notes many instances of slave owners losing their temper, including the infamous story of Hadrian striking one of his enslaved workers with a stylus, leading to the loss of the eye (and Hadrian's later guilt at his actions); Seneca *De Ira* 3.40.1–3 I will discuss immediately below.

76. The penalties were severe for a person who persuaded a slave to go to the statue of the emperor to make his owner seem disreputable; the owner could bring a charge under the *actio servi corrupti* (see chapter 4) as well, as it seems, criminal charges, see D. 47.11.5 Ulpian, *Duties of Proconsul*, book 5.

but the other retellings of the case do not mention a release from slavery.[77] Around this time, however, we begin to find evidence of jurists considering such flights to seek refuge at the statue of the emperor in discussions of what constitutes a runaway slave (they do not).[78]

Later emperors also at times took matters into their own hands. For example, Ulpian reports that the Emperor Hadrian relegated (i.e., banished) a married woman (*matrona*), Umbricia, for five years because she treated her enslaved women (*ancillas*) in an exceptionally terrible way (*atrocissime*) for the most trifling reasons (*levissimis causis*). This anecdote is relayed following the jurist's quotation of a rescript of the Emperor Antoninus Pius, which outlined to the governor of Baetica the proper procedure to follow after the enslaved people from the house of one Julius Sabinus sought refuge at the statue of the emperor. He counsels a sale if the conditions are found to be harsher than is fair or if they had to endure excessively humiliating offenses (*et si vel durius habitos quam aequum est vel infami iniuria affectos cognoveris*). Notably, though, the emperor explains why:

> The powers of owners over their slaves certainly ought not to be infringed and there must be no derogation from any person's legal rights. But it is in the interest of owners that those who make just complaint be not denied relief against brutality or starvation or intolerable wrongdoing.
>
> Dominorum quidem potestatem in suos servos illibatam esse oportet nec cuiquam hominum ius suum detrahi: sed dominorum interest, ne auxilium contra saevitiam vel famem vel intolerabilem iniuriam denegetur his qui iuste deprecantur.[79]

Pius makes it clear that the state, or at least his version of it, does not take intervention upon one's property rights lightly, but will do so when the behavior of

77. Seneca recounts the tale of Vedius Pollio earliest and in most detail in *De Ira* 3.40.1–3, but alludes to the story again in *De Clementia* 1.18.2. The story is also mentioned, but in less detail and at times with differing emphases, by Ovid (*Fast.* 6.639–648), Pliny the Elder (*HN* 9.39), Tertullian (*Pall.* 5.6.1–2), and Dio (54.23). I thank Zachary Herz for many insightful conversations about this anecdote; see Herz (2025, 55–63) for the role of this story in the wider history of legal change under the emperors. See also Watson 1987a, 117–29, on protections for slaves from their owners.

78. Seeking refuge at the statue of the emperor in contrast to running away is discussed in chapter 2.

79. D. 1.6.2 Ulpian, *Duties of Proconsul*, book 8. The governor of Baetica is Aelius Marcianus, not to be confused with the later jurist of the same name. See Tuori 2016, 210–12; Liebs 2012, 139–54. Pius also condemns killing a slave without a reason; see G. 1.53 and I. 1.8.2.

one owner has the potential to affect all owners (presumably through violence). Regarding a different form of delinquency on the part of the slave owner, the Emperor Claudius went even further: Slave owners who abandoned their sick slaves would lose their rights over them at least during the remaining life of the slave.[80] Even this passive form of bad slave management was considered enough of a failure that if the slaves recovered from their illness, they were automatically freed. These slave owners lose their property, the abused enslaved individuals, because the owners themselves do not behave as they should. The bad behavior of the owner inserts the state into the owner-slave relationship; the deficient character of the owner is starkly contrasted with the slave who must act as an intermediary of sorts between the owner and the state.

Identity and Status

The cases and situations exhibited in this chapter have emphasized particular qualities or characteristics (such as *fides*, *virtus*, *liberalitas*—the giving of *beneficia*, or *honor*) of which the jurists desired proof before manumission was granted. All of these qualities were a part of and originated within free Roman society. There was no guarantee when purchasing a slave that they would have *fides* or participate in honor culture. The slave who chose to adopt these Roman virtues and display them enhanced the likelihood of their manumission through this performance of citizen virtues. Ulpian relates a case of fideicommissary manumission where a man who was a slave of enemies of the state (*servus hostium*) was meant to be freed. There is a debate whether the slave was unworthy (*indignus*) of Roman citizenship, but Ulpian argues that if the slave has "begun to be one of ours" (*noster esse incipit*) the manumission stands.[81] The manumission is contingent upon the slave becoming Roman (*noster*); the virtues of Roman citizenship could be taught and adopted.

Enslaved people in the Roman world were considered human property and assigned the status of slave under Roman law. This book has attempted to explore the immense diversity and fluidity that existed within slave status, with the cur-

80. While this edict of Claudius is mentioned in several sources (Suet. *Claud.* 25.2; Dio 61.29; and D. 40.8.2 Modestinus, *Rules*, book 6), only the treatment in the *Codex* (7.6.3–3a) which goes into the most detail, specifies that the recovered slave becomes a Junian Latin. Suetonius also mentions that if a slave owner kills their sick slave instead of treating them, they would be charged with murder. On Claudius' edict, see Major 1994.

81. D. 40.5.24.2 Ulpian, *Fideicommissary Manumission*, book 5.

rent chapter examining a space beyond the trappings of legal status in which a slave could choose how to act. This chapter closes by stepping back from particular cases of extraordinary manumission to consider the flexibility of identity that the mind facilitates and its relation to the seemingly static nature of legal status. The attention to the behavior of a person as an indicator of legal status becomes apparent in texts that debate whether someone is a free person or a slave, such as Dio Chyrsostom's Fifteenth Discourse and the juristic literature on the suits for freedom (D. 40.12). Dio's Fifteenth Discourse considers this question when one speaker accuses his interlocutor of being a slave.[82] The accused then asks how the other man can know who is a slave and who is free.[83] Dio, who wrote the discourse during or after his exile imposed by the Emperor Domitian, sets the debate in two parts before an audience at the home of one of the speakers.[84] The first part has the accuser provide different methods of determining status and the accused parrying each one. The second part moves on more generally to consider who is a slave. The conclusion in the end is a very internal sort of slavery that hinges upon having a slave's nature rather than a free person's. My interest in this debate is not based on the conclusion, which strays from legal status of free and slave, but with the path to this conclusion, which addresses a number of particularly Roman facets of the institution of slavery, especially given that the two men are meant to be Athenians. The text contains some specific allusions to both Athenian and Roman institutions and laws.[85]

The first attempt by the accuser to show that the accused is a slave is made along the lines of kinship: The accused's father was a slave. The accused counters that it is impossible to know people's lineage back along the generations, and as such, slavery by birth is not a good determinant of status.[86] The accused then asks what he does or endures to make the accuser so confident that the

82. On Dio generally: Swain 2000 and 1996, 187–241; Harris 1991; and von Armin 1898. On Dio and slavery: Gallinari 1978; Cretia 1961. On Dio and philosophy: Berry 1983; Brunt 1973.

83. Dio Chrys. *Or.* 15.2.

84. Dio Chrys. *Or.* 15.1 notes that the debate on slavery and freedom does not take place where one would expect—at the marketplace or in court, but at home (οὐκ ἐπὶ δικαστῶν οὐδ' ἐν τῇ ἀγορᾷ, οὑτωσὶ δὲ κατ' οἰκίαν).

85. Dio. Chrys. *Or.* 15.3 mentions both the father of the accuser as an Athenian and a member of the Cynosarges. The Roman institutions will be discussed below.

86. Dio Chrys. *Or.* 15.3–18. At 15.3 on people being ignorant (ἀγνοέω) or knowing (ἐπίσταμαι) the status of their sexual partners, "'Have not many women who are citizens, embarrassed by the scarcity of eligible men, been got with child either by foreigners or by slaves, sometimes not knowing the fact, but sometimes also with full knowledge of it?'" ('ἢ οὐ πολλαὶ ἀσταὶ γυναῖκες δι' ἐρημίαν τε καὶ ἀπορίαν αἱ μὲν ἐκ ξένων ἐκύησαν, αἱ δὲ ἐκ δούλων, τινὲς μὲν ἀγνοοῦσαι τοῦτο, τινὲς δὲ καὶ ἐπιστάμεναι;'). Translations of Dio from Cohoon with modifications.

accused is a slave. The question ties status to knowledge and to the particular actions of a person, that is, to a performance of slavehood:

> A. By the gods, what do you know that I have done or that has been done to me, which justifies your saying that you know that I am in a state of slavery?
> B. I know that you are being kept by your owner, attend him, and do whatever he commands or else you take a beating.
> A. By that reasoning, you can make out that sons also are the slaves of their fathers; for they attend their fathers, often, if they are poor, walking with them to the gymnasium or to dinner; and they without exception are supported by their fathers and frequently are beaten by them, and they obey any orders their fathers give them.

> A. τί δὲ καὶ ποιοῦντά με ἐπίστασαι πρὸς θεῶν ἢ τί πάσχοντα, ὅτι με φῄς ἐπίστασθαι δουλεύοντα;
> B. Τρεφόμενον ἔγωγε ὑπὸ τοῦ δεσπότου καὶ ἀκολουθοῦντα ἐκείνῳ καὶ ποιοῦντα ὅ τι ποτ᾽ ἐκεῖνος προστάττοι· εἰ δὲ μή, παιόμενον.
> A. Οὕτως μέν, ἔφη, καὶ τοὺς υἱοὺς ἀποφαίνεις δούλους τῶν πατέρων. καὶ γὰρ ἀκολουθοῦσι πολλοῖς τῶν πενήτων καὶ εἰς γυμνάσιον βαδίζουσι καὶ ἐπὶ δεῖπνον, καὶ τρέφονται πάντες ὑπὸ τῶν πατέρων καὶ παίονται πολλάκις ὑπ᾽ αὐτῶν, καὶ πείθονται ὅ τι ἂν ἐκεῖνοι προστάττωσιν αὐτοῖς.[87]

The language of the first part of the passage emphasizes the idea that one can know (*epistamai*), or gain the skill of recognizing, a slave by their actions. The determinants of status (if someone is free or slave) have moved from blood to behavior, as it is the actions that the would-be slave performs for his owner that cement in the mind of the accuser their certain slavehood. The accused counters this by asserting that sons often behave much in the same way to their fathers. The examples turn from the general tasks of a slave to the specific discussion of a father's power over the life of his son. Both Roman jurists and modern scholars have noted that there is little legal distinction between owner and slave and *paterfamilias* and son.[88] It is not my intention to dwell upon this

87. Dio Chrys. *Or.* 15.18.
88. See, for example, Jolowicz and Nicholas 1972, 118–20, 238–39, 471, at 118, "The complete power of the Roman father over his children has become proverbial, and the Romans knew that it was an institution particular to themselves." See also G. 1.55.

other than to point out that it is a particularly Roman phenomenon, and that Dio refers to it a number of times.[89] While the accused is a literary construction, he is cast as a "cunning" type, exploiting the well-known lack of distinction between son and slave to dispute his status.[90] In the speaker's difficulty with properly reading the performance of status, Dio is mirroring the issues that Roman jurists face when discussing suits for freedom.

The suit for freedom (*causa liberalis*) is a trial that takes place when someone contests their own legal status (free, slave) or that of another person.[91] There were two types of suits for freedom: an enslaved person could claim they were actually free (a "from slavery to liberty" proceeding—*ex servitute in libertatem*), or another person could claim that someone in a state of liberty was actually a slave (a "from liberty to slavery" proceeding—*ex libertate in servitutem*). The type of proceeding mattered a great deal as the burden of proof was always on the claimant and as such inspired hearty discussion among the jurists.[92] The jurists determined this proceeding by whether the person whose status was in question was "in a state of liberty without fraud" (*sine dolo malo in libertate fuisse*). Ulpian explains how this was assessed:

> Our expression "in a state of liberty" should be taken to mean not that the man subject to a trial for freedom is to show that he is a freeman, but that he was in a state of liberty without fraud. But let us consider what "without fraud" means: for Julian says that all who think themselves freemen have been in a state of liberty without fraud, provided that they behave as freemen, although they could be slaves. But Varus writes that a man who knows himself to be a freeman, while he is in flight, is not regarded to be in a state of liberty without fraud. But once he has ceased to hide as if a fugitive, and now behaves like a freeman, he begins from that moment to be in a state of liberty without fraud. In fact, he says that the man who knows himself to be a freeman but behaves as a fugitive is behaving as a slave because he is in flight. It should then be known that a freeman can be in a state of liberty fraudulently and a slave can be in a state of liberty without fraud.

89. See explicitly, Dio Chrys. *Or.* 15.20.
90. On "trickster slaves" (with reference to Plautus and Aesop), see Stewart 2012, 172–89 and Hopkins 1993; and while the relationship between the accuser and the accused is unclear, see Richlin 2017, 476–77, on using Eugene Genovese and James C. Scott to interpret slaves laughing at their owners.
91. On the *causa liberalis* generally, see Sciortino 2010; Herrmann-Otto 1999; Franciosi 1961; Nicolau 1933; Buckland 1908, 652–75. An *adsertor libertatis* would represent the enslaved person as a slave did not have the ability to bring a suit, see Buckland 1908, 655.
92. See discussion of being "in possession of liberty" and suits for freedom in Lenski 2012.

> Quod autem diximus "in libertate fuisse" sic est accipiendum non ut se liberum doceat is, qui liberale iudicium patitur, sed in possessione libertatis sine dolo malo fuisse. Quid sit autem "sine dolo malo fuisse," videamus. Nam Iulianus ait omnes, qui se liberos putant, sine dolo malo in libertate fuisse, si modo se pro liberis gerant, quamvis servi sint. Varus autem scribit eum, qui se liberum sciat, dum in fuga sit, non videri sine dolo malo in libertate esse: sed simul atque desierit quasi fugitivus se celare et pro libero agere, tunc incipere sine dolo malo in libertate esse: etenim ait eum, qui scit se liberum, deinde pro fugitivo agit, hoc ipso, quod in fuga sit, pro servo agere. Igitur sciendum est et liberum posse dolo malo in libertate esse et servum posse sine dolo malo in libertate esse.[93]

Ulpian cites two earlier jurists in his discussion of suits for freedom. Julian, working at the end of Dio's time, and Alfenus Varus, a jurist of the first century BCE, roughly agree that the crux of showing that one is in a state of liberty is to behave as a free person and to do so without fraud. The objective status (*liber, servus*) was not what was at stake in the determination of whether someone was in a state of liberty (*in libertate esse*).

For Julian someone is in a state of liberty if they think (*putare*) they are free and behave (*se pro libero gerere*) as such.[94] The intention of the person is revealed by their action; there is no certainty in Julian's idea of state.[95] And while in contrast Alfenus Varus speaks about someone certain (*scire*) of their status, the jurists' determination of whether someone is in a state of liberty rests again on behavior: A free person in flight (*in fuga*) appears to be in a state of liberty fraudulently until they stop behaving like a runaway (*pro fugitivo agere*) or a slave (*pro servo agere*). The sixth-century CE compilers of the *Digest of Justinian* broke up this fragment of Ulpian with a text from Gaius, a near contemporary of Dio (and Julian). In a chapter on suits for freedom in his commentary on the edict, Gaius disagrees with the other jurists that a freeman could not behave like a freeman in flight, but nevertheless he is still in a state of liberty fraudu-

93. D. 40.12.10, 12 Ulpian, *Edict*, book 55 (Lenel fr. 1296). This fragment is interrupted by the *Digest* compilers with a text from Gaius. While the passage of Ulpian is considered genuine (see Sciortino 2010, 217n550; more generally on this passage, see 217–22), the phrase *in possessione libertatis* is most likely a later gloss (see Moatti 2016, 543, 543n83). I discuss this text at length in Giannella 2020.

94. Immediately following the text of Ulpian quoted above (D. 47.10.15.34–44) about whether slaves can suffer *iniuria* in their own name, Ulpian cites the jurist Mela who holds that the owner of a slave behaving like a free person (*pro libero se gerere*) cannot suffer *iniuria* from a violent attack on the slave, D. 47.10.15.4 Ulpian, *Edict*, book 77. On the use of *pro* in legal fictions and questions of status, see Ando 2015.

95. See Moatti 2016, 532, 546–47, on intention (*voluntas*) being explicitly tied to action and see especially 549 and 558 on the importance of performativity as a method of reading status.

lently.[96] Both Julian and Gaius have a somewhat softer view than Varus' hard line. This shift is possibly related to the principle of "favoring liberty" (*favor libertatis*), which came to prominence in the second century CE and urged that when status was unable to be determined (or manumission was voided because of a procedural issue), the ruling should lean toward freedom.[97]

These passages reveal the importance of behavior or performance as a means of understanding whether someone is in a state of slavery or freedom. The question of a person's freedom lies in the realm of the mind and their behavior shows their belief in their status as a free person. This is contrasted with a person who knows that they are a slave but is behaving like a free person in bad faith. Certain markers, like running away, are particularly revelatory as they seem to be for the jurists an essential component of slave status and antithetical to free status. The matter first circles around the issue of whether the person in question bears themself or acts like a slave, just as Dio's accuser explains that he knows his interlocutor is a slave because he is "kept by his owner, attends him, and does whatever he commands, or risks being beaten."

The earlier passage from Dio underscores the uncertainty of judging status by actions because of the difficulty in distinguishing between the power of an owner over his slave and that of a father over his son. However, the jurists here are more concerned with an internal knowledge—a particular person knowing that they are free and deceptively not behaving as a free person. The concern with deception is also seen in Dio, when his would-be slave relates a story of a man who passes himself off as a dead freeman. This tale of passing begins when the man accused of being a slave asks his accuser if he had considered that not all people in a state of slavery were slaves.[98] Dio's account exposes the errors and fraud that arise in the determination of status: a free person can find themself in slavery, a slave in freedom. Twisting the confusion between sons and slaves, Dio relates the story of Callias' groom, and while the story takes place in Athens of the past, the reason for telling the story fits with the evolving meaning of slave status in Dio's time.

---

96. D. 40.12.11 Gaius, *Urban Praetor's Edict, Chapter on the Suits for Freedom*, (Lenel fr. 74), "Although in the time of flight he behaved as a freeman, certainly we will say he is in the same situation" (*Licet fugae tempore pro libero se gesserit: dicemus enim eum in eadem causa esse*). The text is inserted in between "*. . . pro servo agere*" and "*Igitur sciendum est . . .*"
97. On *favor libertatis*, see Honoré 2012; Ankum 2007; Brunt 1998, 144–48; Castello 1956.
98. Dio Chrys. *Or.* 15.13.

At the same time, even the son of Callias was thought to have been in slavery for a long time, in Thrace after the battle in which the Athenians suffered a defeat at Acanthus. As a result, later when he escaped and reached home, he laid claim to the estate left by Callias and caused a great deal of trouble for Callias' kinsmen. In fact he was lying, I think, for he was not the son, but the groom of Callias, although he was similar in appearance to Callias' son, who had died in that battle; and he also spoke Greek accurately and could read and write.—But there have been innumerable others who have suffered this fate.

ὁπότε καὶ ὁ Καλλίου υἱὸς ἔδοξε δουλεῦσαι πολὺν χρόνον ἐπὶ Θρᾴκης μετὰ τὴν μάχην ἣν Ἀθηναῖοι περὶ Ἄκανθον ἡττήθησαν· ὥστε καὶ ὕστερον διαφυγὼν καὶ ἀφικόμενος ἠμφισβήτει τοῦ κλήρου τοῦ Καλλίου καὶ πολλὰ πράγματα παρεῖχε τοῖς ξυγγενέσιν, ἐκεῖνος μέν, οἶμαι, ψευδόμενος—ἦν γὰρ οὐχ υἱός, ἀλλ' ἱπποκόμος Καλλίου, τὴν δὲ ὄψιν ὅμοιος τῷ τοῦ Καλλίου μειρακίῳ, ὃ ἔτυχεν ἐν τῇ μάχῃ τελευτῆσαν· ἔτι δὲ ἡλλήνιζεν ἀκριβῶς καὶ γράμματα ἠπίστατο· ἀλλὰ ἕτεροί γε μυρίοι τοῦτο πεπόνθασιν·[99]

Dio's accused slave reveals how status confusion could arise. It was believed that Callias' son, a freeman, was in a state of slavery (*douleuō*); Callias' groom takes advantage of this rumor. The groom fraudulently impersonates a free person and along with the added benefit of looking like Callias' son, the groom could speak Greek accurately and could read and write. While of course some slaves could speak, read, and write the language of their owners, it was perhaps more unusual for a groom. These skills are, while certainly not exclusive to the free population, suggestive markers in this particular performance of freedom. Here the *familiaritas* that Seneca speaks of is used by the groom to pull off his performance as Callias' son, that is, to conduct himself as a free person fraudulently.

To return to the beginnings of this book, the groom's impersonation of Callias' son realizes the jurists' fears about the runaway slave. The rationale behind the fixation of the jurists on this particular form of fraudulent liberty can be seen if we recall a passage of the jurist Caelius (quoted by Ulpian) in the commentary on the Edict of the Aediles. Here Caelius gives a reason for the constant concern about runaway slaves, "Likewise, rightly [Caelius] says flight is an appearance of a kind of liberty, since he is freed from the power of his owner in

99. Dio Chrys. *Or.* 15.15–16.

that moment" (*Idem recte ait liberatis cuiusdam speciem esse fugisse, hoc est potestate dominica in praesenti liberatum esse*).[100] The concern about runaway slaves can be understood as a financial one—it is straightforwardly a loss of property for the owner despite retaining ownership over the slave. But unlike the cases of manumission discussed in this chapter in which enslaved people may make use of their knowledge of Roman social structures and culture in order to encourage or even at times negotiate for their freedom, here the slave takes the decision out of the hands of the owner. The jurists, as we saw before, consider flight inherently servile and beyond the realm of an honest free person, but the runaway slave tests the jurists' methodology of behavior as a determinant of status. The lack of definitive markers of status increases the possibility of someone fraudulently passing as free. The runaway slave being in the appearance of a kind of liberty is almost a warning if we think about the groom's ability to pass as free because of his appearance and behavior.

The juristic literature on suits for freedom and Dio's Fifteenth Discourse speak about status explicitly and show that a person's behavior affected what status others understood them to be. The virtues of a good slave are potentially different than the virtues of a good citizen, but the virtues that bring about the manumissions discussed in this chapter are the ones the state desired in a Roman citizen. This performance of citizenship, however, further troubles ownership and the boundaries of status at Rome: A slave who performs citizenship first performs liberty. In this way, a slave displaying citizen qualities is, in a sense, taking liberties because in those moments they choose to behave with *fides* or *virtus* without explicit direction from their owner. At first sight, there does not appear to be much of a difference between the fugitive slave in the *species cuiusdam libertatis* and the slave performing liberty, which complicates how slave status was understood. The distinction between the fugitive slave and the slave performing citizenship lies in the realm of the mind.

100. D. 21.1.17.10 Ulpian, *Curule Aediles' Edict*, book 1. This passage, and the runaway slave in general, are discussed in detail in chapter 2.

Epilogue

From Mind to Memory

In 61 CE, one of the more notorious events in the history of Roman slaving occurred: four hundred enslaved individuals were put to death, likely by crucifixion.[1] Their owner had been killed by one of their fellow slaves and law dictated that when a slave killed their owner, all the slaves of the household were to be killed. The *SC Silanianum* had been the law of the land since 10 CE, and before that was custom from Rome's earlier days.[2] The justification for the law, and presumably the custom, was deterrence and to encourage informing on fellow enslaved people.[3] Cases of so-called master-murder are usually treated with high-handed moralism in the ancient sources, both toward the actions of the enslaved and those of the owner that led to their demise.[4] Nevertheless, this case attracted particular attention because of the sheer number of enslaved people who were to be killed. The prospect of mass execution led to protests in the streets and a hearing in the Senate, during which the eminent jurist Gaius Cassius Longinus argued that, despite the innocence of most of these enslaved people, the law should be followed. The Emperor Nero concurred, and the enslaved members of the household were led off to their deaths.

---

1. The punishment is not stated in the text of Tacitus, but this was the typical penalty; see Kuhn 1982, 692–93, 719–23.
2. The practice is mentioned in Cic. *Fam.* 4.12.3 (SB 253). On the development and expansion of the *senatusconsultum*, see Harries 2013.
3. Ulpian says as much in the preamble to his discussion of the law, D. 29.5.1pr Ulpian, *Edict*, book 50.
4. See, for example, Pliny's description (*Ep.* 3.14.1) of Larcius Macedo, murdered by some of his slaves in the bath, as "in general an arrogant and savage owner, the kind who remembered too little, or perhaps too well, that his father had been a slave" (*superbus alioqui dominus et saevus, et qui servisse patrem suum parum, immo nimium meminisset*).

The incident is related to us by Tacitus, who gives a very brief explanation for the death of the owner and then reports on the reactions of the people of Rome, the Senate, and the emperor. Attributing the death of the owner to "servile boldness" (*audacia servilia*),[5] he relates the following account:

> Not long after, a slave killed his owner, the urban prefect Pedanius Secundus, either because an agreement for manumission was revoked after the price had already been settled or because the slave was consumed with passion for a male prostitute and would not tolerate his owner as a rival.
>
> Haud multo post praefectum urbis Pedanium Secundum servus ipsius interfecit, seu negata libertate, cui pretium pepigerat, sive amore exoleti incensus et dominum aemulum non tolerans.[6]

Tacitus' use of *exoletus*, the term for an adult male prostitute, puts his moralizing on display: Sex with an *exoletus* was problematic behavior for an elite Roman following the sexual *mores* of the time.[7] The other possible cause for the murder also shows Pedanius in a negative light; this is a man who does not stick to his word. Once a manumission price was set, it was poor form to renege on it. On a larger scale, manumission as a tool for compliance does not work if slave owners get in the habit of revoking what was promised.

This case was sensational in its day not for these failures on the part of the owner, or even his death, but for the hundreds of deaths that were to follow. The murder of Pedanius and its aftermath serve as a microcosm for the whole body of enslaved persons and the Roman institution of slavery itself, presenting both mass violence and the diversity of experiences of enslaved people paired with anonymizing rightlessness. It brings us also to the question of death in the context of slavery. As noted in the previous chapter, most enslaved people, did not reach freedom in their lifetime and death is always an undercurrent, at the very least, in any instance of enslavement. It is worthwhile then to conclude by briefly considering death in our framework of the mind as a limit of slave ownership.

---

5. At *Ann.* 14.40 where Tacitus relates it to another audacious incident perpetrated by a senator.
6. Tac. *Ann.* 14.42.
7. On the use of the term *exoletus*, a "technical term denoting a mature male prostitute," see Williams 1999, 90–93 (quote at 91). The term *exoletus* pertains to the age of the prostitute rather than their sexual role.

I have argued that the mind was a fundamental aspect of slave ownership in ancient Rome and simultaneously the locus of many problems that were exclusive to the reduction of human beings into property. The three parts of this book—at the slave market, at work, and at the end of enslavement—represent moments of critical scrutiny and inquiry into the mind of the enslaved by the jurists and other ancient authors. These moments reveal pressure points on ownership specifically because this was a legal framework for the domination of people against their will, people who could reasonably be expected not to act in ways the slaveholding class might anticipate (the "factual insecurities" of slave ownership). Looking closely at these moments of beginning, connection, and rupture together unearths not just the legal structures that buttressed Roman slavery but also the reliance on extralegal and social underpinnings that made this system work effectively for slaveowners for centuries.

These moments are significant because such scenarios provide content for legal discussions about standards and models for the evaluation of slaves. The reading of legal texts in concert with the direct counsel or anecdotal evidence from literary sources creates a broader picture of how Roman writers both were preoccupied with and attempted to understand the mind of the slave. These writers not only acknowledged the agency and autonomy of their slaves, but they explicitly relied upon these qualities in the work they demanded from slaves. For their part, slaves could use this autonomy either to the benefit or the detriment of the owner. This was at least in part why the slaving class perseverated over controlling their slaves and knowing their minds—a task driven partly by their very awareness that this was not entirely possible. This ontological failure of the owner to know the mind of the slave leads to interference with the traditional performance of ownership: mastery through force. The slaveholder must instead lean on familial and affective ties, negotiation, and social obligation to attempt to ensure compliance, if not true knowledge or trust. I contend it was in these moments, in the realm of the unknowable interior of the slave, that ownership was most challenged. As the murder of Pedanius Secundus and its fallout exemplify, this argument does not dismiss the brutality of enslavement or the constant threat of violence; there is no suggestion that owner and slave could ever be two contracting parties equal before the law. As a crucial juncture marking the end of enslavement, this chapter's emphasis on death is twofold. First, as most enslaved people died while in slavery, it is worth considering this end to the enslaved life. In addition, while death is universal, its forms and meanings are not, and this epilogue considers the loss that accompanies death from the perspective of the owner and the enslaved as a final fault line of slave ownership.

Writing about slavery and death in colonial Jamaica, Vincent Brown contends that "the death of the enslaved was more than disappearances, absences, or extinctions; the deaths generated new stories and understandings to account for the enormity of the social disturbance."[8] Atlantic slavery differed from Roman slavery in a multitude of ways, and the rates of death in colonial Jamaica were certainly higher than those found in the Roman period; nevertheless, it is valuable and meaningful to look to our Roman example from Tacitus and consider what this instance of mass death produced. Taking the deaths of the enslaved members of Pedanius Secundus' household as a brief case study, this epilogue begins with a final look at the construct of "the mind of the slave" by thinking about how these deaths affected first the enslaved population, but also slave owners and heirs along with the wider populace, the Senate, and the emperor. Death is a rupture for slave ownership as it removes the utility of the slave from the enslaver or heir (future enslaver). In this case, the law marshals death and the prospect of death both to influence the minds of other enslaved people into desired behavior and to foment anxiety and fear in the minds of enslavers and the general free populace at the literal expense of the heir. Finally, in a book that has privileged the voices of the slave-owning class, the second half of this chapter will turn to a different frame of the mind of the enslaved. Through a brief discussion of epitaphs of enslaved and formerly enslaved people, the book concludes with instances of self-fashioning and the desire for freedom of expression and the control of one's own memory.

We are not given the name of Pedanius Secundus' assailant, nor are we told what became of him—but if he had managed to escape, it seems plausible that Cassius would have mentioned it in his speech as another outrageous aspect of this murder. It is possible then that he was executed with the other members of the *familia*. The two details that we receive about him are presented as alternatives: he was on the cusp of freedom, or he desired an unnamed person who worked as a prostitute. Before turning to the speech of Cassius that supplies more information about these details, we can probably add that the assailant was in some way close to his owner, given that Pedanius had agreed to free him and that he had a substantial enough *peculium* to purchase this freedom. Even if the *exoletus* was the impetus for the murder, we can assume that the basic

8. Brown 2010, 41.

premise of Tacitus' account (i.e., that he was the kind of enslaved person who could purchase his freedom) was relatively close to reality.

In his speech to the Senate, Cassius implores the senators to carry out the execution of the four hundred slaves and mocks the fictions that allowed the Roman slave system to work so effectively for centuries of slave owners:

> Or, as some do not blush to imagine, did the killer avenge an outrage against himself, because he had settled [on a price with Pedanius] from his father's finances or a chattel slave of his grandfather was being taken away from him? From now on, let us proclaim that the owner seems to have been killed justly.

> An, ut quidam fingere non erubescunt, iniurias suas ultus est interfector, quia de paterna pecunia transegerat aut avitum mancipium detrahebatur? Pronuntiemus ultro dominum iure caesum videri.[9]

Cassius takes aim at the potential reasons for grievance that led to the murder of Pedanius. Strictly speaking, a slave owned nothing according to civil law. He had neither the money to buy his freedom (the *paterna pecunia* referred to here) nor the right to a private relationship (with the *avitum mancipium*). But as we have seen, Roman slavery operated under these exact premises. The *peculium* was controlled by the slave, and slave unions were tolerated or encouraged because they incentivized compliance. Although Pedanius, in the role of the vicious master, went against good slaving practice, which everyone recognized, Cassius points out that outrage—having rights and feeling wronged—belongs to the slaving class, not the enslaved.

More can be gleaned from the somewhat oblique descriptions *paterna pecunia* and *avitum mancipium*. Unlike the representation of motive in Tacitus' description, which emphasizes the language of contract (*pangere*) and a specific type of sex worker (*exoletus*), Cassius stresses family relations: the money of his father, the slave of his grandfather. While these family ties are not legally binding, they are known and clearly have meaning. The language here is ambiguous, but the emphasis on the family of the assailant suggests that he was likely a homeborn slave. This could mean that Pedanius himself was his natural father, or the kin of the assailant had been in the *familia* of Pedanius for generations. In either case, Cassius' description of the *exoletus* as being the slave of his

9. Tac. *Ann.* 14.43.5.

grandfather suggests that this *exoletus* was also part of the *familia* and presumably executed with them.

The assailant, as a homeborn slave with a large *peculium*, was likely educated and could well have engaged in high-level work like account management. Turning to the alternative, Cassius' speech gives us one more salient detail as to the possible persona of the assailant: He was able to enter Pedanius' bedroom unimpeded.[10] The assailant may have been a victim of Pedanius' predation as well, since the use of the term *exoletus* potentially masks Pedanius' behavior more generally within the *familia*. Pedanius' lack of regard for the manumission agreement or for the possible lover of an enslaved person was certainly well within a slave owner's legal rights, as both Cassius attests and Pedanius carries out. Nevertheless, as we see in this particular break of ownership, the results were catastrophic at home and disturbing throughout the city, which rather reflects the social and extralegal realities of Roman slavery.

There is an understandable temptation for the historian to interpret a death like that of the enslaved assailant of Pedanius Secundus as a moment of heightened agency and the ultimate act of resistance against a dehumanizing regime.[11] The assailant surely would have known that his own death was the likely outcome of his actions, especially since we can infer from Cassius' speech that the murder of Pedanius was not in the heat of the moment. Perhaps he did not imagine the death of the rest of the *familia* (though stopping this sort of behavior was exactly the point of the *SC Silanianum*, and its efficacy would have relied on enslaved people being aware of this—part of the reason why execution by crucifixion was a useful tool of domination was its visibility). The two motivations ascribed to the assailant of Pedanius were personal, but of two very different natures. And perhaps this resistance narrative can be read bleakly and individualistically when considering the first motivation for the murder (i.e., freedom or death).[12] The second motive, however, reads more like the assailant

10. Tac. *Ann.* 14.44.1.
11. Perhaps the clearest moment of this comes from Frederick Douglass' autobiography. Douglass had been sent by his enslaver to a "slave-breaker," but after six months of beatings he experiences a moment of realization that he was not afraid to die and defends himself, Douglass 2014, 165–199, with Gilroy 1993, 63. Recent scholarship on slavery studies has pushed back on the framework of agency: see Hartman 1997 generally but most directly at 52–56; the introduction of Marisa Fuentes' *Dispossessed Lives* meditates on the issue of agency, 2016, 1–12 (discussed just below); and fundamentally, Johnson 2003. For a different perspective on enslaved agency, and focused on the ancient world, see Vlassopoulos 2021, especially 189–99.
12. There are, as far as we know, no revolts of enslaved people who sought abolition in antiquity. This has been well noted by scholars of ancient slavery, see, e.g., Vlassopoulos 2021, 188 and Garnsey 1996, 75–86.

was an actor who eventually reached a breaking point while navigating through complex webs of power and dependency.

The rest of the archive of enslavement in this passage is largely unrecoverable. As noted, we have the reaction of the plebs, the speeches of the Senate, and a pronouncement from Nero, but the four hundred enslaved people who were put to death as a result of the *SC Silanianum* remain offstage. We learn nothing more about them other than that some of their number were apparently women and children; hardly surprising for a *familia* of this size.[13] Turning to legal sources, the jurists had quite a lot to say about this *senatusconsultum* generally and engaged in typical juristic debates, such as who counts as part of the *familia* with respect to the *senatusconsultum*. Ulpian cites Pomponius saying that judges usually considered those within earshot of an assailed owner to be "under the same roof" (*sub tecto*) and that they thus should be punished.[14] Children (*impuberes*) were generally excused from this penalty.[15] Enslaved people who were elderly, deaf, blind, unable to move because they were bound, or unable to speak (if the only means of assistance were shouting) were also all excused in the juristic literature of the *senatusconsultum*, though these exceptions are provided by emperors and jurists from the second and third centuries.[16] If these exceptions did exist in the first century, Tacitus makes no mention of them being granted in the case of the *familia* of Pedanius Secundus. The people put to death in an elite household would have been account managers, kitchen workers, gardeners, scribes, bedchamber workers, wet nurses, and potentially natural-born children of the owner, as well as countless others.

At first glance, this massive loss of life affirms what we know already about the institution of slavery: it reduced an entire class of people to rightlessness, it is a reminder of how slaves were treated indiscriminately and regarded as insignificant relative to free persons. It was also at times economically paradoxical.[17]

13. Tac. *Ann.* 14.45.1.
14. D. 29.5.1.26 Ulpian, *Edict*, book 50 and see discussion in Harries 2013.
15. For children, see D.29.5.1.32–33 Ulpian, *Edict*, book 50 and D. 29.5.14 Maecianus, *Criminal Proceedings*, book 11 for an exception to the exception: a boy who was nearly fully grown (*puer nec multum a puberi aetate aberat*) was executed because he was asleep at the foot of the bed when his owner was killed and did nothing even after the danger had passed.
16. Bound: D. 29.5.3.6; elderly: D. 29.5.3.7; deaf: D. 29.5.3.8; blind: D. 29.5.3.9; and nonspeaking: D. 29.5.3.10 (D. 29.5.3 is a fragment from Ulpian's 50th book on the *Edict*).
17. In terms of this paradoxical economic loss we might contrast this with the Zong massacre (1781) in which more than 130 enslaved Africans were drowned when the crew of the slave ship *Zong* began to run out of drinking water and threw them overboard. When they reached Jamaica, the owners of the ship sued for the insurance they had taken out on the enslaved Africans. The jury did find for the owners of the ship—they were to be given the insurance money for the murdered

These people did not die because of their own actions; they died because they did *not* act, that is, they did not stop a death they may not have known was going to take place. From the likely perspective of the vast majority of the *familia*, their own deaths were seemingly random and out of their hands. The *familia* was, simply put, innocent.[18] If this massacre did indeed deter other enslaved people from attacking their owners or encouraged household members to inform on one another, it is impossible to know at what rate.[19] We have plenty of anecdotal data of master-murder continuing, like Pliny's account of Larcius Macedo who was murdered in his bath by some of his slaves.[20] But the existence of the *senatusconsultum* is premised on the very idea that enslaved people should, and would, talk about the fate of *familiae* like that of Pedanius Secundus. Murdering an owner was likely the greatest factual insecurity of slave ownership, but unlike many other factual insecurities, this one was legislated on.[21]

Scholars such as Marisa Fuentes have challenged viewing the lives and actions of enslaved individuals strictly through the framework of resistance or agency, instead emphasizing that the specific circumstances of enslavement are crucial to understanding enslaved people's actions.[22] The death of the four hundred was not an act of resistance, but that does not suggest that it was without meaning. Even in death, the mind of the slave raises problems for ownership. The fear of the mind that plots, acts, or chooses to remain silent runs rough-

---

Africans—but Lord Chief Justice Mansfield overturned on appeal, not because it was necessarily illegal to murder enslaved people, but because it had come to light that they would not have run out of drinking water if the crew were not so incompetent—they got lost several times. The Zong massacre is well studied; see Walvin 2011 and Baucom 2005 as well as the series of papers from "The *Zong*: Legal, Social and Historical Dimensions" symposium published in the *Journal of Legal History* 28 (3) (2007) for the 200th anniversary of the abolition of the British slave trade.

18. Cassius concedes as much in his speech, but argues that, like decimation, this is still necessary for the public good, Tac. *Ann.* 14.44.3.
19. Gamauf 2007, 145, on this question.
20. *Ep.* 3.14.1, cited above in note 4.
21. On factual insecurities, see introduction.
22. Fuentes lays out this discussion in the introduction of her book *Dispossessed Lives: Enslaved Women, Violence, and the Archive* where she examines the lives of enslaved and freewomen in eighteenth-century Barbados. As she notes at 8, "Much of the previous historical scholarship on slavery influenced by the crucial civil rights and Black power activism of the 1960s and 1970s focuses on enslaved resistance, a vital (and decades long) effort to gain insight into the 'agency' of enslaved people and to refute earlier depictions of the enslaved as passive and submissive. The agency of enslaved and free(d) people of color, however, was more complex than the 'liberal humanist' framework allows. We need to examine the excruciating conditions faced by enslaved women in order to understand the significance of their behaviors within the confounding and violent world of the colonial Caribbean." See 8–11 of her introduction as well as chapter 4 of her book. Fuentes is building on, in part, Saidiya Hartman's *Scenes of Subjection: Terror, Slavery, and Self-Making in Nineteenth-Century America.*

shod over the property protections that ownership affords. The very creation of the *senatusconsultum* points to the terrorizing effect that the slave plot, real or imagined, has on the logics of the slave system. The *senatusconsultum* behind the deaths of the *familia* is remarkable as an incident of state intervention into ownership rights. It seems unlikely, in the case of Pedanius Secundus, that his heirs would be in favor of the loss of capital that was incurred with the deaths of the four hundred enslaved people.[23] It is especially unlikely, given that even those out of earshot or otherwise unable to assist were put to death, contrary to what at least later jurists prescribed in their interpretation of the *senatusconsultum*. Ulpian's commentary on the *senatusconsultum* also underscores how the jurists took master-murder as a highly unusual moment where the testamentary wishes of the owner could be ignored; in particular, even enslaved people whom the owner named in their will to be freed were put to death.[24] In general, provided the will was sound, testamentary wishes were relatively inviolable, but here the personal and financial value of these enslaved people is weighed against the concerns of the greater slave society.

The prospect of the erasure of this entire *familia* shaped the actions of the plebs, and the bodies of the *familia* members themselves would have been seen; they were, upon their deaths, horrifyingly and purposefully visible.[25] Tacitus' brief account of the affair indicates that the matter would not have been raised in the Senate without the uproar of the plebs, who blockaded the Senate house and threatened sedition in order to protect so many innocent people. The Senate, for its part, also had some members who apparently felt squeamish at the prospect of this sentence for so many individuals, but most of the members did not think that they should deviate from standard course.[26]

The speech of the jurist Gaius Cassius in favor of upholding the law and putting the whole household to death makes up the majority of Tacitus' account of the murder. Cassius indicates that their Roman ancestors treated the minds

23. Cassius refers to this loss on the part of the heirs by appealing to the public good of, essentially, scaring other enslaved people straight, Tac. *Ann.* 14.44.3.

24. D. 29.5.3.16–18 Ulpian, *Edict*, book 50.

25. There are striking visual parallels to the response to the 1811 slave revolt. Starting in LaPlace, Louisiana, Charles Deslondes and around five hundred enslaved people marched on New Orleans, killing two enslavers and burning plantations as they went. They were stopped by the militia and federal troops after two days. Those that did not manage to escape were given a perfunctory trial before being shot in front of the plantations at which they were enslaved. They were decapitated and their heads were put on spikes as a warning to other enslaved people. In 2016 the Whitney Plantation Museum commissioned the artist Woodrow Nash to create sixty-three ceramic heads to commemorate this loss.

26. Tac. *Ann.* 14.42.

of their slaves with suspicion (*suspecta . . . ingenia servorum*) even though they were born locally; but in their current day, their households were entirely composed of foreigners with different customs and alien or no rituals. And while Cassius concedes that there was sure to be some injustice (*iniquus*) given the current slaving system of the Romans, they must rule over their households, which he refers to as cesspools (*conluvies*), in such a way as to cultivate fear.[27] Finally, the Emperor Nero weighs in and rebukes the people with an edict, in addition to surrounding the road leading the condemned to death with detachments of soldiers.[28] A senator suggested to Nero that the freedpersons of the household be deported from Italy,[29] but Nero draws the line there. There were sometimes questions as to what would happen to freedpersons, but here it appears that their citizenship protected them from this fate.[30] The death of these four hundred enslaved individuals persisted as an instrument of deterrence, potentially affecting the minds of other enslaved people, while the original act of master-murder served to fuel owners' anxieties about wayward or liberatory thoughts in their slaves' minds.

What does death bring then? In his distillation of the constituent elements of slavery, Orlando Patterson laid out the relationship between slavery and death:

> Perhaps the most distinctive attribute of the slave's powerlessness was that it always originated (or was conceived of as having originated) as a substitute for death, usually violent death. . . . The condition of slavery did not absolve or erase the prospect of death. Slavery was not a pardon; it was, peculiarly, a conditional commutation. The execution was suspended only as long as the slave acquiesced in his powerlessness.[31]

Patterson's rendering of slavery as a commutation of death in warfare comes in part from the Roman juridical idea that slavery's origin lay in the enslavement,

27. Tac. *Ann.* 14.44.3.
28. Tac. *Ann.* 14.45.2
29. Tac. *Ann.* 14.45.2
30. Cic. *Fam.* 4.12 (SB 253): Sulpicius Rufus reports to Cicero in a letter of 45 BCE that after their owner Marcus Marcellus was murdered outside his tent, only a few of the slaves and two freedmen remained. The majority had fled in terror because even though Marcellus had not been murdered by his *familia*, they were uncertain what would happen to them. And see Plin. *Ep.* 8.14, which again raises the question of the liability of freedpersons at the death of their former owners; see Harries 2013, 63–66, for a treatment on the matter.
31. Patterson 1982, 5.

rather than execution, of prisoners of war.[32] The assailant of Pedanius Secundus perfectly exemplifies Patterson's idea. But when we extend this to the *familia* of Pedanius Secundus, we must understand that these other household members did not stop acquiescing in their powerlessness in any place but the mind of their enslavers. Perhaps one or two did help Pedanius' assailant or turned a blind eye, but the majority did not.

Death in Rome did not mean freedom. While it is possible that some enslaved people hoped for death to end their experience of enslavement, ownership endured regardless. In some ways it might appear absurd to pose the question of death in a book arguing that the mind was an essential part of successful ownership: The death of an enslaved person would render the mind, and most likely the body, beyond service.[33] What remains, however, is the question of memory: Who is commemorated and who gets to speak for the dead? It has often been noted that freedpersons were particularly interested in the epigraphic habit;[34] we might understand this then as a desire to control the narratives that existed not only for freedpersons but also some enslaved individuals.

A striking instance of this narrativization through death is the *columbarium* tomb type that became popular during the Augustan period; the majority of people commemorated in these *columbaria* were either enslaved or freed individuals. As Dorian Borbonus has persuasively shown, the *columbaria* are particularly noteworthy for their early uniformity—this is perhaps suggestive of the desire for collective identity among enslaved and formerly enslaved people. The *columbaria* were also unlike Republican tombs, which had an inscription outside indicating the elite owner of the tomb rather than the identities of those whose remains were inside. Each *columbarium* niche had a small epitaph below it, identifying and individualizing the niches for later visitors. While only a small amount of text would fit on the epitaphs, Borbonus notes that enslaved people were four times as likely to have their profession listed as freed people were. This indicates that work was a basic part of self-fashioning for enslaved men, and a means of offsetting the "identity void" that came with not having a legal family name or relations, along with other markers of identity and status.[35]

32. D. 1.5.4.2 Florentinus, *Institutes*, book 9.
33. On the corporeal exceptions, see chapter 4 on noxal liability and below on the refusal to hand over the body for burial.
34. The phrase comes from MacMullen 1982, on freedpersons; see MacLean 2018 in general, but especially 21–27.
35. Borbonus 2014, 127, is building on the work of the work of Joshel 1992, 28–32, 49–56.

This phenomenon is perhaps best exemplified by the case of Musicus Scurranus, an imperial slave who was the treasurer (*dispensator*) of the *fiscus Gallicus* in Lugdunensis. He died at Rome and was commemorated in Columbarium 3 of the Vigna Codini by sixteen of his underslaves (*vicarii*) who are named. All of the men—but not the one woman—have their occupation listed as well. Venustus the dealer (*negotiator*) is listed first; then Decimianus the cashier (*sumptuarius*); followed by three secretaries (*a manu*), Dicaeus, Mutatus, and Creticus; two silversmiths (*ab argento*), Epaphra and Anthus, are mentioned mixed in with *vicarii*, who appear to have provided more domestic services. Musicus had a personal physician (*medicus*) Agathopus, along with two bedchamber assistants, Communis and Hedylus (listed as an *a cubiculo* and a *cubicularius*, respectively); two attendants (*pedissequus*), Pothus and Facilis; a valet (*ad vestem*), Primio; and two cooks (*cucus/cocus*), Tiasus and Firmus. The list of sixteen is rounded out by a final name, a woman, Secunda, who does not receive a profession.[36]

Musicus was about as high level an enslaved person as one could find: He was in charge of a treasury and commanded a vast retinue. His epitaph tells us that the sixteen named *vicarii* were with him when he died in Rome. It is unlikely that this was the burial he had imagined he would have, as it seems clear from his staff that he was in Rome on business when he died. Presumably these *vicarii* were acting not at his command, but out of some sense of duty or affection (and his owner, the emperor, did not object). The only descriptor we find that is not a profession is that he was well-deserving (*benemeritus*).[37] The viewer might be impressed that his *vicarii* wanted to commemorate him and that he had so many, but equally we learn about as much about the *vicarii* as we do about Musicus. We might speculate that he had a doctor with him because he was ill, or perhaps because he always traveled this way. And we might wonder who Secunda was to Musicus. It has been suggested she was his "mistress,"[38] and her placement at the end might highlight (or downplay) her position in Musicus' life. Perhaps it says something about Musicus that he could travel with a *vicaria* whose purpose on the journey did not need to be stated. Whatever the case, unlike the male *vicarii* whose professions are listed, the epitaph does not reveal much about Secunda.

---

36. *CIL* 6.5197 = *ILS* 1514. I take the example of Musicus Scurranus as well as the following case of Pompeia Ammia from the excellent book of Dorian Borbonus on *columbaria* and collective identity; see Borbonus 2014, 127. See also Bruun 2014, 617–18.
37. MacLean 2018, 53–54, on *bene merens* with respect to freedmen and former owners.
38. Bruun 2014, 617.

Sometimes women did fare differently. A freedwoman, Pompeia Ammia, was commemorated by her husband in the same *columbarium* as Musicus. Rather than leaving the reader to infer, she is described in relation to her family: named as a mother of four children, two sons and two daughters, a mother-in-law to a husband of one of her daughters, and a grandmother to their child.[39] More about her life can be gathered: Pompeia's husband and son-in-law were likely freed by the same person, or at the very least someone from the same family, and it appears that she and her husband had three children together. She had another child, likely prior to her marriage, as this daughter, Calena Aeliana, does not share the *gentilicium* of Pompeia's husband (Arellius) or of Pompeia herself. In part at least because she was a freedwoman, Pompeia's memory was in the hands of her husband.

Some enslaved people were able to commission epitaphs for their close kin and also identified themselves along familial lines. In one such case a sister, Psyche, and a wife, Optata, put up an epitaph for their brother and husband Sophrus, an enslaved accountant in the *columbarium* of the Statilii in Rome.[40] The women describe themselves through their family ties to Sophrus, even using *coniunx*, a word for a lawful marriage, to describe Sophrus' union to Optata. A commemorator then could be any number of people, including the person to be commemorated, a family member, or perhaps an ex-owner, owner, or *vicarius*. It is worth keeping in mind that these are all commemorations for enslaved people who were from urban *familiae*. We have nearly no records of the commemorations from the enslaved people that lived, worked, and died on rural estates.[41] These simple epitaphs, with their accompanying remains tucked neatly away in the *columbaria* of great houses, are probably the kind of death and commemoration that the crucified *familia* of Pedanius Secundus had anticipated. They died instead in a spectacularly visible manner, collectively remembered not for their lives but for their deaths, as their corpses were left to decompose and be disturbed.

---

39. *CIL* 6.5280 "To Pompeia Ammia freedwoman of Quintus. She died at 60 years old. Mother-in-law of Arellius Strabo, mother of Arellia Sophe, grandmother to Pupius Arellius Strabo; mother to Lucius Arellius Secundus; mother of Calena Aeliana. Lucius Arellius Orentes put up this epitaph for himself and his wife and all their family."

Pompeiae Q(uinti) l(ibertae) Ammiae decessit ann(os) LX socra Arelli / Strabonis mater Arelliae Sophe avia Pup(i) Arelli / Strabonis mater L(uci) Arelli Secundi mater L(uci) Arelli Optati / mater Calenis Ael(i)anaes titulum posuit L(ucius) Arellius Orentes / sibi et uxori suae et suis omnibus. Text expanded in Brunet 2022, 232.

40. *CIL* 6.6358 = *ILS* 7404, "To Sophrus, accountant and slave of Sisenna Statilius, his sister Psyche and his wife Optata made this" *Sophro Sisennae / Statili ser(vo) tabul(ario) / Psyche soror et / Optata coniunx fecer(unt).*

41. Bruun 2014, 611–12, makes this point.

If a person died enslaved, commemoration of any kind was at the permission, or at the very least not at the objection, of the owner.[42] The extreme of this practice can be seen in the *collegium* of Diana and Antinous in Lanuvium, which Andreas Bendlin has argued was a *collegium* predominantly populated by men who were, or had been, enslaved. This may be evidenced by the number of regulations in the bylaws of the *collegium* that relate to enslaved members.[43] The provisions surrounding the right to a funeral by members of the *collegium* were protective of enslaved people and their commemoration; they were also celebratory of manumission. For example, the regulations safeguard members from any legal claims that an owner or former owner might make upon the enslaved person's death, in addition to stipulating that upon manumission, a member must provide an amphora of good wine. The most striking provision, however, concerns when an owner refuses to release an enslaved person's body:

> Likewise, it was agreed that anyone from this *collegium* who has died a slave, and whose body, unjustly, has not been released for burial by his master or mistress, and who has not left documents, a funeral with an *imago* will be held for him.
>
> item placuit q[ui]squis ex hoc collegio servus defunctus fuerit et corpus eius a domino dominav[e] iniquitat{a}e sepulturae datum non fuerit neque tabellas fecerit ei funus imag[ina]rium fiet.[44]

The dispute over the body brings out the tension between owner and enslaved person even in death. We can only speculate as to why this provision was needed and how the *collegium* determined what constituted an unreasonable (*iniquitas*) failure to release the body. On the other hand, the provision that immediately follows states that if a member of the *collegium* took his own life, he would lose his funeral money.[45] The actual provision is not more specific than "anyone" (*quisquis*), but as it is bookended by the provisions regarding slaves, it likely refers to enslaved members. Bendlin suggests that it may have been, "among other things, to safeguard the master's rights of ownership."[46]

---

42. See Bodel 2008, 212, on freed people preferring to do their own commemoration rather than leaving it to their former owners, basing his argument on Taylor 1961.
43. *CIL* 14.2112. Bendlin 2011, 280–81. Bendlin points to other aspects of the *collegium* that support his argument, see Bendlin 2011, 279–285.
44. col. II.3–4, all text and translation (with slight modifications) of *CIL* 14.2112 from Bendlin 2011.
45. col. II.5–6.
46. See Bendlin 2011, 279. Voisin 1987, 262–63, argues that the ban on suicide fits with a general dis-

The regulations of this *collegium* might appear eccentric, but they are a product of the same construction of Roman slavery that the jurist Cassius scorned in his speech. The *collegium*'s provisions are steadfastly protective of the rights of enslaved members until the decisions of an enslaved member affect their owner's legal rights. While the enslaved person did not legally own the money he paid into the *collegium* and his will for the *collegium* was invalid at law,[47] giving the enslaved person this kind of autonomy was a regular part of the Roman social understanding of slavery. In the face of rightlessness before the law, the enslaved population used the same creative agency so valued in slaves as economic actors to uphold these claims as if legally valid. The provision to use an *imago* or representation of an enslaved person in place of the body bespeaks the hostility underlying the reliance on convention (for slaves) and rights at law (for owners).[48] It benefitted the owner if the enslaved had some say over a process that would not affect most slave owners, namely how and by whom the slave was buried and commemorated. The death of a slave was a financial loss for a slave owner, but there was a penalty if that loss was caused by an enslaved person taking control in a situation that was not profitable to the owner. Withholding the body and the *collegium*'s refusal to assist members who died by suicide are severe punishments with consequences for the slave after death. Unburied enslaved people in this case, or in the case of crucifixion above, suffered from, in the words of Vincent Brown, "the continuation of disorientation on a cosmic scale."[49]

This physical, mental, and spiritual disorientation is present in an epitaph from Narbo and provides a lengthy first-person account of enslavement. It records the life of Gaius Ofillius Aeimnestus, a freedman who was born beyond the borders of the Roman Empire but was at some point enslaved and then freed. In this verse inscription, Ofillius chooses to emphasize his experience of enslavement before reflecting on death:

---

favor of suicide that began to emerge in the period of Trajan and Hadrian rather than a strict economic concern. He then goes on to say that this is tied to discussion at the time of the death of Antinous, which Bendlin rightly dismisses. See also Mentxaka 2003 for a detailed discussion on the clause.

47. See col. I.23–24 with Bendlin 2011, 254n109, on the fiction that must be employed to give the enslaved members anything like the right to make a will.

48. The provision for the *imago* brings a hidden transcript up to the surface, see Scott 1990. See also Brown 2009, 1232, on thinking about the demand for burial through the lens of agency or resistance and difficulties therein.

49. Brown 2009, 1232; Brown is writing about the death of enslaved people aboard slave ships and the usual fate of their bodies—thrown into the ocean where sharks awaited them. There are some parallels to crucified enslaved people in Pedanius' house, their bodies left to animals.

Gaius Ofillius A[eimn]estus, freedman of Gaius, of the tribus Palatina, while still alive, (*sc.* has erected this monument) for himself and his wife Mindia Prima, daughter of Marcus, and his son Gaius Ofillius Proculus, son of Gaius, and [*empty space follows*]. The barbarian land that had given birth to him handed him over to the city of Rome in slavery, so that he undeservedly changed his character. He made every effort to enhance the status of the name given to him by his father on his own part, and at a price he obtained what he was denied at his request. He won over his master by his attentiveness, and he did not experience beatings. He did not have the rewards or the privileges[?] that he could have had.

Why do you rush, stranger, see, there is a place prepared for you to relax. This resting area is open to the people always and everywhere for as many hours as . . . [*the remainder of the text here is too fragmentary for it to be rendered in a meaningful way; a gap follows*].

. . . nor should you feel pained by a dire death. Neither you nor we have been granted to live forever. You believe fate is to blame, because we die as young boys? While you are still alive, to lose one's life is grievous; but as soon as we die, you spurn everything. If you have the entire world under control while you are alive, what difference does it make to Orcus? There is no rich people's canvassing for favors down here.

This monument does not go to the heir.

C(aius) Of[illi]us C(ai) l(ibertus)
Pal(atina) A[eimn]estus
uiuos [sibi] et
Mindiae M(arci) f(iliae) Primae
uxori et / C(aio) Ofillio C(ai) f(ilio) Proculo
filio et
(uac.).
Barbara quem genuit tellus
hunc tradidit urbi seruitio,
ingenium ut flec[t]eret
inmerit[o]. quaesitum ex pat[re]
ut potuit s[i]bi nomen adaux[it]
et pretio [obtin]uit quod prec[e]
non ualuit. officiis uicit

[d]ominum nec uerbera sens[it].
[p]raemia non habuit, pignor[a]
quae potuit. quid properas
[h]ospes, requies tibi nota parat[a]
[es]t. hospitium hoc populo
semper ubique patet horaru[m]
numerum quem suspr[- - -]V[- - -]
quoque senti summam [- - -?]
[- - -] securum [- - -]
- - - - - -

nec duro iam doleas obitu.
nec tibi nec nobis aeternum
uiuere cessit: quod pueri
occidimus, fata quaerenda
putas? dum sis in uita, dolor est
amittere uitam; dum simul
occidimus omnia despicias.
orbem sub leges si habeas [d]um
uiuis, ad Orchum quid ualet?
hic nulla est diuitis ambitio.
[H(oc) m(onumentum)] h(eredem) n(on) s(equitur).[50]

This startling inscription brings us from the mind of a formerly enslaved Roman citizen to the right to be remembered; it also poses a number of questions along the way. After giving his credentials as a freed Roman citizen (*tria nomina*, voting tribe, the letter *L* for *libertus*, and a legally recognized family), Ofillius emphasizes that he had been a part of "the regular, daily traffic in slaves."[51] The land beyond the border (*barbara tellus*) births him in one breath and sells him in the next; what portion, if any, of his pre-enslavement life he remembered is not memorialized here. The stress is instead on his sale into slavery, which forced him to bend his character undeservedly (*ingenium ut*

50. *CIL* 12.5026 = *CLE* 1276 and *CIL* 12.5272= *CLE* 1202. Text and translation (with slight modifications) from Kruschwitz 2022. Long treated as two inscriptions, Belloc 2008 noticed that *CIL* 12.5026 is continued in 12.5272. Arminestus is the traditional restoration for his name; other suggestions include Aphrodisius (Belloc 2008) and Aeimnestus (Kruschwitz 2022).

51. *Adsidua et cottidiana comparatio servorum*—after the classic article by Bradley (1991) entitled such, the phrase is found in D. 41.3.44 Papinian, *Questions*, book 23.

flec[t]eret inmerit[o]).[52] Despite his freedom, Ofillius fixates on his enslavement and how it changed him. He includes a narrative of his experience of enslavement, during which he became able to purchase his freedom through hard work (*officia*) rather than the actualization of physical violence (*verbera*). He emphasizes his individual hard work being something inherent to him also through his desire to amplify the name he received from his father (*quaesitum ex pat[re] ut potuit s[i]bi nomen adaux[it]*). The implication here could be that, while enslaved, he was not treated in the essential way of slaves—that is, being dominated by violence—and he negotiated successfully on a price for manumission, which his owner had denied granting him *gratis*. We might read "he did not receive the rewards or privileges that he could have had" (*[p]raemia non habuit, pignor[a] / quae potuit*) in a similar vein, that he did not accept any favors from his owner—or his owner did not offer any—but the meaning of this phrase is uncertain. An alternative reading of this line could indicate a profession as a moneylender: "any pledges he had, he did not take as rewards."[53]

Beyond this speculative line, Ofillius notably does not state a profession or say anything about his post-manumission life other than giving the name of his voting tribe and his family. We are left to hazard how enslavement changed the *ingenium* of this man: Did he mean that he adapted, or something more sinister? There is a possible undertext here as well: *flectere* can mean "to translate from a word in a different language."[54] The second half of the inscription, much of which was believed to be a different inscription altogether until recently, instead addresses the viewers of the epitaph directly. The use of "boys" (*pueri*) might be taken as a final reminder of Ofillius' former enslaved status, but it seems more likely as a contrast with "to live forever" (*aeternum vivere*): All are boys in the face of mortality. And similarly, the penultimate lines about the favors of powerful men might again refer to the rewards he refused from his former owner, which in death no longer matter. It is impossible to know whether this reading, which seems to meditate on his enslavement and its effects on his life, is the one that Ofillius anticipated for his viewers.

The epitaph ends with a generic phrase found on tombstones: "This monument does not go to the heir" (*hoc monumentum heredem non sequitur*, typi-

52. I follow Kruschwitz in reading *inmerito* as an adverb, but it could be read as an adjective modifying *servitio*.
53. I thank an anonymous reviewer for this alternative interpretation.
54. See Quint. *Inst.* 8.3.36; Gell. *NA* 4.3.3. If this is the case, along with the verse inscription, we might tentatively speculate about this man's profession being in the literary world.

cally abbreviated as it is here *HMHNS*).[55] This was meant to prevent the monument from passing to one's heirs and thus being disturbed or reused by them. The phrase also may have taken on a special force with freedpersons because it emphasizes their citizenship and ability to make a will at law. Despite its regularity then, we must see this detail as a profound statement of the desire to remain and the refusal to bequeath one's memory.[56] The marker of Ofillius emphasizes the right to commemoration and the right to mourn and remember. Perversely, the force of *HMHNS* fits aptly with the four hundred victims of the *senatusconsultum* as well; that "monument," the image of the enslaved *familia* crucified, lived on commemorating death rather than the life of the enslaved. Death and commemoration mark a final moment of rupture in ownership as they represent a moment to think not about legal fact, but to create social and affective meaning.

55. It is found on Trimalchio's tomb, Petron. *Sat.* 71.
56. This is particularly true if we think about the longevity of the monuments, see Mihajlović 2020, at 26, on epitaphs as having "agency in their own right."

Bibliography

Abatino, B., and G. Dari-Mattiacci. 2020. "Agency Problems and Organizational Costs in Slave-Run Businesses." In *Roman Law and Economics*, vol. 1, *Institutions and Organizations*, edited by G. Dari-Mattiacci and D. Kehoe, 273–306. Oxford: Oxford University Press.

Abatino, B., G. Dari-Mattiacci, and E. C. Perotti. 2011. "Depersonalization of Business in Ancient Rome." *Oxford Journal of Legal Studies* 31 (2): 365–89.

Albanese, B. 1959. *Actio Servi Corrupti*. Palermo: Montaina.

Ando, C. 2015. "Fact, Fiction, and Social Reality in Roman Law." In *Legal Fictions in Theory and Practice*, edited by W. Twining and M. Del Mar, 295–324. Cham, Switzerland: Springer.

Ankum, H. 2007. "L'expression *favor libertatis* dans les travaux des juristes classiques romains." In *Extravagantes: Scritti sparsi sul diritto romano*, edited by J. E. Spruit and C. Masi Dora, 457–90. Naples: Jovene.

Arzt-Grabner, P. 2010. "'Neither a Truant nor a Slave': Some Remarks on the Sale of Slaves in Roman Egypt and Other Provinces." In *Proceedings of the Twenty-Fifth International Congress of Papyrology, Ann Arbor, July 29–August 4, 2007*, edited by T. Gagos and A. Hyatt, 21–32. Ann Arbor: University of Michigan Library, Scholarly Publishing Office.

Atkinson, K. M. T. 1966. "The Purpose of the Manumission Laws of Augustus." *Irish Jurist* 1 (2): 356–74.

Aubert, J.-J. 1994. *Business Managers in Ancient Rome: A Social and Economic Study of Institores, 200 B.C.-A.D. 250*. Leiden: Brill.

Aubert, J.-J. 2011. "*Vitia animi*: Tares mentales, psychologiques, caractérielles et intellectuelles des esclaves en droit romain." In *I diritti degli altri in Grecia e a Roma*, edited by A. Maffi and L. Gagliardi, 236–48. Sankt Augustin, Germany: Academia.

Bartholomä, A. 2019. "Legal Laughter." In *The Cambridge Companion to Roman Comedy*, edited by M. T. Dinter, 229–40. Cambridge: Cambridge University Press.

Bartsch, S. 2007. "'Wait a Moment, Phantasia': Ekphrastic Interference in Seneca and Epictetus." *Classical Philology* 102 (1): 83–95.

Bartsch, S., and A. Schiesaro, eds. 2015. *The Cambridge Companion to Seneca*. Cambridge: Cambridge University Press.

Baucom, I. 2005. *Specters of the Atlantic: Finance Capital, Slavery, and the Philosophy of History*. Durham: Duke University Press.

Bauman, R. A. 1989. *Lawyers and Politics in the Early Roman Empire: A Study of Relations between the Roman Jurists and the Emperors from Augustus to Hadrian*. Munich: Beck.

Belloc, H. 2008. "Carrière d'affranchi et funus acerbum: Un rapprochement possible entre deux carmina Latina epigraphica de Narbonne (*CIL*, XII, 5026 et 5272)." *Cahiers du Centre G. Glotz* 19: 322–25.

Bellocci, N. 1997. "Il tentato suicidio del servo: Aspetti socio-familiari nei giuristi dell'ultima epoca dei severi." In *Schiavi e dipendenti nell'ambito dell' "oikos" e della "familia": Atti del 22. Colloquio Girea: Pontignano (Siena), 19–20 novembre 1995*, edited by M. Moggi and G. Cordiano, 377–90. Pisa: ETS.

Bendlin, A. 2011. "Associations, Funerals, Sociality, and Roman Law: The *collegium* of Diana and Antinous in Lanuvium (CIL 14.2112) Reconsidered." In *Aposteldekret und antikes Vereinswesen: Gemeinschaft und ihre Ordnung*, edited by M. Öhler, 201–96. Tübingen: Mohr Siebeck.

Bergamasco, M. 1995. "Le *didaskalikai* nelle ricerca attuale." *Aegyptus* 75: 95–167.

Berry, E. 1983. "Dio Chrysostom the Moral Philosopher." *Greece & Rome* 30: 70–80.

Birks, P. 1985. "The Roman Law Concept of *Dominium* and the Idea of Absolute Ownership." *Acta Juridica* 1: 1–38.

Bloomer, W. 2007. "Roman Declamation: The Elder Seneca and Quintilian." In *A Companion to Roman Rhetoric*, edited by W. Dominik and J. Hall, 297–307. Malden, MA: Wiley-Blackwell.

Bloomer, W. 2011. *School of Rome: Latin Studies and the Origins of Liberal Education*. Berkeley: University of California Press.

Blumenthal, D. 2009. *Enemies and Familiars: Slavery and Mastery in Fifteenth-Century Valencia*. Ithaca: Cornell University Press.

Bobzien, S. 1998. *Determinism and Freedom in Stoic Philosophy*. New York: Oxford University Press.

Bodel, J. 2005. "*Caveat Emptor*: Towards a Study of Roman Slave-Traders." *Journal of Roman Archaeology* 18: 181–95.

Bodel, J. 2008. "From *Columbaria* to Catacombs: Collective Burial in Pagan and Christian Rome." In *Commemorating the Dead: Texts and Artifacts in Context*, edited by L. Brink and D. Green, 177–242. Berlin: De Gruyter.

Bodel, J. 2011. "Slave Labour and Roman Society." In *The Cambridge World History of Slavery*, edited by K. R. Bradley and P. Cartledge, 1: 311–36. Cambridge: Cambridge University Press.

Bodel, J., and W. Scheidel. 2017. *On Human Bondage: After Slavery and Social Death*. Malden, MA: Wiley-Blackwell.

Bonfiglio, B. 1998. *Corruptio Servi*. Milan: Giuffrè.

Bonner, S. F. 1949. *Roman Declamation in the Late Republic and Early Empire*. Berkeley: University of California Press.

Borbonus, D. 2014. *Columbarium Tombs and Collective Identity in Augustan Rome*. Cambridge: Cambridge University Press.

Bradley, K. R. 1984. *Slaves and Masters in the Roman Empire: A Study in Social Control*. Brussels: Latomus.

Bradley, K. R. 1987a. "On the Roman Slave Supply and Slavebreeding." *Slavery & Abolition* 8 (1): 42–64.

Bradley, K. R. 1987b. *Slaves and Masters in the Roman Empire: A Study in Social Control*. New York: Oxford University Press.

Bradley, K. R. 1991. "'The Regular, Daily Traffic in Slaves': Roman History and Contemporary History." *Classical Journal* 87 (2): 125–38.

Bradley, K. R. 1994. *Slavery and Society at Rome*. Cambridge: Cambridge University Press.

Bradley, K. R. 2011. "Resisting Slavery at Rome." In *The Cambridge World History of Slavery*, edited by K. R. Bradley and P. Cartledge, 1: 362–84. Cambridge: Cambridge University Press.

Braconi, P. 2005. "Il 'calcidico' di Lepcis Magna era un mercato di schiavi?" *Journal of Roman Archaeology* 18: 213–19.

Braicovich, R. S. 2010. "Freedom and Determinism in Epictetus' *Discourses*." *Classical Quarterly* 60 (1): 202–20.

Brown, V. 2009. "Social Death and Political Life in the Study of Slavery." *American Historical Review* 114 (5): 1231–49.

Brown, V. 2010. *The Reaper's Garden: Death and Power in the World of Atlantic Slavery*. Cambridge, MA: Harvard University Press.

Bruneau, P. 1975. "'L'Agora des Italiens' servait-elle de marché aux esclaves?" *Bulletin de Correspondence Hellénique* 99: 267–311.

Brunet, L. M. A. 2022. "Grandparents in the Roman Empire: The Evidence of the Latin West." PhD diss., University of Manchester.

Brunt, P. A. 1973. "Aspects of the Social Thought of Dio Chrysostom and of the Stoics." *Proceedings of the Cambridge Philological Society* 199: 9–34.

Brunt, P. A. 1998. "Marcus Aurelius and Slavery." In "Modus Operandi: Essays in Honour of Geoffrey Rickman," edited by M. Austin, J. Harries, and C. Smith. Supplement, *Bulletin of the Institute of Classical Studies* S91: S139–S50.

Bruun, C. 2014. "Slaves and Freed Slaves." In *The Oxford Handbook of Roman Epigraphy*, edited by C. Bruun and J. Edmondson, 605–26. Oxford: Oxford University Press.

Buckland, W. W. 1908. *The Roman Law of Slavery: The Condition of the Slave in Private Law from Augustus to Justinian*. Cambridge: Cambridge University Press.

Camp, S. M. H. 2004. *Closer to Freedom: Enslaved Women and Everyday Resistance in the Plantation South*. Chapel Hill: University of North Carolina Press.

Capogrossi Colognesi, L. 1969. *La struttura della proprietà e la formazione dei iura praediorum nell'età repubblicana*. Pubblicazioni dell'Istituto di diritto romano e dei diritti dell'Oriente mediterraneo, Università di Roma, 42. Milan: Giuffrè.

Capogrossi Colognesi, L. 2016. "Ownership and Power in Roman Law." In *The Oxford Handbook in Roman Law and Society*, edited by P. J. du Plessis, C. Ando, and K. Tuori, 524–36. Oxford: Oxford University Press.

Carlsen, J. 1995. *Vilici and Roman Estate Managers until AD 284*. Rome: L'Erma di Bretschneider.

Carlsen, J. 2010. "Recruitment and Training of Roman Estate Managers in a Comparative Perspective." In "Vilici and Roman Estate Managers until AD 284," edited by U. Roth. Supplement, *Bulletin of the Institute of Classical Studies* S109: S75–S90.

Casavola, F. 1976. "Cultura e scienza giuridica nel secondo secolo d.C.: il senso del passato." *Aufstieg und Niedergang der Römischen Welt (ANRW)* 2 (15): 131–75.

Castello, C. 1956. "In tema di *favor libertatis*." *Studia et Documenta Historiae et Iuris* 22: 348–61.

Cloud, D. 2007. "The *Actio Redhibitoria*: Puzzles and Tensions over Mental Defects and Faults of Character from the Second Century BC to the Sixth Century AD." In "Wolf Liebeschuetz Reflected: Essays Presented by Colleagues, Friends & Pupils," edited by B. Salway and J. F. Drinkwater. Supplement, *Bulletin of the Institute of Classical Studies* S91: S67–S76.

Coarelli, F. 1982. "L'Agora des Italiens a Delo, il mercato degli schiavi?" In *Delo e l'Italia: raccolta di studi*, edited by F. Coarelli, D. Musti, and H. Solin, 119–45. Rome: Bardi.

Coarelli, F. 2005. "L' 'Agora des Italiens': Lo statarion di Delo?" *Journal of Roman Archaeology* 18: 196–212.

Cocatre-Zilgien, P. 2008. "La rédhibition de l'esclave pour cause de maladie en droit romain." *Revue générale de droit médical. Pouvoir, santé et société* (October): 9–81.

Cocco, M. 1970. "Sulla funzione dell'Agorà degli Italiani di Delo." *La parola del passato: Rivista di studi antichi* 25: 446–49.

Cohen, E. 2023. *Roman Inequality: Affluent Slaves, Businesswomen, Legal Fictions*. New York: Oxford University Press.

Cohoon, J. W. 1939. *Dio Chrysostom: Discourses 12–30*. Cambridge, MA: Harvard University Press.

Cortese, E. 1988. *La proprietà e le proprietà (Pontignano, 20 settembre–3 ottobre 1985)*. Milan: Giuffrè.

Cretia, P. 1961. "Dion de Pruse et l'esclavage." *Studii Clasice* 3: 369–75.

Crifò, G. 1993. "A proposito di humanitas." In *Ars boni et aequi: Festschrift für Wolfgang Waldstein zum 65. Geburtstag*, edited by W. Waldstein, M. J. Schermaier, and Z. Végh, 79–91. Stuttgart: F. Steiner.

Cursi, F. 2016. "The Scope and Function of Civil Wrongs in Roman Society." In *Oxford*

Handbook of Roman Law and Society, edited by P. J. du Plessis, C. Ando, and K. Tuori, 596–606. Oxford: Oxford University Press.

Daguet-Gagey, A. 2015. *Splendor aedilitatum: L'édilité à Rome: (Ier s. avant J.-C.-IIIe s. après J.-C.)*. Rome: École française de Rome.

Dalla, D. 1978. *L'incapacità sessuale in diritto romano*. Milan: Giuffrè.

Dari-Mattiacci, G. 2013. "Slavery and Information." *Journal of Economic History* 73 (1): 79–116.

Daube, D. 1946. "Two Early Patterns of Manumission." *Journal of Roman Studies* 36: 57–75.

Daube, D. 1956. *Forms of Roman Legislation*. Oxford: Clarendon Press.

Del Prete, P. 1972. *La responsabilità dello schiavo nel diritto penale romano*. Rome: L'Erma di Bretschneider.

De Vaan, M., ed. 2010. *Etymological Dictionary of Latin Online*. Brill. https://dictionaries.brillonline.com/latin

De Zulueta, F. 1945. *The Roman Law of Sale*. Oxford: Clarendon Press.

De Zulueta, F. 1953. *The Institutes of Gaius*. Oxford: Clarendon Press.

Diederich, S. 2007a. *Römische Agrarhandbücher zwischen Fachwissenschaft, Literatur und Ideologie*. Berlin: De Gruyter.

Diederich, S. 2007b. "Sklaverei in den römischen Agrarhandbüchern." In *Unfreie Arbeit: Ökonomische und kulturgeschichtliche Perspektiven*, edited by M. E. Kabadayi and T. Reichardt, 149–65. Hildesheim: Georg Olms.

Diliberto, O. 1984. *Studi sulle origini della cura furiosi*. Naples: Jovene.

Diósdi, G. 1970. *Ownership in Ancient and Preclassical Roman Law*. Budapest: Akadémiai Kiadó.

Di Porto, A. 1984. *Impresa collettiva e schiavo "manager" in Roma antica (II sec. a.C.—II sec. d.C.)*. Milan: Giuffrè.

Dobbin, R. 2007. *Epictetus. Discourses. Book 1*. Oxford: Clarendon Press.

Donadio, N. 2004a. *La tutela del compratore tra actiones aediliciae e actio empti*. Milan: Giuffrè.

Donadio, N. 2004b. "Sulla comparazione tra *desertor* e *fugitivus*, tra *emansor* ed *erro* in D. 49.16.4.14." In *Scritti in ricordo di Barbara Bonfiglio*, edited by E. Cantarella, 137–77. Milan: Giuffrè.

Douglass, F. 2014. *My Bondage and My Freedom*. Edited by D. W. Blight. New Haven: Yale University Press.

Drexhage, H.-J. 1991. *Preise, Mieten/Pachten, Kosten und Löhne im römischen Ägypten bis zum Regierungsantritt Diokletians*. St. Katharinen: Scripta Mercaturae.

Du Plessis, P. J. 2010. "The Slave in the Window." In "By the Sweat of Your Brow: Roman Slavery in its Socio-Economic Setting," edited by U. Roth. Supplement, *Bulletin of the Institute of Classical Studies* S109: S49–S60.

Du Plessis, P. J. 2013. "Damaging a Slave." In *Judge and Jurist: Essays in Memory of Lord Rodger*, edited by A. Burrow, D. Johnston, and R. Zimmermann, 157–65. Oxford: Oxford University Press.

Du Plessis, P. J. 2015. "Property." In *The Cambridge Companion to Roman Law*, edited by D. Johnston, 175–98. New York: Cambridge University Press.

Edwards, C. 1993. *The Politics of Immorality in Ancient Rome*. Cambridge: Cambridge University Press.

Edwards, C. 2019. *Seneca: Selected Letters*. Cambridge: Cambridge University Press.

Edwards, C. 2023. "Letters from an Invalid Philosopher: The Fallibility of Mind and Body in Seneca's *Epistulae morales*." In *Fallibility and Fallibilism in Ancient Philosophy and Literature. Proceedings of the 24th Conference of the Karl and Gertrud-Abel Foundation, Munich, March 25th–26th, 2021*, edited by T. Fuhrer and J. Soldo, 127–45. Berlin: De Gruyter.

Ernout, A., and A. Meillet. 1967. *Dictionnaire étymologique de la langue latine: Histoire des mots*. Paris: Klincksieck.

Evans Grubbs, J. 2002. *Women and the Law in the Roman Empire: A Sourcebook on Marriage, Divorce and Widowhood*. London: Routledge.

Fentress, E. 2005. "On the Block: *Catastae, Chalcidica* and *Cryptae* in Early Imperial Italy." *Journal of Roman Archaeology* 18: 220–34.

Finley, M. I. (1980) 1998. *Ancient Slavery and Modern Ideology*. Edited by B. D. Shaw. Princeton: Princeton University Press.

Fitzgerald, W. 2000. *Slavery and the Roman Literary Imagination*. Cambridge: Cambridge University Press.

Foreman, P. G., et al. "Writing about Slavery/Teaching about Slavery: This Might Help." Community-sourced document. Accessed October 18, 2023. https://www.pgabrielleforeman.com/writing-about-slavery-guide

Forster, E. S. 1950. "Columella and His Latin Treatise on Agriculture." *Greece & Rome* 19 (57): 123–28.

Franciosi, G. 1961. *Il processo di libertà in diritto romano*. Naples: Jovene.

Frede, M. 2007. "The ΕΦ'ΗΜΙΝ in Ancient Philosophy." *Philosophia* 37: 110–23.

Frede, M. 2012. *A Free Will: Origins of the Notion in Ancient Thought*. Edited by A. A. Long. Berkeley: University of California Press.

Frier, B., and D. Kehoe. 2007. "Law and Economic Institutions." In *The Cambridge Economic History of the Greco-Roman World*, edited by W. Scheidel, I. Morris, and R. Saller, 113–43. Cambridge: Cambridge University Press.

Fuentes, M. J. 2016. *Dispossessed Lives: Enslaved Women, Violence, and the Archive*. Philadelphia: University of Pennsylvania Press.

Fuhrmann, C. J. 2012. *Policing the Roman Empire: Soldiers, Administration, and Public Order*. Oxford: Oxford University Press.

Fusco, S. 2010. "*De iniuriis quae servis fiunt*: Un caso di rilevanza giuridica della persona servi?" In *Homo, caput, persona: La construzione giuridica dell'identità nell'esperienza romana. Dall'epoca di Plauto a Ulpiano*, edited by A. Corbino, M. Humbert, and G. Negri, 427–33. Pavia: Iuss Press.

Gallinari, L. 1978. *Schiavitù e libertà (tre discorsi di Dione Crisostomo)*. Cassino: Garigliano.

Gamauf, R. 2007. "*Cum aliter nulla domus tuta esse possit . . .* : Fear of Slaves and Roman Law." In *Fear of Slaves—Fear of Enslavement in the Ancient Mediterranean (Discourse, Representations, Practices). Rethymnon 4–7 November 2004*, edited by A. Serghidou, 145–64. Actes des Colloques du Groupe de Recherche sur l'esclavage dans l'antiquité 29. Besançon: Presses Universitaires de Franche-Comté.

Gamauf, R. 2009. "Slaves Doing Business: The Role of Roman Law in the Economy of a Roman Household." *European Review of History: Revue Européenne d'histoire* 16 (3): 331–46.

Gamauf, R. 2014. "*Erro*: Suche nach einem Verschwundenen Sklaven. Eine Skizze zur Interpretationsgeschichte des Ädilizischen Edikts." In *Inter cives necnon peregrinos: Essays in Honour of Boudewijn Sirks*, edited by J. Hallebeek, M. Schermaier, R. Fiori, E. Metzger, and J.-P. Coriat, 269–87. Göttingen: V&R Unipress.

Garland, R. 1995. *The Eye of the Beholder: Deformity and Disability in the Graeco-Roman World*. Ithaca: Cornell University Press.

Garland, R. 2010. *The Eye of the Beholder: Deformity and Disability in the Graeco-Roman World*. 2nd ed. London: Bristol Classical Press.

Garnsey, P. 1996. *Ideas of Slavery from Aristotle to Augustine*. Cambridge: Cambridge University Press.

Garofalo, L. 2000. *Studi sull'azione redibitoria*. Padua: CEDAM.

Giannella, N. J. 2019. "The Freedom to Give: The Legal Basis of Seneca's Treatment of Slaves in De Beneficiis." *Classical Philology* 114 (1): 79–99.

Giannella, N. J. 2020. "Free in Fact? Legal Status and State in the Suits for Freedom." In *The Discovery of the Fact*, edited by C. Ando and W. P. Sullivan, 91–111. Ann Arbor: University of Michigan Press.

Giannella, N. J. 2023. "¿Honor entre esclavos? La desigualdad frente a la ley en el Imperio Romano." In *Desigualdades antiguas: Economía, cultura y sociedad en el Oriente Medio y el Mediterráneo*, edited by M. Campagno, J. Gallego, C. G. Mac Gaw, and R. Payne, 193–214. Buenos Aires: Miño y Dávila.

Gibson, R. K. 2020. *Man of High Empire: The Life of Pliny the Younger*. New York: Oxford University Press.

Giglio, F. 2018. "The Concept of Ownership in Roman Law." *Zeitschrift der Savigny-Stiftung für Rechtsgeschichte: Romanistische Abteilung* 135 (1): 76–107.

Gilroy, P. 1993. *The Black Atlantic: Modernity and Double Consciousness*. Cambridge, MA: Harvard University Press.

Gonzalès, A. 2002. "Provenance des esclaves au Haut-Empire. *Pax romana* et approvisionnement." In *Routes et Marchés d'esclaves: 26e Colloque Du GIREA, Besançon, 27–29 Septembre 2001*, edited by M. Garrido-Hory, 65–82. Besançon: Presses Universitaires Franc-Comtoises.

Gordon, W. 1983. "Agency and Roman Law." In *Studi in onore di Cesare Sanfilippo*, 3: 341–49. Milan: Giuffrè.

Graver, M. 2002. *Cicero on the Emotions: Tusculan Disputations 3 and 4*. Chicago: University of Chicago Press.

Greenidge, A. H. J. 1894. *Infamia: Its Place in Roman Public and Private Law*. Oxford: Clarendon Press.

Griffin, M. T. 1976. *Seneca: A Philosopher in Politics*. Oxford: Clarendon Press.

Griffin, M. T. 1986a. "Philosophy, Cato, and Roman Suicide: I." *Greece & Rome* 33 (1): 64–77.

Griffin, M. T. 1986b. "Philosophy, Cato, and Roman Suicide: II." *Greece & Rome* 33 (2): 192–202.

Griffin, M. T. 2013. *Seneca on Society: A Guide to De Beneficiis*. Oxford: Oxford University Press.

Grisé, Y. 1982. *Le suicide dans la Rome antique*. Montreal: Bellarmin.

Groen-Vallinga, M. J., and L. E. Tacoma. 2017. "The Value of Labour: Diocletian's Prices Edict." In *Work, Labour, and Professions in the Roman World*, edited by K. Verboven and C. Laes, 104–32. Leiden: Brill.

Gunderson, E. 2003. *Declamation, Paternity, and Roman Identity: Authority and the Rhetorical Self*. Cambridge: Cambridge University Press.

Habinek, T. N. 1998. *The Politics of Latin Literature: Writing, Identity, and Empire in Ancient Rome*. Princeton: Princeton University Press.

Harper, K. 2011. *Slavery in the Late Roman World, AD 275–425*. Cambridge: Cambridge University Press.

Harries, J. 2013. "The *Senatus Consultum Silanianum*: Court Decisions and Judicial Severity in the Early Roman Empire." In *New Frontiers: Law and Society in the Roman World*, edited by P. J. du Plessis, 51–70. Edinburgh: University of Edinburgh Press.

Harrill, J. A. 1999. "The Vice of Slave Dealers in Greco-Roman Society: The Use of a Topos in 1 Timothy 1:10." *Journal of Biblical Literature* 118 (1): 97–122.

Harris, B. F. 1991. "Dio of Prusa: A Survey of Recent Work." *Aufstieg und Niedergang der Römischen Welt (ANRW)* 2 (33.5): 3853–81.

Hartman, S. 1997. *Scenes of Subjection: Terror, Slavery, and Self-Making in Nineteenth-Century America*. Oxford: Oxford University Press.

Hellegouarc'h, J. 1963. *Le vocabulaire latin des relations et des partis politiques sous la République*. Paris: Les Belles Lettres.

Herrmann-Otto, E. 1994. *Ex ancilla natus: Untersuchungen zu den "hausgeborenen" Sklaven und Sklavinnen im Westen des Römischen Kaiserreiches*. Stuttgart: F. Steiner.

Herrmann-Otto, E. 1999. "*Causae Liberales*." *Index* 27: 141–59.

Herz, Z. 2025. *The God and the Bureaucrat: Roman Law, Imperial Sovereignty, and Other Stories*. Cambridge: Cambridge University Press.

Hill, T. 2004. *Ambitiosa Mors: Suicide and the Self in Roman Thought and Literature*. New York: Routledge.

Hoffer, S. E. 1999. *The Anxieties of Pliny, the Younger*. Atlanta: Scholars Press.

Hollander, D. B. 2018. *Farmers and Agriculture in the Roman Economy*. London: Routledge.

Honoré, A. M. 1961. "Ownership." In *Oxford Essays in Jurisprudence: A Collaborative Work*, edited by A. G. Guest, 107–47. Oxford: Oxford University Press.

Honoré, A. M. 1981. *Emperors and Lawyers*. London: Duckworth.

Honoré, A. M. 2012. "The Nature of Slavery." In *The Legal Understanding of Slavery: From the Historical to the Contemporary*, edited by J. Allain, 9–16. Oxford: Oxford University Press.

Hopkins, K. 1993. "Novel Evidence for Roman Slavery." *Past & Present* 138 (1): 3–27.

Howley, J. A. 2013. "Why Read the Jurists? Aulus Gellius on Reading Across Disciplines." In *New Frontiers: Law and Society in the Roman World*, edited by P. J. du Plessis. Edinburgh: Edinburgh University Press.

Howley, J. A. 2018. *Aulus Gellius and Roman Reading Culture: Text, Presence, and Imperial Knowledge in the* Noctes Atticae. Cambridge: Cambridge University Press.

Howley, J. A. 2025. "Despotics." In *Writing, Enslavement, and Power in the Roman Mediterranean, 100–300 CE*, edited by J. Coogan, J. A. Howley, and C. R. Moss. Oxford: Oxford University Press.

Huemoeller, K. P. D. 2016. "Sex and Slavery in the Roman World." PhD diss., Princeton University.

Huemoeller, K. P. D. 2020. "Freedom in Marriage? Manumission for Marriage in the Roman World." *Journal of Roman Studies* 110: 123–39.

Huemoeller, K. P. D. 2021. "Captivity for All? Slave Status and Prisoners of War in the Roman Republic." *Transactions of the American Philological Association* 151 (1): 101–25.

Hughes, L. A. 2006. "The Proclamation of Non-Defective Slaves and the Curule Aediles' Edict: Some Epigraphic and Iconographic Evidence from Capua." *Ancient Society* 36: 239–61.

Hunt, P. 2016. "Slaves as Active Subjects: Individual Strategies." In *The Oxford Handbook of Greek and Roman Slaveries*, edited by S. Hodkinson, M. Kleijwegt, and K. Vlassopoulos. Oxford: Oxford University Press.

Husquin, C. 2022. "Atypical Bodies: Extraordinary Body Treatment and Consideration." In *A Cultural History of Disability in Antiquity*, edited by C. Laes, 15–30. London: Bloomsbury.

Ibbetson, D. 2005. "High Classical Law." In *The Cambridge Ancient History*, vol. 12, edited by A. Bowman, A. Cameron, and P. Garnsey, 184–99. Cambridge: Cambridge University Press.

Impallomeni, G. 1955. *L'editto degli edili curuli*. Padua: CEDAM.

Isaac, B. H. 2004. *The Invention of Racism in Classical Antiquity*. Princeton: Princeton University Press.

Jakab, É. 1997. *Praedicere und cavere beim Marktkauf: Sachmängel im griechischen und römischen Recht*. Munich: C.H. Beck.

Johnson, W. 1999. *Soul by Soul: Life Inside the Antebellum Slave Market*. Cambridge, MA: Harvard University Press.

Johnson, W. 2003. "On Agency." *Journal of Social History* 37: 113–24.

Johnston, D. 1999. *Roman Law in Context*. Cambridge: Cambridge University Press.

Jolowicz, H. F., and B. Nicholas. 1972. *Historical Introduction to the Study of Roman Law*. 3rd ed. Cambridge: Cambridge University Press.

Jones, C. P. 1987. "Stigmata: Tattooing and Branding in Graeco-Roman Antiquity." *Journal of Roman Studies* 77: 139–55.

Joshel, S. R. 1992. *Work, Identity, and Legal Status at Rome: A Study of the Occupational Inscriptions*. Norman: University of Oklahoma Press.

Joshel, S. R. 2010. *Slavery in the Roman World*. Cambridge: Cambridge University Press.

Joshel, S. R. 2013. "Geographies of Slave Containment and Movement." In *Roman Slavery and Roman Material Culture*, edited by M. George, 99–128. Toronto: University of Toronto Press.

Joshel, S. R., and L. H. Petersen. 2014. *The Material Life of Roman Slaves*. Cambridge: Cambridge University Press.

Kamen, D. 2010. "A Corpus of Inscriptions: Representing Slave Marks in Antiquity." *Memoirs of the American Academy in Rome* 55: 95–110.

Kaser, M. 1940. "Zur Kriminalgerichtsbarkeit gegen Sklaven." *Studia et Documenta Historiae et Iuris* 6: 357–68.

Kaser, M. 1956. *Eigentum und Besitz im älteren römischen Recht*. 2. Aufl. mit Nachträgen. Forschungen zum römischen Recht 1. Abhandlung. Cologne: Böhlau.

King, P. V. 2000. "The Cognitio into Insanity." PhD diss., University of North Carolina at Chapel Hill.

Kirschenbaum, A. 1987. *Sons, Slaves, and Freedmen in Roman Commerce*. Jerusalem: Magnes Press, Hebrew University.

Kleijwegt, M. 2009. "Creating New Citizens: Freed Slaves, the State and Citizenship in Early Rome and under Augustus." *European Review of History: Revue Européenne d'histoire* 16 (3): 319–30.

Knoch, S. 2005. *Sklavenfürsorge im Römischen Reich: Formen und Motive*. Hildesheim: Georg Olms.

Koops, E. 2014. "Masters and Freedmen: Junian Latins and the Struggle for Citizenship." In *Integration in Rome and in the Roman World*, edited by G. de Kleijn and S. Benoist, 105–26. Leiden: Brill.

Koops, E. 2020. "The Practice of Manumission through Negotiated Conditions in Imperial Rome." In *Roman Law and Economics: Exchange, Ownership, and Disputes*, edited by G. Dari-Mattiacci and D. Kehoe, 2: 36–77. Oxford: Oxford University Press.

Krenkel, W. 1984. *Plinius der Jüngere: Breife in einem Band*. Berlin: Auflau-Verlag.

Kruschwitz, P. 2022. "Notions of Barbarians and Barbarian Lands in the Latin Verse Inscriptions." *Medieval Worlds* 16: 163–94.

Kruschwitz, P., and A. Cousins. 2022. "Speech: Lack of Language, Lack of Power: Social Aspects of the Discourse about Communication Disorders in the Greco-Roman World." In *A Cultural History of Disability in Antiquity*, ed. C. Laes, 120–36. London: Bloomsbury.

Kuhn, H.-W. 1982. "Die Kreuzesstrafe während der frühen Kaiserzeit: Ihre Wirklichkeit und Wertung in der Umwelt des Urchristentums." *Aufstieg und Niedergang der Römischen Welt (ANRW)* 25 (1): 648–793.

Laes, C. 2013. "Silent History? Speech Impairment in Roman Antiquity." In *Disabilities in Roman Antiquity: Disparate Bodies a capite ad calcem*, edited by C. Laes, C. F. Goodey, and M. L. Rose, 145–80. Leiden: Brill.

Laes, C. 2018. *Disabilities and the Disabled in the Roman World: A Social and Cultural History*. Cambridge: Cambridge University Press.

Laes, C., ed. 2022a. *A Cultural History of Disability in Antiquity*. London: Bloomsbury.

Laes, C. 2022b. "How and Whether to Say 'Disability' in Latin and Ancient Greek." In *A Cultural History of Disability in Antiquity*, edited by C. Laes, 1–14. London: Bloomsbury.

Laes, C., C. F. Goodey, and M. L. Rose. eds. 2013. *Disabilities in Roman Antiquity: Disparate Bodies a capite ad calcem*. Leiden: Brill.

Leesen, T. G. 2010. *Gaius Meets Cicero: Law and Rhetoric in the School Controversies*. Leiden: Martinus Nijhoff.

Lendon, J. 1997. *Empire of Honour: The Art of Government in the Roman World*. Oxford: Clarendon Press.

Lenel, O. 1889. *Palingenesia iuris civilis: Iuris consultorum reliquiae quae Iustiniani Digestis continentur, ceteraque iuris prudentiae civilis fragmenta minora secundum auctores et libros*. Leipzig: Tauchnitz.

Lenel, O. 1927. *Das Edictum perpetuum: Ein Versuch zu seiner Wiederherstellung*. Leipzig: Tauchnitz.

Lenski, N. 2009. "Schiavi armati e formazione di eserciti privati nel mondo tardoantico." In *Ordine e sovversione nel mondo greco e romano: Atti del convegno internazionale Cividale del Friuli, 25–27 Settembre 2008*, edited by G. Urso, 145–75. Pisa: ETS.

Lenski, N. 2012. "Constantine and Slavery: *Libertas* and the Fusion of Roman and Christian Values." In *Atti dell'Accademia Romanistica Costantiniana XVIII*, edited by S. Giglio, 235–60. Rome: Aracne.

Lenski, N. 2018a. "Framing the Question: What Is a Slave Society?" In *What Is a Slave Society? The Practice of Slavery in a Global Perspective*, edited by N. Lenski and C. M. Cameron, 15–57. Cambridge: Cambridge University Press.

Lenski, N. 2018b. "Ancient Slaveries and Modern Ideology." In *What Is a Slave Society? The Practice of Slavery in a Global Perspective*, edited by N. Lenski and C. M. Cameron, 106–47. Cambridge: Cambridge University Press.

Levin-Richardson, S. 2011. "*Facilis Hic Futuit*: Graffiti and Masculinity in Pompeii's 'Purpose-Built' Brothel." *Helios* 38 (1): 59–78.

Levin-Richardson, S. 2013. "*Fututa Sum Hic*: Female Subjectivity and Agency in Pompeian Sexual Graffiti." *Classical Journal* 108 (3): 319–45.

Levin-Richardson, S. 2019. *The Brothel of Pompeii: Sex, Class, and Gender at the Margins of Roman Society*. Cambridge: Cambridge University Press.

Lewis, D. 2017. "Orlando Patterson, Property, and Ancient Slavery: The Definitional

Problem Revisited." In *On Human Bondage: After Slavery and Social Death*, edited by J. Bodel and W. Scheidel, 31–54. Malden, MA: Wiley-Blackwell.

Lewis, D. M. 2018. *Greek Slave Systems in their Eastern Mediterranean Context, c. 800–146 BC*. Oxford: Oxford University Press.

Liebs, D. 2012. *Summoned to the Roman Courts*. Berkeley: University of California Press.

Long, A. A. 2002. *Epictetus: A Stoic and Socratic Guide to Life*. Oxford: Clarendon Press.

Long, A. A. 2006. *From Epicurus to Epictetus: Studies in Hellenistic and Roman Philosophy*. Oxford: Clarendon Press.

Longo, G. 1961. "D. 11,3." *Bullettino dell'Istituto di Diritto Romano* 44: 199–229.

Longo, G. 1966. *Ricerche Romanistiche*. Milan: Giuffrè.

MacLean, R. B. 2018. *Freed Slaves and Roman Imperial Culture: Social Integration and the Transformation of Values*. Cambridge: Cambridge University Press.

MacMullen, R. 1982. "The Epigraphic Habit in the Roman Empire." *American Journal of Philology* 103 (3): 233–46.

MacMullen, R. 1986. "Judicial Savagery in the Roman Empire." *Chiron* 19: 147–66.

Maestre Maestre, J. M., L. Charlo Brea, and A. Serrano Cueto, eds. 1997. *Estudios sobre Columela*. Cádiz: Universidad de Cádiz.

Major, A. 1994. "Claudius' Edict on Sick Slaves." *Scholia* 3: 84–90.

Maltby, R. 1990. *A Lexicon of Ancient Latin Etymologies*. Leeds: Cairns.

Manna, L. 1994. *Actio redhibitoria e responsabilità per i vizi della cosa nell'Editto de mancipiis vendundis*. Milan: Giuffrè.

Mantovani, D. 2010. "Lessico dell'identità." In *Homo, caput, persona: La construzione giuridica dell'identità nell'esperienza tomana. Dall'epoca di Plauto a Ulpiano*, edited by A. Corbino, M. Humbert, and G. Negri, 3–47. Pavia: Iuss Press.

Martin, R. 1971. *Recherches sur les agronomes latins et leurs conceptions économiques et sociales*. Paris: Les Belles Lettres.

Martin, R. 1974. "Familia rustica: Les esclaves chez les agronomes latins." *Actes du Groupe de Recherches sur l'Esclavage depuis l'Antiquité* 3 (1): 267–97.

Martin, R. 1985. "État présent des études sur Columelle." *Aufstieg und Niedergang der romisches Welt (ANRW)* 2 (32.3): 1959–79.

Maschi, C. A. 1948. "Humanitas come motivo giuridico." In *Scritti in memoria di L. Cosattini*, 263–362. Trieste: Università di Trieste.

McCarthy, K. 2000. *Slaves, Masters, and the Art of Authority in Plautine Comedy*. Princeton: Princeton University Press.

McDonald, G. C. 2009. "Concepts and Treatments of Phrenitis in Ancient Medicine." PhD diss., Newcastle University.

McGinn, T. A. J. 1998. *Prostitution, Sexuality, and the Law in Ancient Rome*. Oxford: Oxford University Press.

McGinn, T. A. J. 2004. *The Economy of Prostitution in the Roman World: A Study of Social History and the Brothel*. Ann Arbor: University of Michigan Press.

McGinn, T. A. J. 2011. "Roman Prostitutes and Marginalization." In *The Oxford Hand-*

book of Social Relations in the Roman World, edited by M. Peachin, 643–59. Oxford: Oxford University Press.

McKeown, N. 2016. "Slaves as Active Subjects: Collective Strategies." In *The Oxford Handbook of Greek and Roman Slaveries*, edited by S. Hodkinson, M. Kleijwegt, and K. Vlassopoulos. Oxford: Oxford University Press.

Mentxaka, R. 2003. "La cláusula 'item placuit: Quisquis ex quacumque causa mortem sibi adsciveri(t), eius ratio funeris non habebitur' de CIL 14,2112 y sus hipotéticos fundamentos." *Revue internationale des droits de l'Antiquité* 50: 218–47.

Metzger, N. 2018. "'Not a Daimōn, but a Severe Illness': Oribasius, Posidonius and Later Ancient Perspectives on Superhuman Agents Causing Disease." In *Mental Illness in Ancient Medicine: From Celsus to Paul of Aegina*, edited by C. Thumiger and P. N. Singer, 79–106. Leiden: Brill.

Mihajlović, V. D. 2020. "Roman Epigraphic Funerary Markers, Ontological Transition, and Relational Work-Nets." In *Beyond the Romans: Posthuman Perspectives in Roman Archaeology*, edited by I. Selsvold and L. Webb, 25–40. Oxford: Oxbow Books.

Moatti, C. 2016. "Les erreurs de statut et l'idée de la liberté dans l'espace judiciaire romain jusqu'au IIIe siècle de notre ère." In "Recht haben und Recht bekommen im Imperium Romanum: Das Gerichtswesen der römischen Kaiserzeit und seine dokumentarische Evidenz," edited by R. Haensch, F. Hurlet, K.-L. Link, S. Strassi Zaccaria, and A. Teichgräber. Supplement, *Journal of Juristic Papyrology* S24: S523–S59.

Montefusco, L. 1996. "Logica, retorica e giurisprudenza nella dottrina degli *status*." In *Per la storia del pensiero giuridico romano: dall'età dei pontefici alla scuola di Servio*, edited by D. Mantovani, 209–28. Turin: Giappichelli.

Morabito, M. 1981. *Les réalités de l'esclavage d'après le Digeste*. Paris: Les Belles Lettres.

Morgan, T. 2015. *Roman Faith and Christian Faith: Pistis and Fides in the Early Roman Empire and Early Churches*. Oxford: Oxford University Press.

Morris, E. P. 1968. *Horace: Satires and Epistles*. Norman: University of Oklahoma Press.

Mouritsen, H. 2004. "Freedmen and Freeborn in the Necropolis of Imperial Ostia." *Zeitschrift für Papyrologie und Epigraphik* 150: 281–304.

Mouritsen, H. 2007. "*CIL* X 1403: The Album from Herculaneum and the Nomenclature of Latini Iuniani." *Zeitschrift für Papyrologie und Epigraphik* 161: 288–90.

Mouritsen, H. 2011. *The Freedman in the Roman World*. Cambridge: Cambridge University Press.

Mouritsen, H. 2016. "Manumission." In *Oxford Handbook of Roman Law and Society*, edited by P. J. du Plessis, C. Ando, and K. Tuori, 402–15. Oxford: Oxford University Press.

Nardi, E. 1983. *Squilibrio e deficienza mentale in diritto romano*. Milan: Giuffrè.

Nicholas, B. 2008. *An Introduction to Roman Law*. Oxford: Oxford University Press.

Nicolau, M. G. 1933. *Causa liberalis: Étude historique et comparative du procès de liberté dans les législations anciennes*. Paris: Recueil Sirey.

Noè, Eralda. 2002. *Il progetto di Columella: Profilo sociale, economico, culturale*. Como: New Press.

Nutton, V. 2008. "The Medical World of Rufus of Ephesus." In *On Melancholy*, edited by P. E. Pormann, 139–58. Tübingen: Mohr Siebeck.

Ortu, R. 2008. *"Aiunt aediles . . .": Dichiarazioni del venditore e vizi della cosa venduta nell'editto de mancipiis emundis vendundis*. Turin: Giappichelli.

Padilla Peralta, D. 2017. "Slave Religiosity in the Roman Middle Republic." *Classical Antiquity* 36 (2): 317–69.

Padilla Peralta, D. 2020. "Epistemicide: The Roman Case." *Classica* 33 (2): 151–86.

Padilla Peralta, D. 2023. "Pharmapolitics and the Early Roman Expansion: Gender, Slavery, and Ecology in 331 BCE." *Classical Antiquity* 42 (1): 159–94.

Palma, A. 1992. *Humanior Interpretatio: Humanitas nell'interpretazione e nella normazione da Adriano ai Severi*. Turin: Giappichelli.

Parlamento, E. 2001. "*Servus melancholicus*: I *vitia animi* nella giurisprudenza classica." *Rivista di Diritto Romano* 1: 325–44.

Patterson, O. 1982. *Slavery and Social Death*. Cambridge, MA: Harvard University Press.

Pigeaud, J. 1989. *La maladie de l'âme: étude sur la relation de l'âme et du corps dans la tradition médico-philosophique antique*. Paris: Les Belles Lettres.

Plass, P. 1995. *The Game of Death in Ancient Rome: Arena Sport and Political Suicide*. Madison: University of Wisconsin Press.

Pormann, P. E., ed. 2008. *On Melancholy: Rufus of Ephesus*. Tübingen: Mohr Siebeck.

Pucci, G. 2005. "'*Detrahis vestimenta venalibus*': *Iconografia della vendita di schiavi nell'antichità e oltre*." *Journal of Roman Archaeology* 18: 235–40.

Reduzzi Merola, F. 2007. "Schiavi fuggitivi, schiavi rubati, '*servi corrupti*.'" *Studia Historica* 25: 325–29.

Reduzzi Merola, F. 2011. "Le vol de l'esclave fugitif et la *corruptio servi*: Entre élaboration jurisprudentielle et définition des délits." In *Figures d'empire, fragments de mémoire: Pouvoirs et identités dans le monde romain impérial (IIe s. av. n. è.-VIe s. de n. è)*, edited by S. Benoist, A. Daguet-Gagey, and C. Hoët-Van Cauwenberghe, 399–406. Villeneuve-d'Ascq: Presses universitaires du Septentrion.

Reitz, C. 2013. "Columella, *De Re Rustica*." In *A Companion to the Neronian Age*, edited by E. Buckley and M. T. Dinter, 275–87. Chichester, UK: Wiley-Blackwell.

Riccobono, S. 1965. "L'idea di *humanitas* come fonte di progresso del diritto." In *Studi in onore di Biondo Biondi*, 2: 583–614. Milan: Giuffrè.

Richlin, A. 2014. "Talking to Slaves in the Plautine Audience." *Classical Antiquity* 33 (1): 174–226.

Richlin, A. 2017. *Slave Theater in the Roman Republic: Plautus and Popular Comedy*. Cambridge: Cambridge University Press.

Riggsby, A. M. 2010. *Roman Law and the Legal World of the Romans*. Cambridge: Cambridge University Press.

Riggsby, A. M. 2019. *Mosaics of Knowledge: Representing Information in the Roman World*. Oxford: Oxford University Press.

Rio, A. 2017. *Slavery after Rome, 500–1100*. Oxford: Oxford University Press.

Rivière, Y. 2002. "Recherche et identification des esclaves fugitifs dans l'Empire romain." *Collection de l'Ecole française de Rome* 297: 115–96.

Robinson, O. F. 1995. *The Criminal Law of Ancient Rome*. Baltimore: Johns Hopkins University Press.

Robleda, O. 1976. *Il diritto degli schiavi nell'antica Roma*. Rome: Università Gregoriana Editrice.

Rodger, A. 1972. *Owners and Neighbors in Roman Law*. Oxford: Clarendon Press.

Rosen, G. 1968. *Madness in Society: Chapters in the Historical Sociology of Mental Illness*. Chicago: University of Chicago Press.

Roth, U. 2010. "*Peculium*, Freedom, Citizenship: Golden Triangle or Vicious Circle? An Act in Two Parts." In "By the Sweat of Your Brow: Roman Slavery in Its Socio-Economic Setting," edited by U. Roth. Supplement, *Bulletin of the Institute of Classical Studies* S109: S91–S120.

Rouland, N. 1977. *Les ésclaves romains en temps de guerre*. Brussels: Latomus.

Saller, R. 1982. *Personal Patronage under the Early Empire*. Cambridge: Cambridge University Press.

Salway, B. 2010. "*Manicipium Rusticum Sive Urbanum*: The Slave Chapter of Diocletian's Edict on Maximum Prices." In "By the Sweat of Your Brow: Roman Slavery in Its Socio-Economic Setting," edited by U. Roth. Supplement, *Bulletin of the Institute of Classical Studies* S109: S1–S20.

Schadewaldt, W. 1973. "*Humanitas Romana*." *Aufstieg und Niedergang der Römischen Welt (ANRW)* 1 (4): 43–62.

Scheidel, W. 1990. "*Agricola, colonus, cultor, rusticus*: Beobachtungen zum rechtlichen und sozialen Status der 'Landwirte' in Columellas Schrift *de re rustica*." *Maia* 42: 257–65.

Scheidel, W. 2005a. "Real Slave Prices and the Relative Cost of Slave Labor in the Greco-Roman World." *Ancient Society* 35: 1–17.

Scheidel, W. 2005b. "Human Mobility in Roman Italy, II: The Slave Population." *Journal of Roman Studies* 95: 64–79.

Scheidel, W. 2011. "The Roman Slave Supply." In *The Cambridge World History of Slavery*, vol. 1, *The Ancient Mediterranean World*, edited by K. R. Bradley and P. Cartledge, 1: 287–310. Cambridge: Cambridge University Press.

Schiller, A. A. 1930. "Trade Secrets and the Roman Law: The *Actio Servi Corrupti*." *Columbia Law Review* 30: 837–45.

Schumacher, L. 2010. "On the Status of Private *Actores, Dispensatores and Vilici*." In "By the Sweat of Your Brow: Roman Slavery in Its Socio-Economic Setting," edited by U. Roth. Supplement, *Bulletin of the Institute of Classical Studies* S109: S31–S47.

Sciortino, S. 2010. *Studi sulle liti di libertà nel diritto romano*. Turin: Giappichelli.

Scott, J. C. 1990. *Domination and the Arts of Resistance: Hidden Transcripts*. New Haven: Yale University Press.

Sherwin-White, A. N. 1966. *The Letters of Pliny: A Historical and Social Commentary.* Oxford: Clarendon Press.

Sirks, A. J. B. 2015. "Delicts." In *The Cambridge Companion to Roman Law*, edited by D. Johnston, 246–71. Cambridge: Cambridge University Press.

Stein, P. 1958. *Fault in the Formation of Contract in Roman Law and Scots Law.* Edinburgh: Published for the University of Aberdeen by Oliver and Boyd.

Stewart, R. 2012. *Plautus and Roman Slavery.* Malden, MA: Wiley-Blackwell.

Straus, J. A. 1971. "Le pays d'origine des esclaves de l'Égypte romaine." *Chronique d'Égypte* 46: 363–66.

Straus, J. A. 2004. *L'achat et la vente des esclaves dans l'Egypte romaine: contribution papyrologique à l'étude de l'esclavage dans une province orientale de l'Empire romain.* Munich: K. G. Saur.

Swain, S. 1996. *Hellenism and Empire: Language, Classicism, and Power in the Greek World, AD 50–250.* Oxford: Clarendon Press.

Swain, S. 2000. *Dio Chrysostom: Politics, Letters, and Philosophy.* Oxford: Oxford University Press.

Swain, S. 2008. "Social Stress and Political Pressure: On Melancholy in Context." In *On Melancholy*, edited by P. E. Pormann, 113–38. Tübingen: Mohr Siebeck.

Swanson, K. W. 2020. "Race and Selective Legal Memory: Reflections on *Invention of a Slave*." *Columbia Law Review* 120 (4): 1077–1118.

Taylor, L. R. 1961. "Freedmen and Freeborn in the Epitaphs of Imperial Rome." *American Journal of Philology* 82: 113–32.

Temkin, O. 1971. *The Falling Sickness: A History of Epilepsy from the Greeks to the Beginnings of Modern Neurology.* 2nd. ed., rev. Baltimore: Johns Hopkins University Press.

Thibodeau, P. 2016. "Greek and Roman Agriculture." In *A Companion to Science, Technology, and Medicine in Ancient Greece and Rome*, edited by G. L. Irby, 519–32. Chichester, UK: Wiley Blackwell.

Thibodeau, P. 2018. "Ancient Agronomy as a Literature of Best Practices." In *The Oxford Handbook of Science and Medicine in the Classical World*, edited by P. T. Keyser and J. Scarborough, 463–80. New York: Oxford University Press.

Thumiger, C. 2017. *A History of the Mind and Mental Health in Classical Greek Medical Thought.* Cambridge: Cambridge University Press.

Thumiger, C., and P. N. Singer, eds. 2018a. *Mental Illness in Ancient Medicine: From Celsus to Paul of Aegina.* Leiden: Brill.

Thumiger, C., and P. N. Singer. 2018b. "Introduction. Disease Classification and Mental Illness: Ancient and Modern Perspectives." In *Mental Illness in Ancient Medicine: From Celsus to Paul of Aegina*, edited by C. Thumiger and P. N. Singer, 1–33. Leiden: Brill.

Thurmond, D. L. 1994. "Some Roman Slave Collars in the *CIL*." *Athenaeum* 82: 459–93.

Tomlin, R. S. O. 2003. "'The Girl in Question': A New Text from Roman London." *Britannia* 34: 41–51.

Toohey, P. 2013. "Madness in the Digest." In *Mental Disorders in the Classical World*, edited by W. V. Harris, 441–60. Leiden: Brill.

Tougher, S. 2013. "The Aesthetics of Castration: The Beauty of Roman Eunuchs." In *Castration and Culture in the Middle Ages*, edited by L. Tracy, 48–72. Cambridge: D. S. Brewer.

Treggiari, S. 1991. *Roman Marriage: Iusti Coniuges from the Time of Cicero to the Time of Ulpian*. Oxford: Clarendon Press.

Trenchard-Smith, M. 2010. "Insanity, Exculpation and Disempowerment in Byzantine Law." In *Madness in Medieval Law and Custom*, edited by W. J. Turner, 39–55. Leiden: Brill.

Trentin, L. 2011. "Deformity in the Roman Imperial Court." *Greece & Rome:* 58 (2): 195–208.

Trümper, M. 2008. *Die "Agora des Italiens" in Delos: Baugeschichte, Architektur, Ausstattung und Funktion einer späthellenistischen Porticus-Anlage*. Rahden, Nordrhein-Westfalen: Verlag Marie Leidorf.

Trümper, M. 2009. *Graeco-Roman Slave Markets: Fact or Fiction?* Oxford: Oxbow Books.

Tuori, K. 2016. *Emperor of Law*. Oxford: Oxford University Press.

Valiño, E. 1967. "Las *actiones adiecticiae qualitatis* y sus relaciones basicas en derecho Romano." *Anuario de Historia del Derecho Español* 37: 339–480.

Van Hooff, A. J. L. 1990. *From Autothanasia to Suicide: Self-Killing in Classical Antiquity*. London: Routledge.

Veyne, P. 1981. "Suicide, fisc, esclavage, capital et droit romain." *Latomus* 40 (2): 217–68.

Veyne, P. 1993. "*Humanitas*: Romans and Non-Romans." In *The Romans*, edited by A. Guarina, 342–69. Chicago: University of Chicago Press.

Vlassopoulos, K. 2011. "Greek Slavery: From Domination to Property and Back Again." *Journal of Hellenic Studies* 131: 115–30.

Vlassopoulos, K. 2021. *Historicising Ancient Slavery*. Edinburgh: Edinburgh University Press.

Voisin, J.-L. 1987. "Apicata, Antinous et quelque autres [Notes d'épigraphie sur la mort volontaire à Rome]." *Mélanges de l'École française de Rome* 99 (1): 257–80.

Volkmann, H. 1990. *Die Massenversklavungen der Einwohner eroberter Städte in der hellenistisch-römischen Zeit*. Stuttgart: F. Steiner.

Von Armin, H. 1898. *Leben und Werke des Dio von Prusa, mit einer Einleitung: Sophistik, Rhetorik, Philosophie in ihrem Kampf um die Jugendsbildung*. Berlin: Weidsmann.

Wacke, A. 1994. "Die adjektizischen Klagen im Überblick. Erster Teil: Von der Reeder- und Betriebsleiterklagen zur Direkten Stellvertretung." *Zeitschrift der Savigny Stiftung für Rechtsgeschichte: Romanistische Abteilung* 111: 280–362.

Wacke, A. 2001. "*Manumissio matrimonii causa*. Die Freilassung zwecks Heirat nach den Ehegesetzen des Augustus." In *Fünfzig Jahre Forschungen zur antiken Sklaverei an der Mainzer Akademie, 1950–2000*, edited by H. Bellen and H. Heinen, 133–57. Stuttgart: F. Steiner.

Walvin, J. 2011. *The Zong: A Massacre, the Law and the End of Slavery*. New Haven: Yale University Press.

Warmington, E. H. 1938. *Remains of Old Latin, Volume III*. Cambridge, MA: Harvard University Press.

Watson, A. 1965. *The Law of Obligations in the Later Roman Republic*. Oxford: Oxford University Press.

Watson, A. 1968a. *The Law of Property in the Later Roman Republic*. Oxford: Clarendon Press.

Watson, A. 1968b. "Morality, Slavery and the Jurists in the Later Roman Republic." *Tulane Law Review* 42 (303): 289–303.

Watson, A. 1971. *Roman Private Law around 200 BC*. Edinburgh: Edinburgh University Press.

Watson, A. 1987a. *Roman Slave Law*. Baltimore: Johns Hopkins University Press.

Watson, A. 1987b. "Seller's Liability for Defects: Aedilician Edict and Praetorian Law." *Iura* 38: 167–75.

Watson, A. 1996. "Trade Secrets and Roman Law: The Myth Exploded." *Tulane European and Civil Law Forum* 19: 19–29.

Welwei, K.-W. 1988. *Unfreie im antiken Kriegsdienst*. T. 3: Rom. Stuttgart: Steiner.

Welwei, K.-W. 2000. *Sub corona vendere: Quellenkritische Studien zu Kriegsgefangenschaft und Sklaverei in Rom bis zum Ende des Hannibalkrieges*. Stuttgart: F. Steiner.

White, K. D. 1970. *Roman Farming*. Ithaca: Cornell University Press.

Wibier, M. 2016. "Cicero's Reception in the Juristic Tradition of the Early Empire." In *Cicero's Law: Rethinking Roman Law of the Late Republic*, edited by P. J. du Plessis, 100–122. Edinburgh: Edinburgh University Press.

Wiedemann, T. E. J. 1981. *Greek and Roman Slavery*. Baltimore: Johns Hopkins University Press.

Williams, C. A. 1999. *Roman Homosexuality: Ideologies of Masculinity in Classical Antiquity*. Oxford: Oxford University Press. 2nd ed., 2010.

Wohlers, M. 1999. *Heilige Krankheit: Epilepsie in antiker Medizin, Astrologie und Religion*. Marburg: N.G. Elwert.

Wolff, C. 2009. *Déserteurs et transfuges dans l'armée romaine à l'époque républicaine*. Naples: Jovene.

Woolf, G. 1998. *Becoming Roman: The Origins of Provincial Civilization in Gaul*. Cambridge: Cambridge University Press.

Wright, J. 2020. "Preaching Phrenitis: Augustine's Medicalization of Religious Difference." *Journal of Early Christian Studies* 28 (4): 525–53.

Zimmermann, R. 1996. *The Law of Obligations: Roman Foundations of the Civilian Tradition*. Oxford: Oxford University Press.

Index Locorum

Legal Sources

Literary Sources

Epigraphical and Papyrological Sources

Index of Persons and Places

Index of Terms

Printed and bound by CPI Group (UK) Ltd, Croydon, CR0 4YY
16/09/2026
14963491-0006